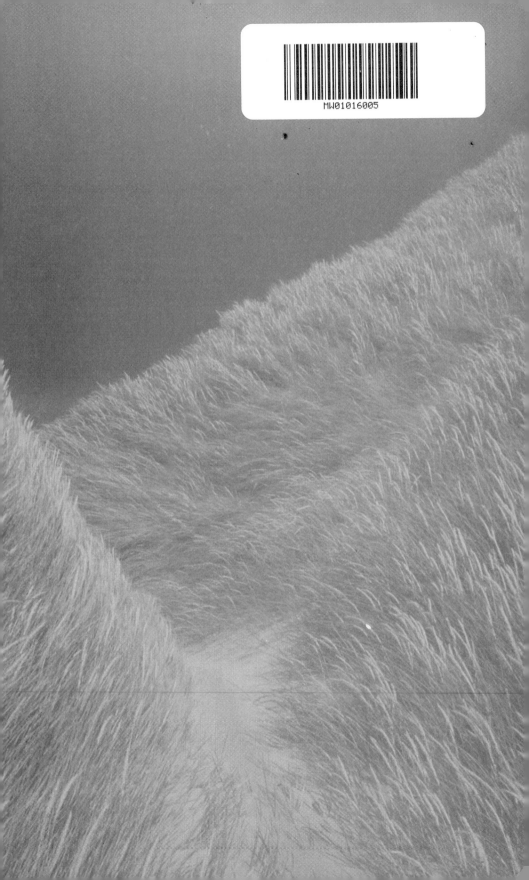

Born in Oamaru, Fiona Farrell was educated at the Universities of Otago and Toronto, where she graduated in Drama. She has published two collections of poetry, two collections of short stories and four novels, three of which have been shortlisted for the Montana New Zealand Book Awards. *The Skinny Louie Book* won the award in 1993, while *The Hopeful Traveller* (2002) and the popular *Book Book* (2004) were also nominated for the international IMPAC Award. Her poetry and short stories have been widely anthologised. She has received the Bruce Mason Award for Playwrights, the Katherine Mansfield Fellowship in Menton, and in 2006 spent six months in Donoughmore, Ireland, as one of the inaugural recipients of the Rathcoola Residency for New Zealand and Australian writers and artists.

THE
BEST
NEW ZEALAND
FICTION

VOLUME 4

EDITED BY FIONA FARRELL

V

A VINTAGE BOOK
published by
Random House New Zealand
18 Poland Road, Glenfield, Auckland, New Zealand
www.randomhouse.co.nz

Random House International
Random House
20 Vauxhall Bridge Road
London, SW1V 2SA
United Kingdom

Random House Australia (Pty) Ltd
20 Alfred Street, Milsons Point, Sydney,
New South Wales 2061, Australia

Random House South Africa Pty Ltd
Isle of Houghton
Corner Boundary Road and Carse O'Gowrie
Houghton 2198, South Africa

Random House Publishers India Private Ltd
301 World Trade Tower, Hotel Intercontinental Grand Complex,
Barakhamba Lane, New Delhi 110 001, India

First published 2007

© 2007 introduction and selection, Fiona Farrell
For copyright details of individual stories see page 7

The moral rights of the authors have been asserted

ISBN 978 1 86941 877 9

Cover and text design: Katy Yiakmis
Layout: Elin Bruhn Termannsen
Cover photograph: Juliet Nicholas
Printed in Australia by Griffin Press

Contents

ACKNOWLEDGEMENTS

The stories listed below were first published or broadcast as follows:

'The Stone' by SANDRA ARNOLD — Radio New Zealand National, October 2006.

'Win a Day with Mikhail Gorbachev: A Melodrama in Four Parts' by TIM JONES — *Full Unit Hookup*, Summer 2002.

Fiona Farrell

Introduction

THERE WAS A SONG — one of those slack-jawed, gun-totin' monologues drawled by someone called T. Texas Tyler — about a soldier caught in church with a deck of cards. 'Soldier,' says the Sargent, 'Put away those cards!' And the soldier, who may have talked real slow but was not born stupid, explains that the Ace reminds him that there is but one God, and the Deuce of how the Bible is divided into two parts, and the Five recalls those wise virgins who trimmed their wicks and the five foolish virgins who didn't see the point in a whole lot of trimmin', and the Queen reminds him of the Queen of Heaven, and the Ten is . . .

I have never edited a collection before. I spend my days writing in a hut in a paddock because I like trying to make something beautiful out of words. But I recieved an email from Random House last year when I was in Ireland, asking if I would edit the 2007 volume of *The Best New Zealand Fiction*. It was spring, and words and confidence were rising like sap. Of course, I said. Anything at that moment seemed possible. Back in New Zealand, I read the magazines, scanned websites, listened to Radio New Zealand, wrote to writers whose work I already knew and loved, contacted others whose work I was coming across in odd places for the first time, and assembled twenty stories that for me best express the distinctive power and beauty of New Zealand fiction.

So here they are, arranged in alphabetical order of authors' names, and, following convention, I must now explain the principles of selection: I must, like T. Texas Tyler addressing the provost marshall, 'satisfy you, sir, with the purity of my intentions'.

1. 'THE FREE BOX' reminds me that fiction is patchwork. Every motif, every technical device, every word is a scrap with a long history, passed down, worn smooth, frayed, stitched into one pattern then another. We talk of fiction using words that refer to fabric: we spin a yarn, weave a plot, follow the thread, tie up loose ends, employing an imagery natural to generations intimately familiar with the process whereby something as natural and inchoate as fleece or flax fibre could be shaped into something

useful like a cloak or a bag, to hold food or keep a body warm. This story makes from its tiny patchwork of words a structure strong enough to contain a circus act and a free bin alongside something deeper, and older. There is the young woman flying and the narrator following her with a beam of light, as all storytellers pick out their individual subjects from the dark. There is the encounter with the father crossing the road, which is just the road at Newtown, but there's the echo of that dusty crossroads near Thebes and that story that has taken on the mantle of myth. Why? Because it catches at the pain of the child encountering the random father. And, here, that pain is relieved by a perfect, simple, loving gesture.

2. 'THE STONE' reminds me that fiction is geography. Stories are laid down like sediment over a landscape. In Ireland the layers lie as thick as blanket bog; in New York and London, writers tunnel through heaps of debris like those Chinese villages near buried in computer components or plastic bags, in search of the odd, the eccentric, the disregarded, the something that is shiny-new. In New Zealand, the layers sit more lightly but more densely than they did fifty years ago. In this collection, Auckland will become a little more distinct — Gisborne, Tokoroa, Colombo Street, Dannevirke, Nugget Point. Nor will it be the statistician's landscape we had to draw in school, with its dots for hundreds of sheep and its green hatching for forestry plantations, but a landscape invested with feeling. In this story, the setting is alien, a dry valley of grief. And in this arid place, there is catharsis: a vision of shared fate that transcends country and culture to encompass all the sentient world, in that wonderful final image of a female turtle plodding up the sand to begin the cycle of birth, life, death all over again.

3. 'THE GOOD AND GENTLE' reminds me that fiction is political. But then, every story in this collection reminds me of this fact. They have all been written on a skinny archipelago with a long and complicated and quarrelsome history. And whether Maori or Pakeha, it is fairly safe to bet that most of these writers are only a few generations away from illiteracy. My great-grandmother couldn't write her own name, signing receipts for marriage, births and deaths with a shaky cross. A generation or so earlier my entire paternal line — a scrum of Farrells, Slavens, Dalys and O'Tooles — vanishes without a trace into some colonised, famine-starved Irish bog. The reason I haven't joined them in leading a short and brutalised life is down to politics, and in particular to the shift in public conscience that led to the election of the 1935 Labour government. That this collection exists at all is due to free health-care and education and bossy Plunket nurses and those little bottles of stale milk at the school

gate and a thousand other tiny political things. Race, class and gender are its themes, as they are the themes for all fiction written in this small post-colony.

But then, fiction has always had its roots down deep in politics. Decades ago, Dale Spender described how the novel evolved alongside modern empirical science in a newly enlightened Europe. Released at last from the circular tunnels of medieval religiosity, men were freed to speculate, explore and experiment, while women, who had to remain at home rather than heading off to the South Seas and elsewhere, set about their own explorations. They developed a new literary form, the 'novel', to test reality, producing literally hundreds of these little self-contained hypotheses — though most have been forgotten. Academia has largely chosen to ignore them, nominating for serious attention just those few examples that were written by men. This has obscured the fact that, at its root, fiction was an expression of oppression, of that eternal truth that the mind can roam free though it be in chains.

It is the medium of isolates, unlike the communal consensus of drama that was its popular precedent. It evolved in an era that promoted individualism, when women, as any Jane Austen heroine knows full well, were required to forsake home and kindred if they were to achieve full adulthood through that daunting economic and social contract modern readers blithely dismiss as 'falling in love'. Something sweet and palest pink. In the act of reading, the isolate finds diversion, but also reassurance, inspiration and the samizdat knowledge of joining an invisible community of like minds.

To return to Brown's story: it is superbly both good and gentle, but at its core there is the woody intransigence of race and class with which we live. Fiction in New Zealand has its barriers, and by and large writers stick to their own side rather than risk inauthenticity, tokenism or cliché. The neo-colonial Alexander McCall-Smith brand of whimsy in which black women characters are co-opted into some provocative conservative fictional fantasy, for example, doesn't get much mileage in New Zealand. But fiction is also the way we find out about what lies behind barriers and concealed beneath that New Zealand reluctance to make a fuss or to say what we really think in public. It is how writers here have made vivid the fine detail of existence, the pin-pricks too trivial to warrant protest or legislation but which rub a bitter blister on the soul. The little jokes. The tiny revelatory discourtesies. Fiction is where the small stuff gets sweated. It's where the tables can be turned and the bosses rendered fools. This colonial legacy is often credited as one of the reasons the Irish have produced their great literature, and why the contemporary driving energy in literary England is immigrant-based. Friction creates fiction, the medium of the disenfranchised.

4. 'The Feijoa is Brother to the Guava' reminds me, in its dazzling welter of words, flooding like small change from a pokie machine, that fiction is verbal. The language of New Zealand fiction changes in response to subtle shifts of influence — from the frilly Wordsworthian effusions of Maoriland to the clean, Deco lines of Mansfield, through the New Deal working-man monotone of Sargeson to Frame's transformative synthesis of narrative and metaphor to seventies feminist introspection to the cinematic cut and edit of more recent writing: a rich fusion of Europe, America and the Pacific to which each writer puts their signature rhythm and phraseology. Sometimes when I have been working on this collection, a page has floated off the desk onto the floor. It has been simple to put it back, even when the page lacks name or title: the author's style — the pace of their sentences, their characteristic phrases, their manner of rendering dialogue — is as much a thumbprint as subject matter.

5. 'The Body' reminds me that fiction is anthropological. It satisfies human curiosity about the secret working of other lives. I am entranced by this strangely real family: the children making potions, the adults making theirs, the attempt to get out of it, wherever that may be, to see beyond. It is as though there is dark space surrounding these characters, who don't exist except as lines and circles on a piece of paper, but who live as if spotlit by the searing gleam of the author's imagination.

6. 'WhatSmartGirlsKnow' reminds me that fiction is cross-referential. No book is an island. Like this archipelago on which we live (I've read somewhere that there are 450 islands making up New Zealand), the stories in this collection set up their own angle and echo to one another. One story yells, another tugs at the sleeve. Themes recur and are rephrased. I like the fact that alphabetical accident has placed two subtle and wonderful stories about families side by side here: death and sexual tension are worked over in those twin poles of New Zealand fiction, the city and the beach.

7. 'I've been Thinking about You, Sister' reminds me that fiction is half emotion, half intellect. Ihimaera punts this fact straight into centre field. There will be no easy slump into empathy here. There's a writerly 'I' present and he's irritated, presuming an audience prone to sentimentality. I feel got at and tested, as if a liking for his early work is a failing. Then he does it again: makes me cry at the old man with his shiny white trainers sitting in an airport lounge and the old woman running to her brother's

grave. It is like watching Brecht for the first time, a battle between the impulse to engage and the requirement to analyse: a brilliant juggling act in which the reader is tossed from hand to hand. On the one hand, you think about the writer, colonialism, stereotyping. On the other hand, you feel the absolute beauty of love and loyalty.

8. THIS EXTRACT FROM *Manifest* reminds me that fiction is primal. At school we were taught that a story must have a beginning, a middle and an end. But we need far less prompting to begin detecting narrative. We possess an instinct for story, derived no doubt from the innate capacity to speculate of the hunter planning to waylay an animal, and the gatherer considering the possible scenarios consequent on ingesting some unfamiliar berry. This is one of two extracts from novels in this collection. There is no middle, no end here. Just glimpses from a wider canvas, like details from a massive painting glimpsed beneath plaster: an old man in his car, two boys squabbling. But how quickly in such wonderfully skilled hands we are drawn into this fictional world! How readily we start guessing at the links that will make up the story.

9. 'WIN A DAY WITH MIKHAIL GORBACHEV' reminds me of fiction's capacity to be richly satirical, in its marvellous blend of *Hello!* magazine celebrity gossip, with a splash of clichéd Russian identity and a twist of sci-fi. The whole can be analysed as commentary on the way language and the media shape our view of history, or enjoyed for the sheer delight in watching a marvellously inventive writer playing about with style.

10. 'HEAVEN FREEZES' reminds me that fiction is, at heart, optimistic, confirming order. A strange blue light arcs over these characters, shedding a sense of transcendence, of nature lending significance to ordinary human experience. During the period when this collection has been coming together the newspapers and television have been preoccupied with sex as pain: women have been reduced to holes to be penetrated with batons, bottles or whatever, and men reduced to brutes competing over an inanimate body. Just another episode in the nightly narrative of abused babies, beaten women, a girl raped then run over in a parking lot off Manchester Street . . . There can be no conclusion to these tales. They trail away into despair and a cynical shrug. Or they become the hook for formula cop shows, calculated to hold an audience through those awkward gaps between plugs for insurance or cars. But in Kidman's story, love and sex are slow and complex. Fiction restores a tender empathy, and some faith that it might be worth being human after all.

11. 'My Friend Freddy' reminds me that fiction does not deal in reality but in credibility. It is what drew me to fiction in the first place: the freedom of it, the infinite variety of possible conclusions, the way it flirted with unlikelihood. Mathematical problems and scientific experiments were predictable and dull by comparison: the answer would inevitably be sixty-seven and the litmus paper would inevitably turn pink. How could they compare with Emma making a mess of her life? Or the Mayor of Casterbridge making the single mistake that brings down catastrophe? Or, for that matter, a Machiavellian sheep in a superb classic fable about self-preservation? And what would a collection of New Zealand writing be without one of those?

12. 'Red Christmas' reminds me that fiction, like the blues, like street art, is innately subversive. Who can tell what is happening in the mind of that woman seated on a train reading? What revolution might that man be contemplating as he turns the page? No wonder fiction has been proscribed and burned. No wonder there is a constant struggle for control via the genteel restraints implicit in publishing, reviewing, marketing and academic gatekeeping. This story should spark a revolution, like those operas in nineteenth-century Europe that drove their audience out onto the streets to storm palace and prison. Of course it won't. But in the reader's mind small lights switch on, as, with warmth and delight in the strength of children and in small kindnesses this story illuminates those abstract nouns violence and poverty more powerfully than any number of reports. I write this in a week when adults are taking to the streets to defend the right to hit a child, bringing with them their own children, who hold up banners reading 'I'd rather be smacked.' New Zealand is turning its weirdly brutal side to the camera.

13. 'The Last Good Day of Autumn' reminds me that fiction occupies the crumbling bank at the very moment when stagnant routine breaks through and narrative begins to flow. Detail is gathered into the growing flood: here a tourist shop becomes entangled, along with canoes on a river and an old man in a wheelchair. And these details, simple in themselves, begin to surge with metaphor and some deeper import.

14. 'The Bugger' reminds me with superb concentration of the tease and tension of fiction. The hang-on-let's-see-what-happens-next of it, the turning of the page, the wait for the next chapter, the next episode. Fiction plays games with our sense of time, setting up parallel worlds that ignore the creeping tedium of Big Brother reality for quick quick slow: sometimes accelerating to leap over swathes of time, sometimes steadying,

as this story does, to observe the classical unities of time and place.

15. 'Velocity' reminds me of the regionality of fiction. There's a deadpan rural voice any New Zealander recognises as local. It goes along with a distaste for weakness and a refusal to emote, which we have been trained to recognise as genial when it is often deeply cruel. New Zealand has its regional specialities. The English can do manners, whether village murderer or London immigrant street gang, and the Irish can do verbally inventive, and the French can do intellectual surreal, but New Zealanders can do small-town dark, and here it's done brilliantly, with a pigeon.

16. 'In the Palace Gardens' reminds me of the fiction written by New Zealanders living abroad: the way it always seems to come down to just the issues discussed in this perfectly classical story told against the measured crunch of feet in snow: Nature with a capital N, and Man with a capital M. While darting about among the trees is a memory of family and home and nature that doesn't require any kind of capital initial.

17. These extracts from Sarkies's novel, *Two Little Boys*, remind me of the buzzy energy of fiction when the voices feel new and strong and vivid and the whole structure is roaring along, taking me with it on a wild ride, and there's a soundtrack playing and a kind of cinematic rush but it's better than a movie where I'm sitting on the outside watching people do whatever they do, because I've actually been let inside these characters and I'm looking out. And what is even better is that these characters are creating their mayhem around Nugget Point.

18. 'a working model of the sky' reminds me of the quiet complexity of fiction, where random events are brought together to an effect that eludes exact definition. It cannot be reduced to some hundred-word pitch. It's a matter of style and pace and tone: a kind of exquisite music.

19. 'A War Story'. Any writer recognises the grip on the wrist, the stranger who leans in suddenly and says, 'Here's a story. You could write about this.' This beautiful, spare narrative reminds me that one of the functions of fiction is to record, to reinforce memory, to avenge.

20. 'Crash' reminds me that New Zealand fiction is indeed dark — but it is the darkness of the bush where the light, when it does penetrate, is all the brighter for its confined focus, and where you know that, if you keep climbing high enough, you will emerge into tussock and clear sky. In New Zealand, there is a kind of darkness to our history, perhaps some brutal

luggage brought in from other repressive places, perhaps the inevitable aftermath of colonial invasion. But last year I went up to a writers' festival in Canada, a place with a similar history and a similar chiaroscuro to the fiction. A French Canadian writer was trying to describe his struggle with words. He was having trouble expressing himself in English, his head grasped in his hands, his face anguished. Suddenly he exploded into voice: 'Why does no one,' he said, the words thickly flavoured with the vinegar tang of joual, 'talk about beauty? Because that is what writers do: we try to make beauty!'

And that is it, really. Beauty. Beautiful structures, made entirely of air. That's what this collection is. And, like T. Texas Tyler, I believe that should be enough to satisfy you.

Fiona Farrell
May 2007

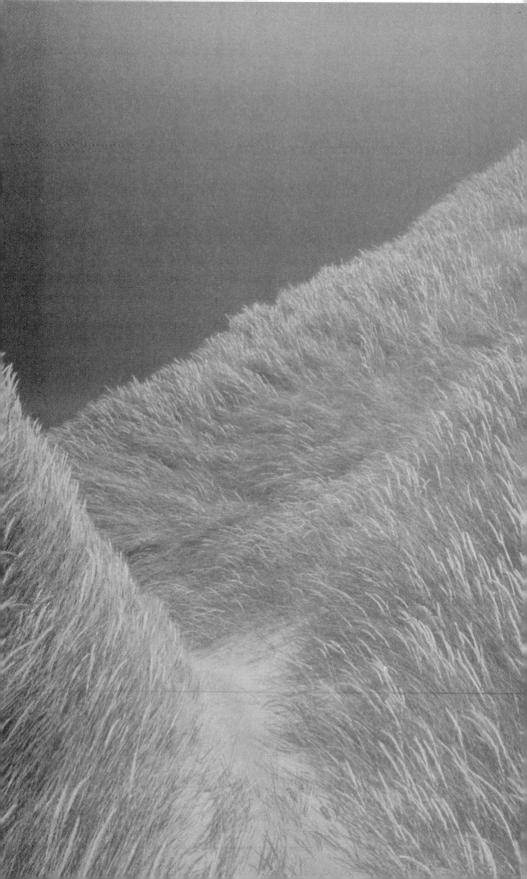

MICHELLE ARATHIMOS

The Free Box

THE DAY BELLE SAW HER father was the day we became best friends.

We'd known each other before, but after that there was something between us, some unspoken thing that was there when we were around other people, something I understood about her that they didn't. Belle was a circus performer; we'd met at the Women's Circus, where I was doing lighting and she was on trapeze. Everyone loved Belle. She was cute and small and neat; she flipped and somersaulted on the bar like nothing I'd ever seen.

When I saw Belle that first night I thought she looked like a tulip. She had these big green-brown eyes and a delicate little mouth, and her skin was pale and smooth. I was in charge of training the lights on her and it was strange, I can tell you, flicking them from gold to red to gold again, changing the colour of her skin as she pranced on the trapeze. The crowd was going off, but she seemed impervious to it all, contained, lithe in her lycra and spinning like a toy.

She came to meet me afterwards.

'I'm Belle,' she said, extravagantly, generously. She shook my hand. Her spandex was hot pink, and she wore fishnets underneath. When she spoke you felt she was giving you a present.

'Tora,' I said. I was dusty from the beams, and hot. I looked down.

'It's hard work, eh, on the lights?' Belle said. 'I did some lighting a couple of years ago, but I gave it up. Too many men in the industry.'

'Yeah, I know!' I said. I was surprised. 'The producers and the managers — they're mostly guys. No one thinks I can lift anything.'

'But you're great!' Belle said. She smiled. 'That's what I came to say: the lighting was totally spot on. You timed it with the changes in the music and everything!' She sighed dramatically. 'God, you don't know how long I've waited for a lighting person like you.'

I noticed a blue sequin glued to her cheek at the corner of her eye.

The day Belle saw her father she'd come around to my house for a cup of tea. I'd been stencilling words onto T-shirts I was planning to sell at the local fair. I had on painty jeans and a bandana. Belle arrived with biscuits, and as we ate them I showed her the T-shirts.

'I just *love* this one, Tora,' she said, holding one up. '*2 Rad 4 Brands.* That's awesome.'

'Thanks,' I said, looking down at the shirt. It was just a T-shirt.

'I'd love to make more stuff,' Belle said. 'Like you. Patches and stuff.'

'Hey, did you know there's a free box outside that place down the road?' I asked. 'At that new op shop? I had a look yesterday. There's heaps of free material and stuff.'

'A free box!' Belle grinned. 'We should totally go check it out.'

The day outside was clear and still. It seemed earlier than it was, like the air wasn't dirtied by people's breathing yet. There was no wind. The blossoms were coming out on the trees along my street and we heard a howler monkey call as we left the house, from the zoo one street away. Even the council flats at the end of the road looked clean and crisp, lucid in the light.

'So how *are* you?' Belle asked.

I sighed. 'I'm having a hair crisis,' I said.

Belle looked at me. 'You want to shave it off again?'

'Yeah. I don't know what it is — I just get this urge. But then whenever I do it I get hassled at work.'

Belle did a little skip. She was wearing a petticoat and a turquoise cardigan. Her hair was cut in a pixie style and she'd dyed it fire-engine red.

'It's just fashion,' she said. 'Humans are essentially superficial, right? Don't worry about it! Do whatever you want, Tora. I think you'd look great with a shaved head!' She flung her arms wide and did a few tap-dance steps on the street, her shoes crunching on some broken glass. She spun. She laughed.

'It's political,' I said. She rolled her eyes, still dancing, arms out to the world.

We were coming back along the main road when we saw him.

We'd passed the point where the shops petered out into old houses, past the mural of the stars and moon on the side of a building, past the second-hand bookshop and the community centre. Someone had sprayed graffiti on its wall: *It could be worse, you could be on fire.* We were stepping lightly past the TAB, with the cigarette butts and beer cans on the verge outside, and the Asian food store with the smell of samosas wafting out. Belle was carrying a huge pile of fabric she'd got from the free box, polkadotted and striped and patterned material wrapped around with a scarf. I had a smaller pile. We were going to make patches and sew them on things.

'We're so *resourceful*,' Belle said to me. She winked.

'I would have been good in the depression,' I said.

We started to cross the road. There was a man crossing towards us, a nondescript man muffled up in layers of clothing as if he was cold. He had a beanie pulled low over his eyes, and a huge baggy jacket, loose pants. He was staring at Belle. People tend to stare at Belle. She hadn't noticed. I waited for him to call some random insult, or a pick-up line. You can get anything around here.

We were halfway across the street when he spoke.

'Hello,' he said.

He didn't speak to me but directly to her. We were pretty close to him by then, standing almost face to face.

Belle looked at him. Then she stopped walking and stood there, still, fabric trailing from her arms.

'*Dad*,' she said. '*Dad*.' I watched her face empty of everything — the things she had been about to say, what kind of patches she would make, the moves she would perform tonight at the circus, everything. The smile slowly left her face. 'I didn't recognise you,' she said.

'Hi,' the man said. 'Hi, honey.' His voice was low and gentle: I could hardly hear it over the traffic sounds. 'I thought I'd see you sometime, Belle,' he said. 'I thought I'd run into you one of these days.'

Belle stepped forward suddenly and clasped him, the scraps pressed between their bodies, his big dark coat against her red hair. A car turned into the street and nosed towards us. It tooted its horn.

'Come on,' I said to them. 'Come on! We have to get off the street.'

They moved as if hypnotised. They didn't look at me.

'I meant to call you,' Belle said. 'I meant to . . . I had this phone number, but then it didn't work and —'

'It's okay,' the man said. I couldn't see any resemblance between them, but then I saw their eyes were similar, his a little darker brown than hers. I realised he was crying.

When I turned to look at Belle there were tears on her face too.

'It's okay, Belle,' the man said again. 'What you been up to, honey? What you been doing?' He spoke quietly.

Belle gasped a little. 'You know, Dad,' she said. Her face wasn't scrunched up or red at all; the tears were just something happening naturally, like breathing. 'This and that. Performing. Travelling a bit.

I live down there,' she said, pointing with one arm and clutching her bundle with the other. 'How about you?'

'I'm all right,' Belle's father said. 'I've been working — it's a little job, really, but it's something. I'm local again, so . . .' He reached into his pocket, scribbled something on a piece of card. He was still crying, those Belle-eyes watery in his face. 'So here's my number,' he said. 'Honey, if you want to give me a call. When you're ready.'

He gave it to her.

'Thanks,' said Belle. 'Thanks, Dad.'

He kissed her cheek and walked across the road, away from us.

Belle looked at me as if she were waking up, and saw me there, waiting.

'Tora! Sorry,' she said. 'I'm so sorry, I just —'

'No, Belle, don't be stupid,' I said. 'It was your *dad*. I don't mind! God!'

We started to walk. The tears kept running down Belle's face in the clear light, like jewels. I put my arm around her.

'I haven't seen him in three years,' she said. 'And you know the horrible thing? It's not even like we had some big fight or anything. I went down south and then he had to move,' she said. 'He had some debts or something — got in trouble with the police. He's a bit random, my dad. And it's not like he talks to Mum.' She took a breath. I looked at her. She was hugging the scraps of fabric to her chest.

'I kept meaning to call him but then it got awkward, you know, because I'd left it so long.' She stopped suddenly. 'Oh God,' she said, 'I forgot to say I missed him, didn't I? I forgot to tell him!'

'It's all right,' I said. 'I'm sure he knows.' He'd spoken to her so softly, weeping in the middle of the road.

We started walking again. I could smell the blossoms on the trees near my house.

'He looked so different,' she said. 'For the longest time, standing there, I didn't know who he was.'

We'd been walking together but now I let her go and looked at her. She was stepping without seeing the footpath, the material bunched up under her chin, looking up at the sky.

'Let me carry that for you,' I said. I reached over and gathered up the fabric. She let it go, not looking, and the material cascaded into my hands.

She rubbed her face with the back of her hand. She swung her arms.

I hefted the load up, trying not to drop it. All the bright colours, the musty smell.

'Thanks,' she said. 'I didn't realise.' She smiled at me. 'I didn't realise how heavy it was.'

SANDRA ARNOLD

The Stone

THREE HUNDRED KILOMETRES SOUTH-EAST OF Muscat, Egyptian vultures glide above the Eastern Hajar Mountains, and burnt-toffee peaks slice into the milky sky. Gravel plains and arid valleys lie on the inland side, a vast sandy plain on the east, and to the south the rolling red sand dunes of the Wahiba Desert. Herons and cormorants wait at the edge of the Arabian Sea, which glitters with hard, blue light.

The dirt road drops vertically into the ravine and rises almost as steeply up the other side, where clumps of dun-coloured houses squat on the cliffs. A battered utility truck, stuffed with turbaned, white-robed villagers, hurtles out of a cloud of red dust straight towards us. It misses our rented Landcruiser by a centimetre. The men — one of whom is hanging on to a goat — shout greetings, laughing at our ashen faces. I clutch the stone in my hand. Rob blows out his breath. 'Bloody hell!'

Still shaking, we crawl through the narrow, winding streets of the village of Bimmah, steering warily around donkeys and goats that wander at will. Just as oblivious are the women in bright red, green and orange dresses and veils who saunter across the track with baskets on their heads. Blood is spattered over several doorsteps from the Eid al-Adha sacrifices and runs into congealed puddles in the gutters. Outside one house a family is helping to carve up a goat strung from a tree. For some reason it makes me think of Amina.

Amina comes from the Al Mahri tribe, which was reputed to have lived in the city of Ubar before it suddenly disappeared, centuries ago, into the desert sands. In the 1990s explorers, with the help of NASA satellites and Bedouin folklore, located the ruins. It was an underground river, the archaeologists said, which had steadily eroded the limestone on which the city had been built, that had caused it to collapse. Amina disagreed. It was the wrath of God, she said, punishing the inhabitants for their undisciplined lifestyle.

When she returned to the Language Centre last week, after only two weeks of her maternity leave, none of the men gave any sign of noticing her grey face streaked with tears; nor did they lift their heads from their books when she kept leaving the class to disappear into the prayer room. Fayza, Amal, Thuraya and Fatma stayed behind when the men left for their coffee break.

'She is from Salalah, Ms Alexa,' said Amal, 'but even for a woman from that region this is not normal behaviour. Two weeks! We are worried about her. In our hostel we hear her crying all night but when we try to talk to her about it she denies it and says she is okay.'

I promised I would talk to her myself, and asked Amina to come to my office.

In answer to my questions she said, 'My father says I must finish my Academic English course.'

'But you're twenty-five,' I said. 'Isn't that decision yours and your husband's?'

She wiped her face with the sleeve of her abaya. She alone, of all the female students, had no embroidery on her sleeves to relieve the plainness of her black robe. And where her classmates' robes were fitted at the waist, Amina's — from Saudi Arabia, she informed me — concealed her tall, graceful figure as effectively as a body-bag. Which was why none of us at the school had realised she had been pregnant, let alone that she had given birth.

'If I don't pass my exams,' she wept, 'I won't be able to go to Australia to do my postgraduate study. My whole family's depending on me. It's just that I didn't know I would feel like this. I thought I could just hand him over to my mother.' Her tears splashed onto my desk. 'But I can't stop thinking about him.'

'Could you fly back home at the weekends?' I asked.

Amina tucked a stray hair under her hijab. Her fingers were long and slender. Like Beth's, I thought.

'Not till after the exams.' She took a tissue from the box I gave her and mopped her eyes. 'But I can still feel his skin next to mine. My whole body aches to see him, smell him, touch him.' She glanced up at me. 'Can you understand what I mean, Ms Alexa? Am I imagining this?'

'Yes, I do understand what you mean,' I said. 'And no, you're not imagining it.'

Her face relaxed. 'So you have children too?'

I nodded.

'How many?'

I hesitated. In New Zealand, friends and colleagues had avoided this topic for the past two years. Since my arrival in Oman I had often wondered what I would say if someone asked me this question. Now that someone had, I didn't know how to answer. Amina was watching me, waiting.

'Three,' I said.

Her smile broadened. 'Are any of them my age?'

'Beth — my youngest,' I said, 'would have been the same age as you now.'

Amina looked into my face for a long time.

'I'd like to see her photo,' she said at last. 'Will you bring me one?'

I promised I would.

The woman carving up the goat sees me watching and waves. I stare at her pink satin dress. 'The blood!' I remark to Rob. 'How on earth will she wash it off?'

Rob squeezes my knee with his hand.

Between the villages of Bimmah and Shab we spot a tiny cove of white sand between low cliffs. Behind the beach lie the ruins of an ancient mud-brick town that had been part of a thriving port when Marco Polo visited.

'Perfect timing,' says Rob. 'It'll be getting dark soon.'

There's plenty of driftwood around to make a fire, and while I boil up the kettle and heat our food Rob sets up the tent. We sit cross-legged on the rapidly cooling sand and eat our meal in silence as the sky turns navy and a huge orange moon rolls above the sea. The surf breaks with tiny sparks of luminescent light. There's no sound but our breathing. Since Rob found the stone this morning he's hardly said a word. I move closer to him and turn the stone in my hand, pushing its sharp edges into my skin.

This morning we'd watched the sun rise over the sea, because on this day of all days we needed to see colour spill over the earth. We walked past deep holes dug by nesting turtles and over the tractor-tyre tracks that their flippers had gouged in the sand. We found piles of broken eggshells at the bottom of the holes.

'Let's hope one of the little buggers made it to the sea,' Rob said. 'Then after twenty-five years it'll find its way back to where it was born.' He picked up a stick and drew a heart in the sand around a cluster of empty shells.

'What a waste,' I said, estimating that there were around two hundred eggs.

'Just part of a cycle,' Rob said, writing our initials inside the heart.

We peeled off our clothes and waded gingerly over the stones until we were up to our necks in the sea. Seabirds circled and dived. The sun blazed. Floating on my back in the warm salty water I thought of a friend who once described the hours he had spent in the sea after his boat had capsized in a storm. As he waited to be rescued, the world became the boat he was clinging to, and only that moment had any substance. He felt, he said, outside of time. I never fully understood what he meant, until now.

Outside of time. On this day. At this time. Two years ago. In New Zealand.

Beth asks for music to be put on. She discusses a racehorse with Vincent and tells him she wants to train a white horse when she gets better. She asks me several times who came through the door and I say there's no one else here, just the seven of us. She touches everyone and checks their names, then asks Melanie, 'What sound does a bear make when it's stung by a bee?' We think it's a riddle but Beth says she doesn't know the answer either. I ask her why she thought of it and she says she has no idea.

The two nurses decide to leave, as she seems so much better now. She can breathe and she's laughing and joking. Her face is a better colour. I say goodbye to them on the porch. When I go back into the living room Melanie is telling Beth she and Vincent will stay overnight, so Rob and I can get some sleep. Beth smiles and thanks her, then nestles the side of her face into the chair and closes her eyes. As I sit down opposite her I see that her chest is still. We put our faces close to her mouth and nose and feel the tiniest whisper of air. Rob finds a pulse in her neck, beating very faintly. My heart is beating so hard I think it will burst. Vincent and Melanie slip outside and wait on the veranda. The nor'wester roars through the trees, whipping up the autumn leaves. Rob and I hold Beth's hands.

Beneath the hills, wild horses graze in the moonlight. The lead mare lifts her head and pricks her ears. The colts and fillies stop chasing one another's shadows. Foals stand closer to their mothers. The old ones stop grazing. They all watch the lead mare, and wait. The earth holds its breath. Beth's pulse flutters like a moth's wing, and is gone. I go outside to tell Vincent and Melanie and they say they know because the wind has died.

I don't sleep that night, and next morning I move around as if trapped in glass. In the middle of a conversation with Olivia and Sam a sound slides from my throat. It rises to a wail. Wave upon wave of wailing, from a place deep inside in my body. I have never heard such a sound in my life and I can't believe it's coming from me. Rob, Olivia and Sam can do nothing but hold me. A fantail taps on the window. As Beth's friends start arriving, the fantail circles around their heads.

I floated in the water like a foetus, my arms curled around my knees. Rob knelt on the sand with the sea up to his chin. He gave a long, shuddering sigh like the exhalation that comes after learning that the expected bad news is good news. Or the relief when a truck misses your car by a fraction.

The surf hissed. A seagull flew over our heads, its long, mournful keening breaking the silence of the deserted beach.

'Do you remember,' I said, 'when I was in labour? You suggested playing Scrabble to keep my mind off the contractions. I thought you were joking! Then you put your hand in the bag of letters and brought out a B.'

Rob nodded.

'I knew then our baby would be a girl.'

Rob laughed. 'If we'd had a boy you'd have convinced yourself the B was for boy.'

'No. I knew it was B for Beth.'

'Coincidence,' Rob said, 'just coincidence.' Then, 'Ouch! These bloody shells are sharp!'

He reached down into the water and brought up a flat, oval stone that fitted into the palm of his hand. 'No wonder it cut me. It's covered in limpets.' He turned it over. His brow creased as he stared at it in silence.

'What's wrong?' I asked.

He held out the stone. In the middle the limpets had dropped off, leaving behind a raised pattern of white calcification. Shaped into a perfectly formed B.

Now, sitting under the stars on the beach in front of our campfire, I hold the stone between my hands and stare into the flames.

'In ancient Persia when someone first saw oil trickle out of the desert they didn't understand what it was,' I say. 'They thought it was some kind of water, and when it ignited they believed the fire was sacred. They didn't believe the flame just went out. They thought it died, like the soul leaving the body.'

Rob touches my arm and points to the sea. The little sparks from the agitation of the algae have become flashes of light that run along the length of each wave. The sea is ablaze with white fire. As we stare, struck dumb by the beauty, a large, dark shape emerges from the water. A giant turtle. She drags herself across the sand, stopping to check out sites to dig a hole, then makes her way to our tent and starts digging beside it. With a sigh, she begins the long process of shovelling out sand with her front flippers. Hardly daring to breathe, we edge closer, and by the light of the moon we watch the turtle lay her eggs.

After two hours the exhausted creature covers her nest with sand. Her task completed, she turns around and heads back to the sea. We follow, hand in hand, and watch her swim away. Pieces of moon float on the water where she disappears beneath the waves.

BEN BROWN

The Good and Gentle

'WHERE'S THAT OLD MAN GOING?'

Aunty was beside herself, which was formidable. One version of Aunty alone was enough to scare the crap out of most people.

'Ah . . . church, Aunty. It's Sunday, eh.'

'Don't you give me your bloody lip!' She scowled. 'Why didn't you stop him?'

I didn't answer. I thought the question was rhetorical and anyway, Aunty was already off down the road, hiking up her skirts to allow those mighty legs a greater mobility.

'Jesus bloody Christ . . . *Koro! Whakatuu te Motoka!*' she bellowed, slowly closing the distance between herself and the old man's HT Holden Kingswood 186, which is not as impressive as it sounds. The old man never got out of low gear when he was driving, and even then the clutch got a harder workout than the accelerator. The old man was a car-killer, eh. There's a graveyard full of his car wrecks somewhere, died in agony every one from burnt-out gearboxes and clutches.

But that's not what Aunty was going apeshit about. The old man was nearly blind with age these days, however old he was, and nobody really knew — not his children, not even himself, born in the years before the Pakeha bureaucracy arrived up here to certify his birth, or even give him a driver's licence.

Anyway, Aunty could yell about it till the heavens fell: the old man wouldn't hear a thing without his hearing aid, which he never wore with his best suit on, for reasons known only to himself. But Aunty knew all that, eh.

She's just one of those people who's got to yell about everything, I guess.

The old man always wore his best suit when he went to church. Potae as well — one of those gangster hats that old-timers like to wear; and lately he wore sunnies to take the pressure off his eyes.

'He'll be right,' chuckled the bro. 'The ancestors were navigators, eh. He knows where he's going.'

Aunty's feet raised the dust from the gravel road as they pounded after the old man. It was a straight run of maybe four hundred metres from the front gate to the church. The old man only had two corners to negotiate — left out of the driveway, left again into the church domain. He'd been walking and driving it blind and sighted forever — from the little Maori house to the little Maori church down the little Maori road.

'Ten bucks says she won't catch him,' said the bro.

'You're on,' I said. 'Gizza toke, eh?'

The bro had just fired up. He passed the joint. Skunky shit. I coughed the lining from my lungs and got head-spinny.

First taste of the new harvest.

'Pay up!' said the bro in a cloud of smoke.

We could see the Kingswood pig-jump its way over the verge of the church domain, with Aunty a good twenty metres behind him but *still* hard out, almost like the old man knew she was there all the time and was giving it just enough gas to keep in front of her.

'Jeez, that's wicked gear, eh,' one of us said.

'I reckon . . .' said the other.

'Kia inoi, tatou.' Let us pray, intoned the minister.

Most of the scattered congregation knelt to comply, praying by rote according to the liturgy.

The old man's head was bowed already, although not in any way supplicant to the churchman's command. Karakia was almost a natural state of being for him. His gods were many and he knew them intimately, by name and countenance.

He neither stood nor knelt throughout a service, but sat with his head at rest upon his clasped hands. His nearly blinded eyes were closed behind his sunnies. His lips moved in a silent korero. Tupuna conversed. Atua shared his pew. The twelve heavens were open to him. Christ walked with his grandfathers. The dead called from the mountain, he mihi'd them all — his wife and lost children, his brothers and sisters . . .

The bro and me had finally cracked it. The Big Score . . . almost. All we had to do was shift the stuff. We'd lined up a deal with a crew down in the city. Delivery tonight: a hundred pounds of primo for two hundred and fifty grand — discount for cash. The city crew would put it through their tinny houses and make an easy million.

We were smoking some of it now, parked up on the veranda of the old man's house, home to the bro and me for all our twenty-five whaangai years as grandsons and brothers. We were the old man's moko. Aunty lived in the only other house on the old marae, way too close sometimes.

The old man's house stands where a wharepuni used to rest a hundred years ago. That's how old the old man's house is. Behind the house there's a fruit grove — apples, pears and peaches; further on a garden full of spuds and kumara, giving out to fallow paddocks rising to the mountain.

We know the hills — not in the same way as the old man, who knows them as cousins and uncles and aunties — but we know their tracks and their trails and their sunniest faces, hunting pigs and possums and anything else that can trash a plot.

We grow weed behind the mountain, deep in the bush and close to one of the streams that vein the lower foothills there, marking the rohe. The bro and me been growing the stuff since we left school ten years ago. Started small, a few plants here and there sorta thing. Seemed like easy money, eh.

Was, too.

It's the only job we ever had.

Awa, maunga, whenua.

All you need.

The old man left the church in his own time, always last by an hour or two. The *Paipera Tapu* before him remained unopened, the liturgy unsaid.

The warm wood of the church to him was a whareao, pillared at each corner with the ancestors, timbered from these breathing hills around him, awhi mai, awhi mai . . .

All his worlds reposed herein, whakapapa to the very earth, as real to him as the mantric drone of the churchman to the pious and devout, *te po* at the fringes in manifold shades, *Io* at the topmost heaven, *Tariao* the morning star, father, son and wairua tapu . . .

He knew his daughter would be in the driver's seat. Every time he got away from her she wound up in the driver's seat. These days, church was the only place he drove to.

'Silly old bugger,' she spat — with him deaf to it in the dim light of his seeing, yet not as blind as she thought he was — before dropping a wheelie on the church domain out of sheer footsore exasperation, fishtailing back down the road, getting it sideways for the gate . . .

The bro and me nearly pissed ourselves laughing as Aunty came careening back down the road and into the driveway. You could hear her going off above the straining 186 as a cloud of gravel dust descended in her wake.

The old man was unfazed. With his sunnies on and that smile on his face, he looked like Ray Charles singing 'What'd I say?'.

Aunty was still blasting the old man when they got out of the car. He just nodded aroha and thanks to his belligerent daughter and shuffled up the steps and into his house to have a cuppa.

'What the bloody hell are you two idiots laughing at?' she roared.

We were set. Just waiting for nightfall to make the run to the city. The gear was stashed in knotted-up rubbish bags in the back of the ute, along with the shotties. We'd done business with these guys before, but a hundred pounds is a hundred pounds. We weren't about to be ripped off, eh. The shotties were loaded and they weren't there just for effect.

Nightfall was half an afternoon away so we kicked back on the veranda couch, smoked joints and watched the shadows lengthen.

He's ahi kaa, the old man. The fire has burned within him since Mahuika first drew out her fingernails to Maui's trickery, since the Potiki first raised up the land, so he has smouldered here before this mountain.

Here the spider speaks to him. The river foretells with its babble. The mood of the mountain informs. A quiet breeze reveals to him a pause in animosity of storm upon the forest in the war of ancestors, where brother battles brother for the land beneath his feet, whose mauri even now rises within him and calls him taku tama.

All his life he has sustained the remnants of this old marae. The mana of the lands around it, river, mountain, hinterland, resides in him, te ahi kaa, the burning fire, the unextinguished flame . . .

A suit was kicking me awake — nothing violent, you understand, just kinda tap-tap-tap against my leg with a shiny shoe. Another suit was doing the same thing to the bro, eh. He had nice shoes as well — the suit, not the bro. The bro's shoes were shit.

'He takes a bit of waking, eh,' I mumble, knowing cops when I see them.

'Having a nice kip there, matey?' the D that kicked me awake asks pleasantly, and with a smile.

We must've crashed out for a couple of hours.

'I was, yeah . . .' I said, trying to rub the stone from my eyes and get my instant shit together.

A hundred pounds of weed and two loaded shotguns . . .

The bro woke up . . . eventually.

He took one look at the smiling detectives standing over us on the veranda and the four armed uniforms and two drug-dog handlers waiting on the lawn in front of the house, with Scooby Doo and Lassie getting hyped up on the ends of their leashes, and said, 'Aw, fuck it, maaan,'

'We've been talking to a mate of yours in the city,' said the D who woke the bro, and who was holding up the ounce we'd been sampling before we crashed out. The bro said, 'We never seen that bag before, officer . . . You musta put it there, eh.'

The D stuck his nose in the bag but he didn't need to. It reeked. He laughed. Scooby Doo and Lassie started salivating.

'Good season, was it, fellas?'

We didn't say.

The first D started up again. I'm gonna call him Slick. He kinda was.

Slick says, 'Okay, here's a search warrant . . . Duly showing it . . . Acting on information received bla-bla-bla . . .'

The uniforms dispersed.

The bro called out to them, 'Hey, you look out for Grandad, eh. He's . . . old . . .'

'Don't worry about Grandad. Worry about yourself.'

Don't know which one of them said that.

Slick does all the talking now.

'Like my colleague said, boys, we picked up an acquaintance of yours in town on what we'd refer to as an *unrelated matter* . . . You could say you're the victims of an unfortunate coincidence in many ways, fellas . . . Ah well, shit happens . . .'

A hundred pounds of weed and two loaded shotguns . . .

'. . . so anyway, it turns out this guy's got himself in some deep do-do with one of the gangs — you boys know them, by all accounts . . . you've been dealing with them for years . . . that's what *this* guy's saying . . .'

A hundred pounds of weed and two loaded shotguns . . .

'. . . rather bust you doing the deal, of course . . . We could haul the lot of you in and you'd all get seven or eight years and it'd be my shout down the pisser when they lock you up . . . but guess what . . .'

Slick expected an answer, so we said, 'What?'

This seemed to please him, so he continued.

'Well . . . *this* guy says they're gonna do the dirty on you and blow you boys away later on tonight . . . So whadaya think that means, eh?'

A hundred pounds of weed and two loaded shotguns . . .

Slick was enjoying his story so much we said we had no idea what it meant, just to hear the rest of it. We needn't have worried; he was going to tell us anyway.

'It means,' Slick went on, 'that we have to decide whether to let you dickheads show so we can maybe watch it turn to shit and then do someone for murder . . . I mean, career-wise, it's an attractive thought

— a couple of *resolved* murders always looks good on a cop's CV, y'know — or do we come up here instead for a nice Sunday drive in the country and bust a couple of scumbag dealers, *ironically*, saving them a bit of grief in the process? Whadaya reckon about that, eh, *Rangi* . . . you know what *ironically* means?'

He said *Rangi* like the phone *rang* but no one answered it. He was looking at me when he said it.

I reckoned a lot of things right then but all I said was, 'My name's not *Rangi*, eh.'

Slick was just getting started, though, and he continued his ramble as if I'd said jack-shit, dismissing me with a waggle of an indifferent finger and a quick, impatient look.

'But *wait* . . . there's *more*, son . . . Y'see . . . if we happen to find a *significant* amount of — saaaay, *cannabis* — in the course of our search . . . I dunno, maybe *a hundred pounds*, for example . . . well, there are *consequences, Rangi* . . .'

He got in my face and showed his teeth.

'You could lose the lot, shit-head! Go to jail. Lose your house. Lose your land. Whadaya reckon that would do to the old man . . . eh, *Rangi*? Knowing his grandsons lost him his precious *feh-noo-aah*?' Hanging the question by the neck.

We said, 'Fuck you!'

Slick spat back, 'Fuck you too, girls.'

'No drugs t'speak of. Two shotguns in a ute out back — made safe. Sarge's got 'em. The dogs were pretty interested but all we found was a couple of roaches in th'ashtray . . .' One of the dog handlers was reporting back to Slick. 'Y'might wanna have a look at *that*, though . . .' He was gesturing toward the back of the house, but we couldn't see anything from where we were sitting.

Slick eyeballed us. 'Don't fuckin move!'

His partner leaned on one of the veranda posts, watching us with a shit-eating grin, to make sure we didn't. Slick headed around the back of the house to see what the dog handler was talking about.

Scooby Doo and Lassie got put back in the dog van.

A couple of roaches in the ashtray?

Where the . . . ?

The bro and me looked at each other with empty-space expressions.

It didn't take the uniforms long to search the house. There was nothing to find in there. We had fuck all stuff in four square rooms. We lived simply and without clutter.

The Sarge wandered past with a shotty in each hand on his way to one of the marked police cars parked out front, where he opened the boot to secure the weapons and ammunition.

The bro calls out, 'We got licences for those, eh.'

'Not any more you haven't,' snarled the Sarge.

Slick came back. He was having a bit of a laugh to himself.

'Met your grandad, fellas . . . Nice old codger. Looks like Ray Charles in those sunglasses. Deaf as a fucking post, though. Likes t'keep himself busy, eh?'

'Yeah . . . that's him all right . . .'

'Yeah yeah . . . I can see that . . .' Slick was being agreeable again. 'Raking up leaves n'stuff out th'back there . . . Keeping the place tidy . . . Been burning rubbish all afternoon, by the looks of it, while you two losers . . .'

Slick shook his head. He was showing his teeth again, but they were smiling this time. 'Lights a pretty fierce fire, that old man.'

The suits were conferring. Sarge was having his say as well. We hadn't shifted from where the cops first woke us up.

Slick gave us the hard word.

'You little wankers are *so* fucking lucky . . . And you've got that old man to thank for it . . . I should haul his raggedy arse in for obstruction!'

He paused to let that sink in, before continuing. 'We're taking that bag and we're taking those roaches and you're gonna lose your shotguns . . . And you still might get busted if I can be fucked with the paperwork for a shitty ounce . . . But it means your fucking cards are marked either way . . . So if you two come back to my city and start selling drugs again then I'm allowed t'shoot you and I fucking *will* . . . And I'll get away with it because I'm the cop and you're the wasters! And not a word to those bastards you were doing business with . . . Got it?'

'Sweet as, man.' We meant it.

And there were other cities.

That was it. They left in three cars and a dog van, cascading a trail of dust behind them, dwarfing even Aunty's ride.

We just sat there.

Two stunned mullets.

'Fuck me,' said the bro.

The old man came shuffling out onto the veranda. He didn't look our way but he was talking to us.

'*No more, eh, boys,*' he uttered quietly into the settling dust, and then he turned around and shuffled back into the house, closing the door behind him.

DAVID EGGLETON

The Feijoa is Brother to the Guava

THE BOARDING HOUSE IS AT the bottom of a gully that slopes down from the long ridge of the Great North Road. Here, below the shantytown reef of roofs, the old villas and cottages are just wooden crates, a lot of them done up by developers now, but a few are untouched and slowly subsiding into the undergrowth.

Rat Central is what we call this place. Rodents scurry beneath the floorboards. Birds rustle in the ceiling. There's the thrumming noise of TV's yacker and radio's hard sell coming through the walls — the noise of the hidden residents cocooned away in their sunless and stagnant rooms. I suppose I'm one of them.

The people who live here, well, we've brought our ghosts with us. We're the inhabitants of a looped loserville that's been halfway gaffer-taped together and called mended. Supposedly. Sit out on the veranda among the furtive smokers and you'll get the hard-done-by stories, one by one.

Louisa has survived one of the last practising backstreet abortionists and she still nurses a grudge, stamping around the house in jandals and the same faded op-shop frock every day. Trevor's an ex-wharfie who got crushed in an industrial accident. He hops along, hunched and humpbacked and bullnecked, his tilted chin jutting upwards, his beady eye on you just like a scavenging seagull. He's developed a squawk, too, spluttering about the compo he blew in a couple of years.

Ben's a young fellow who says he's been weirded out by his strange upbringing — his family were in a strange cult that worshipped the tree frog in a hippy commune out in the Coromandel. Now he distributes Bible pamphlets up on K' Road. He's got the jive of crazy hands and the patter of a born-again preacher, but his eyes always look panic-stricken and shun your gaze and his true god is Prozac.

Adrian's a wrinkly from a bygone era. Tells me that as a teenager he worshipped at the 1960s shrine of an unholy trinity of pop — Janis, Jimi and Jim. In those days he wore platform shoes and bell-bottom loons and had seventeenth-century hair tumbling in curly locks, and he bowed to the greater glory of Led Zeppelin. 'Hey Henry, it's been downhill ever since,' he cackles at me. Adrian quit school to play bass in a covers band and occupy a succession of rented rooms that were heavy with the fug of marijuana. Then he became a casualty of one too many psychedelic brainstorms after an acid trip. He spent years in the bin. Now he says he's just ghosting — a hangover from the suitcase wasteland of '70s back numbers. But his face crinkles into a gnomic smile as he tells you this — like a piece of cardboard that has been unfolded and refolded many times.

Me, too: I'm a denizen of struggle street, been educated in the school of hard knocks. Left home early — didn't get on with the olds. Ended up in a gang. We used to settle business with boots and fists. Yep, back then I was strutting tall among my misfit mates, agents of misrule. But to be always fighting, you know, it's life in a collapsed scrum. I ended up staggering around like a punching bag, one full of broken springs and miscellaneous lumps of metal. Had to get out of that.

Anyway, upshot was I decided to go solo, become a stairdancer, take the back way into office buildings during lunch-hour and give them a going over. Yeah, I was a good thief — put the stuff down my pants, inside my coat, in a bag, down a sock, up my sleeve. Used to be always out casing some joint, or else living it up. But then I got caught, eh. Not on the job — I had this old puttabomb of a car, and anyway the cops pulled it over, found all this property in it. So I went to jail.

Still pretty young and green back then, but I came out a boobhead, fully fledged and staunch as. Did some more burgs and went back inside. That's when I started to change my attitude, but. Because by that time I was a hard case, chemically dependent something chronic. Had seven devils on my shoulder and Hakana the Great on my back. Yeah, was pinged-out and frittered sideways, bro. Talk about suck it and see. I looked in the mirror and saw a death's head staring back. So in prison I slowly kinda got educated — had to. Not boobhead university exactly, but just the steady influence of social workers and agencies and all that.

I took courses in psychology. Got to know the mental fallback positions, all the psychological default modes, how to push the right buttons for the parole board. Anyway, in the end they stuck me in this boarding house and I've been here a long time now. I travelled to Hellangone and came back, so I reckon this could be a place to make a stand — or tread water.

I was going past a dairy the other day — one of those ones with fruit boxes out the front? And I saw this sign up, caught my eye. It said: 'The feijoa is brother to the guava.' Underneath it was this polystyrene tray of bright green fruit, glossy and green, but when I stopped for a closer look I saw they were all speckled with little bruises like they were going rotten. Dairy owner came out and said there was nothing wrong with them. They were sweet as. I looked him up and down, then kept on going.

Down here in the gully, days, weeks, months pass and nothing much happens. We idle away the days on our pensions and benefits. Nod to the rats scuttling beneath the floorboards. Same old same old. So what I've taken to doing is roaming up out of the gully — the valley of discontent where we fumble with the ladder of our twelve-step fellowship — and roaming into the tangle of surrounding streets. Kinda tracing out a crisscross pattern on the map. I roam the city's overpasses and ravines. From Grey Lynn to Kingsland to Eden Terrace, over to Grafton and through the Domain, just roaming all day long, dogging my own footsteps.

Up on Great North Road, wandering past the endless jamborees of car sales yards with those fronds of plastic pennants along the skyline, it's like the whole place worships the car. And in summer, when each day seems to tread on the next one's heels, sticky with humidity, you feel you're wading through the fermentation process of something toxic. What is it? It's smog, dude, with the smell of fried garlic spiking the exhaust fumes. Look around, you can see it, like smoke in a bottle, a pall of fluorocarbons misting up the atmosphere. Auckland's petroleum dream shown up for what it is — a petrochemical seepage created by all that traffic filtering through its innards. And as you walk you go on sucking that bad medicine into your lungs — some rush, eh?

Anyway, along I tramp to Karangahape Road, where I did my time as a squeegee merchant, cleaning windscreens, cadging loose change. Now it's the money merchants who've hit the real estate jackpot, and Skid Row these days overlooks building-site panoramas. It's a sweet spot for skyscrapers. That's where they're putting New Zealand's shiny new front teeth. But all you can see for the moment, peering down into the foundations, is a mosaic of steel rods, access ducts, conduits, wires, pipes and drains. The noise of machinery is the manic pulse of the city. Too much noise. I press ahead, zoned out, tuned into a blank frequency, blocking out the blare, the grumble and growl of buses and trucks.

Cars wait at the stoplights like runners in a race, crouched for the gun. Inside, drivers' eyes are darting at the rear-vision mirror, while fingers absently probe an ear cavity or nose cavity, or drum the steering wheel, and a leaden foot drags at the brake. At green, with a surge, a beat-up Beamer Death Ray guns the crossing and screeches right into Queen Street, making my skin crawl. That'll be Kingsland George with his out-of-it young streeties. Makes my skin crawl.

Maybe I'll turn away into the park, do some texting, meet with a buddy from the old days, just to catch up. A token pull at a bottle of hooch and a yak, or if it's Zeph there, shaking his dreads, we might set fire to a spliff, inhale his feverish realm of cloud castles and dragon-slayers, until the cicadas begin to shrill like a billion cellphones, sunlight starts swarming through the eucalyptus, and the whole luminous feverfew of the place begins burning its chlorophyll magic into my thinking, and before I get too pasted, I have to get up and push on, past the phoenix palms, across the tufty grass, across the greensward, towards downtown, towards the waterfront, because, yep, I've got to keep moving: a side-effect of my medication.

Out on the Waitemata, yachts are puffing out their white sails over their rushing keels with a crackle like that of hot popcorn expanding. The windjammed canvas could be the shirts of passing tourists billowed out by the breeze, or a restaurant tablecloth caught by a gust and flicking off slow flies while knives and forks clatter to the ground. And I'm just some patchouli-soaked and tattooed crusty crim left to loiter here by the Viaduct Basin, not a tealeaf stairdancer any more, only a trance-dancer sluggishly chasing my shadow through the concrete jungle, killing time.

Going up Queen Street, I ankle past a busker with a one-string Chinese lute, and then two Japanese girls playing recorders, and then a CD's skittery racket emanating from a record store. In the helter-skelter, pedestrians bob and weave, and men in suits shoot their cuffs on their way into a corporate conference, and hoodies laughingly playfight in Vulcan Lane, and fistic men slope into a side-street gym.

Climbing the great lump of Albert Park, I have to park myself on a bench by the fountain to rest, and then, as thunderclouds roll in, I get up and set off down towards the Domain. Sheltering beneath a corrugated iron overhang, I listen to a downpour that sounds like the rattling of glass marbles on the corrugated iron, and suddenly there's rain everywhere, the tentacles of some kind of monster jellyfish bladder up from the sea. Flinging out from the sea like a thing uprooted, it's shark-grey all the way and spilling forth a jackpot of rain — ka-ching ka-ching!

The traffic has to be blinded by it. The vehicles zooming onto the motorway up the Grafton Gully on-ramp are beginning to slow and thicken until they're going at five clicks an hour in a dirty great tailback that must reach forward to the Otahuhu off-ramp or thereabouts. Blood clouds and magenta swirls of rainbow hover above the grey scrim of rain that skims the isthmus, wrapping the road-trains of traffic in traceries of mist and drizzle, until, with everything rinsed and steaming, the storm is rolling away as suddenly as it arrived.

It'll soon turn humid again — even those flying buttresses of cumulus swanning into view are damp and fungoid in the crevices. It's like a big boat, a waka, eh, this place — Auckland, I mean, blurred between sea and sky. Sometimes the sky seems to be at your feet, reflected in all those puddles, and all the water views might be in the sky. You feel after the afternoon rain as if you're floating along in a big bubble, here on the mysterious isthmus of Oceania. Yeah, lenses of water around the rotundas of hills, the big volcano tips with their scoria quarries. Living here, we are all kind of flowing ourselves, over the lava flows, down towards the tidal lagoons over Orakei basin way or Herne Bay way, and then over toward Penrose — that's portage country, where they used to carry their waka across. Man, I love it, love to patrol around this littoral — it's like the decking of a boat that's cresting waves. Go crawling up the side of Mt Eden and there's the twenty-first century below you: you can address it from up there, bro, from the lookout over to the container stacks of the port, stacked like so many cardboard boxes in a shoe shop. You could be in the crow's nest of a windjammer about to cruise out, the whole city below you— city of sails — setting sail, off to drop anchor in some new harbour, following those brilliant last rays out over the Waitakeres.

Somehow, dinnertime nearly always finds me fetching up at the Mission for a feed. There's a good crowd there. It's a chance to see who's still around. I was thinking of my mate Grizzo — haven't seen him about lately. He was a buzz, that fella — came from down country. Yep, I was inside with him. Good to watch your back, look out for you. Yep, Grizzo with his pebble-thick glasses and tattooed heft of chest, part Mr Magoo, part Mr Magog-man, bro! He was a goer. He'd pub-crawl till he chundered, that bloke, then stagger up from his knees and sway forward to the next bar, intent on a rumpus. He'd go till he was blacked out. Go till he was blotto. Where is he now? No one knows. He's disappeared like so much bulldust. Actually, I heard he'd disappeared up into the hills of Taranaki with some sheila to run an ostrich farm. I dunno, could be.

The bar tragics, the marathon drinkers, the couldabeen youse — you want a good ending for them, you want them to have fluked it. You think of them as barnacled and battered whales that have somehow managed to elude the driftnets and harpoons and swum away into the sunset, to some undersea grotto. Hey, bud, time to chow down on a reality sandwich. It's way more likely they kidney-punched themselves into an early grave, done in by their own demons.

Like those kids out there I bump into huffing from glue bags. They pop up from under a bridge or somewhere, join the crawling king snake of the street, hustle you with hands out, then slouch from sight. They are, like, way beyond problem children — salvation for them is a tinny house and being a gang prospect. Or maybe getting taken up by Kingsland George, that whisky-breathed old perve in his Beamer. See him around a lot, especially after dark, his reedy voice a harmonica of wheedling tones. Only time I've seen him lug his heavy gut out of the car is when he's on a triumphal march into a bottlestore up on Ponsonby Road.

Sparkly old Ponsonby Road. Road for ponces, all right. It's prospectus of Ponsonby to you, mate. Cost you an arm and a leg for a good possie. Stroll along there after dark and get stampeded by the well-heeled snatching a prime spot in a restaurant. All the aromas catch your nose — perfume, spices, vinegar, garlic, grilled steak. And a sort of charcoal glow everywhere, like they're barbecuing the fat of the land.

Peer through the windows at the candle-lit flicker within. Blackboards with chalked-up wine lists being aligned with the chink of happy testimonials from glass and plate and uproarious scrum-downs of glad-handers around tables. All that chatter. They'll be swapping goss about the confetti blizzards of the internet, or the celebs on the box, or about the doings of their kids or what the neighbours are up to with the back yard. Lotta hooha about nothing — the town's grapevine ripening sour knowledge. But nobody's asking me.

So I plod past the bars where the believers in the possibility of the serendipitous congregate. After a few drinks, all these textbook examples of animal magnetism recklessly eyeball one another, hormonal fixes kicking in. Clusters of young women smirk delightedly at their own wardrobe malfunctions; gaggles of smiley-faced blokes chase along.

Stand outside the old post office up Three Lamps, for instance, among the pavement smokers, and listen to the affable volubility floating out of the bar it's been turned into, launched on a tide of beery bonhomie. And that farewell chorus you get: *You call me — I'll call you — you call me — I'll call you — call me* . . . All the funfair of the ringtones, whippedy-do.

Used to be into that myself once. Nah, it's a lot of hooha about nothing. Spare me the reruns. The stone-cold truth is, I'm happier down among the dump-bin divers, the wind-drifters, the vagrants. Been buffeted by that yadda yadda too long; I'm glad to be over all that aggravation.

The sky is grey in the violet night and their sparks are wooshing away from me, and the neon skyline is blazing, and it is breathy and fevered up here among the crowds on Ponsonby ridge. I've got to move on — business in town — so I plunge down into the dark of Freemans

Bay, along back streets where it's dark enough on this Pacific night to dig the grave of a knave.

The nocturnal ambience has the velvety feel of great whirring moth wings, and out of a momentary deep pool of stillness and quiet rises the yee-haw of a donkey siren chasing down a fire. Could be some greasy spoon combusted, or some shanty-town bungalow gone up. Then the midnight song of a car burglar alarm starts. Brings back memories. Up ahead now the tower of Cyclops, its big concrete shaft glowing with a cold, blue light. Out of moon craters of blackness, glass-sided wands poking up grids of light. A graveyard of big apartment blocks emerges in front of me, each apartment with its little balcony window all in rows like trapezes for acrobats of light to dance up. Sure, sure.

I've arrived. The casino. Stop, first, to draw out my monies from a cash machine. Goes in at midnight, and tonight's the night. Then up inside to where night and day dissolve into a continuous ever-glowing present, and it's hushed like the hush of rain, so you can concentrate. And here I sit, alongside the good, the bad and the sun-starved, a commodore of spindrift, my deck a squat stool through which I keel the seawrack on wings of surf and time. I'm inside Cyclops' tower, where the pokies rattle their jackpot shackles, and a billion chains of stardust glitter, and a tuning-fork hum crackles through your pockets to a salsa beat. You gotta squash doubt here, bud. Wait for a winning streak. And mayhap, after all the beeps and gurgles seem to have been churning forever, the blinking signs will halt on a regurgitation. A blurting of rodeo trumpets. A slurry of coins. The rinky-dink ice-cube clink of cool dollars. So, this time I beat the one-armed bandit to the draw.

I look up and around at the wry-mouthed coin-spinners ranged beside me, still lost in speculation, hot-breathed and malodorous, with hands that clutch at buttons, hands out on the ran-tan, a night on the pokies. Get a nod or two. I tot up my winnings, a few hundred, and quit while I'm ahead. Been a good night.

Outside, it's chill, but the air's clean, kinda purified, and the darkness has begun to dim and pale. Wakas of stars are paddling away. And against the matador's cape of dawn the constellation of Taurus has entered the arena. But it's fading, too, as I head for home, and, as I walk, on a red-eye flight out of darkness into mango orders of messy sky come the booty-licious colours of sunrise, clearing in thinnest air from yellow, red and orange to the blue juice of day. The city stirs in her sleep.

CHARLOTTE GRIMSHAW

The Body

THEY WERE CRAMMED IN THE car: Bennie who'd had to be dragged because he didn't want to look at a dead body, the other three children bouncing and chattering, Emily driving and her mother, Beth, reading the map.

'You've gone wrong,' Beth announced.

Emily turned the car around. They drove slowly, peering at signs.

'There,' said Beth in triumph.

They parked. There was a languid silence. They were in Mt Wellington, on a street of shabby wooden houses. Number one, on the corner, was a tiny bungalow with a porch and a scruffy lawn in front. It was hard up against the concrete warehouse that had its entrance on the main road.

Emily looked behind. Bennie, her nephew, was grimacing behind his hands, shaking his head. He was a big boy, nearly ten. She tried a wry, ironic tone: 'It's meant to be good to see the body. It assists in "closure".' She scratched quote marks in the air.

And Beth, who felt strongly on the subject, having been denied a look at her father when he'd died, and having *dreamed he was alive* for years afterwards, chimed in: 'It's crucial!'

But Bennie said, 'I didn't know her.'

'You met her,' Beth said good-naturedly.

He sighed. Deep gloom was Bennie's natural state.

They coaxed him from the car, watched by Antonia, his younger sister, and Paul and Caro, Emily's children. Bennie stood jigging, his hands in front of his mouth. There was a wide, strained smile on his face.

On the porch were two empty beer crates and an old couch. There was a big pile of shoes.

'I'm not taking mine off,' Emily said.

The door opened. The Reverend Matiu stood at the door in his socks. 'Aah, kia ora.' He stretched out his hands, kissed, made sounds of welcome and professional sorrow.

The children took off their shoes. Beth, looking guilty and vague, took hold of Bennie and yanked him into the hall, keeping hers on.

Emily followed. The Reverend looked pointedly at her feet, then stepped back, allowing her to pass into the sitting room. The room was dim and very small. Net curtains covered the windows. A floral couch against one wall, a three-bar heater and a small TV mounted on a bracket high in a corner. In the middle of the room was the open coffin, in which Emily's Aunt Jenny lay tucked up in a white lacy nightie. She'd been brought here, to her son Don's house, from the hospital where she'd died. Her hair was snowy white; her face was swollen and faintly shone, as though glazed.

Bennie took one look and retreated, covering his down-turned mouth.

'Ugh,' he said.

Chrissie greeted them. She was Emily's first cousin, and the Reverend Matiu's wife.

'Come and see Mum. You can talk to her — see?' She patted her mother's still forehead. 'We're glad you came, aren't we, Mum?' she said to the corpse.

Beth went close to the body, her fists clenched, eyeing it beadily as she might have looked at a good piece of beef at the Remuera delicatessen: 'She looks very nice, Chrissie.'

'She's never left alone,' the Reverend Matiu said. 'We talk to her, keep her company until she goes. In the Maori way.'

'That's right, eh, Mum?' Chrissie said. 'Never leave you alone.' She stroked the dead white face. 'I'll make some coffee, eh?'

She took the children into the kitchen. The Reverend withdrew with a discreet cough, leaving Beth and Emily with the body.

Beth sank down, sighing, on the couch.

Emily said, 'The Reverend's taken over.'

'I don't suppose she minds.'

They looked guiltily at the coffin.

'We're not Maori; Jenny's not. Why do we have to do things the Maori way, just because Chrissie married one?'

'How about that coffee?' Beth said.

Emily bent to look at a photo on the wall. 'What about not leaving her alone?'

'Oh . . .' Beth waved her hand. 'We're going for coffee, all right?' she said to the body.

Emily followed her from the room.

Jenny's son, Don, was in the kitchen. He wore his peaked cap pulled low over his eyes. Two young Maori women came forward. Don gestured, awkward, looking away: 'Aunt Beth, my cousin Emily — this is my girlfriend, Hine, and her sister, May Rangi.'

Hine was slim, sharp and pretty; May Rangi was heavy, puffy-faced, her hands and arms marked with crude tattoos.

Hine went to the sink. 'I'll make coffees for youse. Chrissie's feeding the dogs.'

Through the door to the back yard Emily could see Caro standing near a slavering Rottweiler. The Reverend appeared.

'We're having coffee,' Beth said. 'Jenny doesn't mind.'

Matiu smiled in a forgiving way.

'She can hear us from here,' Don said, from under his hat. He looked sideways at Beth and let out a giggle. Beth grinned.

Matiu pursed his lips. 'Ah, times of strife, eh,' he said into the air.

'It's very sad,' Beth said. 'We did have some nice times at the end.' She wiped away a tear.

'Kia ora,' Matiu said softly.

The dog barked. Caro shrieked.

'Is that dog all right with kids?' Emily asked.

'Get away, you bugger,' Chrissie growled from outside. She crossed the yard wielding a big bone. The dog followed swiftly. There was another shriek.

'No, good as gold, mate,' Hine said comfortably. 'It's the other one you've got to watch, but he's got a muzzle on. Take no chances with him.'

May Rangi laughed. 'He's a bad one.'

Emily went out to the small concrete yard, bordered on one side by the warehouse wall and on the other by a corrugated-iron fence. On a wooden picnic table were three institution-sized cooking pots, one of which contained cuts of raw meat and bones. There was a barbecue, and beside it a cactus grew in a concrete pot. The dogs lay chewing on bones. The sun came into the yard and a gust of wind blew the fly-strips on the door. Caro poked one of the dogs with a stick. It whipped its head around and stared at her, then turned back to its bone with a groan.

'Better not do that.' Chrissie took the stick. Bored, the children trailed inside. She wiped her hands on a stained towel. 'Is Uncle Per . . . ?'

Emily's father, Per Svensson, had been at his sister's bedside when she died — a prolonged, horrible dying: he'd described it to Emily, tonelessly, over the phone. Then he'd gone — not home, but to the studio where he worked. Emily had driven there after the phone call, wondering whether there was something she should do. She'd said, experimentally, 'You must feel very strange.' He didn't reply. She said, 'Should one . . . ?' They were standing at the door. He didn't invite her in. He was holding the cordless phone, pointing the aerial in front of him like a weapon. He looked fierce. She left. Whether he cared or not, she wasn't sure. But he wanted to be *alone*.

And now Emily's brother Larry and his wife Raine arrived. They were Bennie and Antonia's parents. Raine had been to a twee school down south; her vowels had never recovered. 'Gorgeous shirt, Beth,' she said, reaching over to finger the breast pocket. 'Ay'm making a dress in that colour. It's going to have paua-pattern shoulder-pads!' She smiled and smiled, widening her blue eyes.

'Lovely,' said Beth.

Larry stared and tensely grinned, as though he feared something was going to lunge at him and *bite*.

'How are you, Larry?' The Reverend's tone was caressing.

Larry cleared his throat. He said faintly, 'Good, Matiu. Working seven days a week. It's a fairly big job I do. A lot of responsibility.' He stared at the Reverend, defiant, cornered, managing to sound pompous despite the 'thing' that waited and watched . . .

'Poor Jenny,' Raine said. 'The children are with her. But Bennie's hayding in the car. He says he doesn't like bodies.' She let out an abrupt cackle.

In the sitting room the other three children were sitting in a row, their feet up on the edge of the coffin, watching *The Simpsons*.

Raine had one of her rushes of energy. She wrenched open the front door.

'Bennie!' she shrieked. The children looked up, startled.

She marched to the car and dragged him out, loudly telling him off. She hopped about on her thin legs. To the children, she sounded like a strange, harsh bird: Caw! Caw! She pulled Bennie into the room. But he shrugged and veered away and wouldn't look.

'It's only Mum,' Chrissie said, coaxing. 'Don't you think she looks lovely?'

'She looks dead,' he said rudely.

Raine yanked him into the hall. The door slammed. 'Locked him out,' she said. She gave her 'simple seamstress' smile.

Emily pulled back the net curtain. Black clouds were gathering over the street. The sun shone, and there was a strange, green-gold light. Colours were sharpened; for a moment the houses and fences gleamed, pearly-white, and then the clouds crossed the sun and the street went dreary and dark. It was hot. A strong gust stirred the rubbish on the grass. She saw her father's car turn slowly off the main road.

Beth and the Reverend got out a photograph album. There were ancient photos of Per and Jenny, little brother and sister, posed with their mother, playing at the beach. Twins, but different: already pulling away from each other, going in opposite directions. Later pictures: Jenny with her husband, the genial Barry, war veteran, Mason, lawnmower salesman, who'd taken care of his invalid wife until he'd died. Their children, Emily's cousins: Don, Chrissie and Ray. Things had got tough long ago, when Jenny first fell ill. Don ran away to live with the Maoris at the end of the street. At seventeen Chrissie married a drug dealer who carried a gun (but now she was a vicar's wife!). Ray was the solid, dependable one. He lived in America. He was in sales.

Emily went back out to the yard. Don stood looking over the fence, smoking. This was Don at family gatherings: his back to the group, his cap pulled down low, staring out at something, silent, absorbed. Waiting to be released.

The sky had turned dark over the warehouse roof. Emily watched a bird floating on the wind. Beams of sunlight broke through, shining on the twisted, hairy limbs of the cactus. She thought of the death notice she'd read that morning. It had been placed by Chrissie, Don and Ray: *'Mum. You were a breath of fresh air when all else failed.'*

Fresh air. When all else failed? She said it over to herself, frowning.

Don's shoulders twitched. She wondered, with a little thrill, whether he was crying. But he turned and ground his cigarette out on the wall, and in his blue eyes she saw something remote, secret, hard.

Larry burst through the plastic fly-strips, brushing them aside, his chest puffed out, like a lifeguard emerging from the surf. He looked from side to side and announced carefully, 'Hello.'

'How's work?'

He looked high-minded. 'It's fairly demanding, Emily. I'm handling literally millions of dollars of orders. I'm responsible for the whole city now. It'd be easier if I didn't have to spend so much time fixing other people's . . .' His voice trailed off. His eyes grew fixed. He was staring at the cactus. There was a silence.

'That's an interesting plant you've got there, Don. Is it . . . ?' He stood up and fingered the ugly, ridged green stalk.

'Yeah, it's one of those.' Don said. 'Boil it up, drink it, you're stoned out of your tree. Visions. Flying.' He spat over the fence. 'It's not my thing though, eh.'

Larry gave a strained smile. 'Not your thing,' he repeated.

But it was terribly much *his*.

The clouds were rolling in, gathering against one another, dense and black as Emily drove along the Onehunga Mall. There were three children in the car now. Bennie, in disgrace, had been squashed into his parents' car with a group of relatives.

'Something stinks,' Caro whined.

'You were a breath of fresh air when all else failed,' Beth said in a faint voice. There was a heightened silence. They didn't dare look at each other.

Per was in the carpark talking to a slim woman in a blue dress. He leaned close and she threw back her head and laughed out loud.

Beth said thoughtfully, 'Per drives like the wind, doesn't he? Like a fiend.'

'This is Sherry,' Per said, very taken with the tall stranger, who tossed her red hair and shook hands and said how nice to meet noo family. She was sorry it was the loss of Ray's mom that . . .

She was all smiles but Per abruptly tired of talking to her and said, 'Why don't we get started?' He glared around the group. Sherry was disconcerted; Beth looked amused. They began to file into the chapel.

Piped music played. At the front, by the closed coffin, stood a woman in a suit. She was the functionary laid on by Griefcare Funeral Services.

Heat from many bodies in a small space spread through the room. Children's heads drooped, the adults stared, open-mouthed, their eyes glazed. More piped music; they rose to sing. A series of prayers, more singing and then a pause. Emily looked up from a daydream. People were stretching and looking around; the woman in the suit waited with an encouraging smile. 'Now we can all share memories of Jenny's life. Who would like to be the first?'

Movement in the front row. Someone standing. And a sudden ripple — Per half rising, signalling angrily, 'No.'

Beth turned, startled.

It was Bennie, pushing his way along the row, ahead of everyone, about to 'share' something about his great-aunt, whom he had met only once on a hospital visit, when he and the other kids had paid brief unwilling homage before sitting out the boredom in the TV room with a row of tranced old folk. He was determined, frowning, his fists clenched. He turned to face the room.

But Per's ferocious expression made him waver. He paused. The silence seemed to last and last, until, slowly, he made his way back to his place and sat down.

Emily craned to see his face. What an odd boy he was. He hadn't known Jenny at all. What on earth could he have been going to say?

Emily's children came bouncing out with Chrissie's sons, who had made a speech about their grandmother in charming, piping voices.

Per said, 'I didn't mean to be *repressive*. But what was he going to tell us about Jenny? And to push in front of her grandchildren . . .' He looked around. 'I suppose Raine and Larry are annoyed with me now.'

But Larry, striding out of the chapel, had his mind on other things. And Raine, who thought Bennie would at least have been well spoken, unlike some other people, only smiled, jabbed her son lightly and said, 'Zip up your fly.'

'Are you going to the wake?' Emily asked Larry.

'So it seems.' He glanced behind.

Talking to Larry was like interrupting a watchman on a lookout (on a parapet, on a tower of melodrama): he answered but he stared beyond at some dark distant thing. His replies were cursory, secretive, condescending, because you, foolish innocent, didn't understand what was *out there . . .*

Three o'clock. Hot, mid-afternoon gloom. The city waiting for the storm that went on threatening but didn't break. The clouds were so black they looked purple; sometimes they parted for a moment and a shaft of sun lit the green slopes of the mountain. Light and dark on the hillside, shifting shadows.

Emily was driving home. There was a gap in her vision, a black hole with glowing outlines. The pain was gathering, waiting to break through in unbearable streams. She was desperate to get home.

At the wake she had glanced up at the crowd and seen, opening up before her, a long shaft of pure blackness, as if her aunt had carelessly left open a doorway to death, and she was staring directly into it. She'd waited a moment, until she was sure the migraine was really coming, then she'd gone looking for her mother.

And Beth had said, 'Oh, bad luck. You go. We'll bring the children home.'

She drove recklessly, yearning to be upstairs in the empty house, surrendering to it. She was capable of a kind of furious ecstasy during these crises of pain, and of a strange sense of luxury afterwards.

She shouldn't be driving. It was like accelerating into a black tunnel, its edges shimmering with vivid purples, starry greens. The visual distortions came first — the strange light effects, black holes. The pain was the second stage, the full force of the storm. Her eyes throbbed. And the sky, as if in reply, bulged and swelled with its own troubled atmospherics. The clouds hung heavy with rain, sheet lightning flashed; there was a rumble, then a crack, of thunder. She thought the weather had brought the migraine on — the stifling sense of energy, pressure building. And the difficulty of talking to cousins she knew but ought to have known better. Per and Jenny had been twins but remarkably different. There hadn't been many occasions when the families had got together. There were the bare outlines: Jenny's husband was dead; her son Don, since running away to live with the Maoris in his teens now spoke, lived and looked like a Maori, and ran a stall with Hine and May Rangi at the Otara Market. Chrissie, along with the Reverend Matiu, had some line in good works (social work, counselling?). Ray (the boring one) had escaped to the States. They all had children whom Emily didn't know, although Per had mused, after meeting a daughter of Don: 'Funny about the genes. I felt as though I was talking to my *mother.*'

Emily drove with one eye closed. The visual distortion, the agonised hour in the darkened room, then the languid recovery — it was such an intense, private battle. As she turned into her street the sky unleashed itself. Rain spotted then blurred the windscreen, and intensified to a roar. The noise on the car roof was tremendous. The last barrier broke inside her head and the pain flooded in.

Lying on her bed upstairs it occurred to her: this is what dying will be like. And she thought of that first warning at the wake, the shaft of absolute blackness splitting the air, as if a door had opened to . . .

Larry was alone. He got out of the car. Everyone was still at the wake and he had slipped away, saying he wanted to buy cigarettes. Don's house, hard up against the warehouse wall, was small, shabby and deserted. He knocked on the door and called, 'Hello.'

There was a garish pulse of light, followed by an abrupt boom. He stepped off the porch and peered down the south side of the house. The gap between the house and the warehouse wall was too narrow — or was it? Could he squeeze his way along to the back yard? He imagined, with a little shiver of laughter, getting stuck halfway: his smothered cries, scenes of consternation as they returned from the wake. On the other side of the house, a corrugated iron fence blocked the way. Larry dithered, looking at his watch.

Next door was a 'duplex' — two state houses stuck together and sharing a front yard. There was a driveway, a dead car on the lawn, and windows patched with hardboard where the glass was broken. There was no sign of life. He walked along the drive until he was level with Don's back garden. He could see the cactus, up against the barbecue, too far away to reach — he would have to climb the fence. He glanced back at the duplex and thought he saw one of the blinds move. He couldn't wait; they might be calling the police already.

He began to climb the fence. It was rickety and unstable. When he was wobbling on the top of it the iron buckled. He lurched sideways to steady himself, cut his hand, and his jacket snagged. For a second he struggled, teetering, and then he chose to fall forwards — no going back. He landed in Don's yard, his jacket ripped, his hand bleeding.

He peeped back over the fence. A window had opened next door. He ducked down. The sky was black and the green cactus rose — no, *reared* — against it, looking . . . magnificent. He was struck with such an exquisite sense of comedy that he leaned back against the fence and fairly shook. Here he was, preparing to steal (and for what a wicked, immoral purpose) while the family, quite ignorant, were solemnly grinding through Aunt Jenny's wake. He felt in his pocket for the knife, and the fact that he'd swiped it off the refreshment table half an hour before struck him as hilarious. It really was true: he had the most amusing time when he was alone.

He inspected the plant, gauging how he could cut the most off without it being noticed. He was expert at brewing up this kind of cactus; if you did it properly it would keep you high for days. What visions, what splendid vistas. It was like booking the most exotic and dangerous holiday. Absolute secrecy was required, of course. He had a private place where he could brew up — a flat belonging to a friend.

He began to saw. Careful. Mustn't be greedy.

A car door slammed. Larry's scalp prickled at the thought of being discovered. Especially if his father . . . He felt cold at the thought of Per. Mustn't panic. Don't give up now. The stem was tough but he got through it with a last effort. He wrapped it in the torn jacket, climbed the fence, and was up the neighbour's driveway in a flash. He tipped the jacket into the trunk of his car and drove away, stopping at the petrol station for cigarettes and a plaster for his hand.

Raine had been searching for him. He looked strange, pale, almost radiant.

'Larry! Larry!'

The children lifted their heads, startled.

He went obediently towards her.

Beth was in her kitchen, looking out at the storm. The house backed on to a reserve. The trees were tossing in the wind, and the rain lashed down. It was hot and steamy. At the table little Caro was making a potion. She put in detergent, flour, instant coffee, sugar, salt, pepper.

Per had gone to his studio, two doors along. He had been in a rage on the way home. She'd talked about Jenny and it had irritated him. She had felt him wincing and withdrawing. They had all four grandchildren in the back of the car, and only Bennie might have noticed that Per's silence and her talk stood for something. Me banging my head against a brick wall, she thought. Me kicking down his door.

Caro added tea-leaves and Ajax to her mixture. She broke a glass.

'Careful,' Beth said calmly. She picked up the broken pieces. The other grandchildren were downstairs. She had invited all four to stay the night.

It was sad about Jenny. She wanted to talk about it, have the odd luxurious cry. Per knew this, and reacted with cold contempt, as though she were a frivolous tourist traipsing through his private battlefield. What would he say? 'Be sad if you like. I'm not stopping you. You don't need me.'

Now he was alone, locked in his studio. He would never tell her what he really felt. He was hypersensitive, difficult. It was unfair . . .

'I want to cook it,' Caro begged. 'Please.' She wrapped her arms around her grandmother's waist.

Sighing, Beth poured the mixture into a cake tin and opened the oven.

'We'll turn the heat up really high,' she said, sliding in the tin.

Caro nodded. 'We'll feed it to people,' she whispered. 'Make them go funny.'

They sat together at the table, and soon the mixture began to heat up, sending a pungent, unpleasant odour out into the reserve.

Late in the evening, when the storm was at its height, the lights went out. Per walked through the house, trying switches. He went outside. The power was out all along the street. He remembered he'd left a window open in his studio. He felt for his keys, closed the door behind him and ran two houses along. He worked in the top half of this second house, and rented out the bottom storey, which was converted into a flat. He went to the window and looked out at the reserve. As far as he could see beyond the park the city was in darkness. The wind roared, sighed, howled in the big trees. When Jenny was dying he had sat at the bedside and listened to the terrible, harsh gasps, and he had closed his eyes and silently begged it to stop. Please, please stop suffering, die. He'd wanted to block his ears, to put a pillow over her face, and he'd sat, stony-faced and listened, in agony. At some point he'd stood at the window and seen, far away, a ship sailing out past the islands towards the open sea. He'd walked out of the room. The doctor was by the nurses' station. Per said, 'She tried to commit suicide last year. She was brave; it was her choice. They brought her round. *Why?*' And the doctor, a young man, looked at him with weary, intelligent eyes and said, 'She hasn't got long.'

Per stood in the dark. He saw her aged thirteen, coming up the street. Vivid, pretty. Slamming the gate, hurrying, angry about something. Sun on the garden, on the dry stone wall. Late summer. The smell of cut grass. Her dress. Her hands. She frowned and shouted over her shoulder at him, and ran off up the path.

He felt a crushing weight; his chest froze, and a sense of horror came over him. He sank down and sat on the floor in the dark, his hands over his face.

Images ran through his mind. The Reverend Matiu, an Anglican vicar, but still cleaving to the Maori way, talking to the body, never leaving it alone. Strange. It's good to have respect. But to stroke the body and converse with it, to pretend that it can hear? I could have pulled its hair, I could have pissed on it, what difference would it have made? *The damage is done.* Her grandchildren believed she was in heaven. But there's no God, he thought. Matiu's church — all churches are an intellectual slum. We come from dust and return to dust. There's nothing — no door behind the sky. She bored me, irritated me, filled me with guilt. She married a simpleton; I had an intellectual life. But in the dying, emptying face I saw something, felt it, raged against it. The destruction of part of myself.

Per walked slowly back to the house. Beth came up from the lower floor carrying a torch. They lit candles and sat in the living room, watching the white flashes lighting up the trees. The candle flames made shadows on the walls.

Per put two candles on the side table so he could read. He rearranged them, trying to get the best light. She watched him angrily. That's how he is, she thought. He works. He reads. Life goes on. It's as if nothing has happened. It's unbearable.

She threw her book aside. 'How can you read?'

He said stiffly, 'I'll get another candle.'

She turned to him, imploring. 'Say something. Please.' She put her arms around him, squeezing him tight, begging him to understand how she felt.

He sat silent, looking over her head, into the black shapes beyond the glass.

Everything was quiet and still. At 4 am the wind had died. The rain had stopped. Per and Beth were asleep, but downstairs the children sat in a circle around a lit candle, dividing a hoard of sweets.

Caro didn't like the strange shadows leaping on the walls. She moved closer to Chris. There were three green lollipops and one yellow. Yellow was much nicer.

'Don't touch,' commanded Antonia, and Caro whipped her hand away.

They listened. Bennie pulled back the curtain. In the reserve the trees were still, and there was a streak of pale light, like a seam, in the black sky. Antonia counted out the sweets, arranging them in piles. Bennie watched her ironically.

'You're such a control freak, Antonia, ' he said.

They were silent again. Caro kneeled up on Bennie's bed, looking out the window.

'Let's go out there,' she whispered.

'It's wet,' he said kindly.

But Antonia sat up and snapped her fingers. 'Good idea.'

Caro tried to look solemn, but beamed. 'Really? Shall we?' she said loudly. They shushed her.

Antonia crept upstairs. She took two more candles, Per's biggest umbrella and a box of matches. The back door was deadlocked; the lock was noisy. They would have to use the window.

They put on their clothes. Bennie eased the window open and climbed down the trellis. They got Caro onto the windowsill and dropped her down to him. She landed awkwardly, knocking him over. He put his hand over her mouth.

Antonia threw down the supplies, and she and Paul slid down and dropped onto the grass.

'How are we going to get back in?' Paul asked.

Caro stared at the dark trees, which could have been hiding something unseen and terrible. Everything looked different. She tried to make out shapes and outlines but the trees looked to her like huge figures, their arms outstretched, bending towards her. Above the reserve the sky was dark, streaked here and there with stray gleams of light. All around was the rustling and gurgling of water in the drenched grass, and far away a sighing roar, as if they could hear the last of the storm passing out of the city and whirling away, over the dark countryside and out to sea. There were so many sounds, and yet everything was so still; it seemed as if the park was holding itself in check, waiting . . .

'There might be a homeless person,' Antonia said.

There was a sudden rustling in the trees and a series of harsh, coughing barks. They moved close together. They knew it was a possum, but it was such an eerie sound they felt unnerved, until Paul darted forward and hurled a stick. The possum went quiet. They heard it crashing about in the branches, heavy and ungainly.

Caro looked at the sky and saw that the grey seam had grown wider, that a pearly light was coming from it. Inside that opening was the daytime. It was still dark, but the trees were no longer so black and monstrous, and as she watched, a fine, delicate rim of pink appeared on the edge of the clouds. There was a squall of wind and the trees heaved, sighed, subsided.

They walked through the park, away from the houses. Antonia knelt down and lit the candles, setting them carefully on the path. The others sat beside her and she put the umbrella up over them. They huddled in the circle of flickering light. There was a long dreamy silence. They watched the light turning gradually from dark to grey, and soon the colours of the trees and flowers began to show, and there were sparkles of light in the drenched grass. A bright patch gleamed at the edge of a roof and a streak of light came over the corrugated iron and shone on the trees. The clouds had frayed in places and there were pale spots that might soon become blue sky. They listened to a rat scuttling in the bushes, a car starting up in the street, the possum again, further away, making its harsh purr. A bird flew up and wheeled away, cheeping indignantly. Another beam of light crossed the grass, a twig cracked, a second bird started.

Caro looked at the seam in the sky with the daytime inside it. She'd never been outside in the night before. It was beautiful, mysterious, solemn. The darkness changed the shape of things and the dawn changed them back. When I grow up I will go out every night, she thought. And she saw a grey cat sitting on the path, watching her with unblinking eyes. It walked across the park, picking its way delicately through the wet stalks, its fur covered with tiny diamonds of dew.

First thing in the morning, Saturday, Larry went to visit his friend. They boiled up and consumed his stolen prize. Then he went home to work in his garden, a long, steep section that he and Raine had terraced and cultivated. He had made a bird-table, and he watched as the sparrows and blackbirds squabbled and hopped and pecked. The garden was full of life. He moved through it, his head pleasantly buzzing. The sun was hot on his back; he was dazzled in the bright light. He had cut down a small dead tree and was chopping it into pieces in order to carry it down the hill and load it on a trailer. He was enormously strong. The dead wood splintered, chips flew around him. Words came into his head and seemed to hang there, glowing, like paintings in a dark room. Yellowhammer. Kingfisher. Blackbird. The leaves shone; the palms were yellow, buttery. The air was full of tiny insects that scattered, regrouped, streamed through the brightness. Chop. Chop. The air flew apart, whirled to the sound of his axe. He worked fast, singing parts of songs.

When the tree was all in pieces he stopped and looked up. At the top of the hill, a few feet away from him, a man was watching him. He stood against the blue sky, moving slightly. He was all in black. His clothes were so black that they seemed to Larry to be an absence of matter, as if the shape of a man had been cut out of the blue sky, revealing a void behind. Larry stared, gripping his axe. He lifted it slightly. The man made a gesture: careless, scornful, as if to say that nothing could touch him. Then he came slowly down the path.

Larry dropped the axe and backed away. He blinked. The man had gone.

He went inside and locked himself in the bathroom. He looked at himself in the mirror. His pupils were large and dark. He sat on the edge of the bath. After a while, he had a shower.

He walked into the sitting room. Raine was talking to his mother on the phone. She clapped down the receiver and said, 'Ay've got to finish the wedding dress. You pick the children up.'

The wedding dress, commissioned by an old friend from school, was spread over the dining table. The table and floor were cluttered with paper and material and scissors and pins. The material was creamy, slippery, shimmery. It seemed to Larry to have a kind of rippling life in it; if he moved his head it looked like a stream of liquid running over the table and onto the floor of the sunny room. His wife stood with a piece of material over her arm, the sun behind her, lit up like a saint.

He went out and stood in the street and stared at the leaves, the patterns they made, light on dark. He looked at the hard blue sky, the atoms dancing in it. Raine opened the window and shouted from upstairs, 'Take them to the park. And get something for dinner.'

Larry waved vaguely and got in the car. The steering wheel was hot. He enjoyed the acceleration as he shot away from the kerb. After last night's storm the city was fresh and glittering, the sky blue, every outline sharp, with the photographic clarity of a perfect Auckland summer day. Mt Eden was wearing a shimmering halo of paler light. Larry drove and the air parted in front of him, silvery, liquid. He shot through it, as quick as a fish.

Bennie let him into his parents' house. He looked warily around for his father, but Per liked to spend Saturday afternoons in his studio. His mother got up slowly. The children milled around her, Caro with her vivid little face, like a troll . . . they were a cluster of trolls, gnomes, in a warm cave. Antonia did something with a roll of tinfoil; he stared at the trail of silver it left in the air.

They were saying things.

'We went out in the dark. We had to knock on the door to get back in. They got such a surprise. We made a cake. Look!'

Cake. A funny word.

His daughter gnome. Snaky blonde hair. His son, the light on his spectacles, so you couldn't see his eyes. Silver-eye. Wax-eye. Peeping at him from behind the opaque glasses. And the air, the way it parted as he came forward, the weight of the air, not silvery in here but warm and blurred . . .

She handed him a cup. Steam curled and slipped through the light. Careful, he thought. It was harder to keep steady in here.

He crossed to the kitchen and looked out at the trees. There was a trench of dark shadow beneath them. He listened to the drops of sound the tuis made — cluck, click, scratch, a pause, then a 'plonk', like a stone falling into water. Rosellas flew from tree to tree, flashing their bright reds and greens and yellows.

The trolls ran in and out, leaving scatterings of disturbed sound. His mother said something. He sipped his coffee, rigged up a smile, then struggled to get rid of it. He turned its full beam on Paul, who looked disconcerted and ducked his head.

Larry put the cup down, but it hit the edge of the sink and cracked. He stood over his children, fighting down the smile. 'Off we go.'

At the door he wondered whether anyone had noticed the cracked cup. 'The air can be very . . . heavy,' he observed quietly.

He swooped out to the car, hoping this would cover it.

'Where are we going?' Bennie asked.

'Killing time,' he told them. He thought about this phrase. It chimed in his head.

Killing time.

He drove them to the top of Mt Eden. They got out and looked over the suburbs. 'It's so beautiful,' he said. There were puffy clouds in the west; from them the sun shot down beams of light, what the Maoris called the ropes of Maui. He pointed. The children looked obediently, shading their eyes. They lay in the grass watching the clouds move in. The wind blew in the white flowers. Above them, on the ridge, busloads of tourists chattered, smoked and clicked cameras.

The drive down the winding mountain road was exhilarating. He stopped and bought ice-creams, but when they got home he'd forgotten about the supermarket. Raine shouted and complained. He watched her from across the room. She snapped and sparkled. The air flew away from her, sensitive to sound. After a while she went out to buy groceries, taking Bennie with her. He was left alone with Antonia. She turned on the television.

Six dressmaker's dummies lived in an apartment. Three male, three female. They talked; in answer, from somewhere unseen, came waves of laughter. The dummies tossed manes of blow-dried hair. Their mouths opened and closed. Their voices were nasal: quack quack quack. The laughter came blowing back, first a trickle, then a gust, then a real shriek. He listened to the quacking and laughing, and he became aware that Antonia, sitting on the floor in front of him, was part of the pattern; she leaned back and kicked her feet and — 'squeak squeak' — drew her elbows into her sides and giggled into her cupped hands.

He got up. He pointed the remote control and pressed the red button. There was a dry click. The dummies disappeared.

Antonia flew at him, grabbing for the remote, whining, cajoling. She made noises: 'Aw. Aw.' He held her off. Fantail. Silver-eye. Tui. She was as light as a bird.

She stopped trying to grab the remote. She stood up. Her eyes filled. She stared at him with her liquid eyes: a lost look. 'Why are you *smiling?*'

She ran away upstairs. Her bedroom door slammed.

He followed her, light-heartedly tiptoeing up the stairs. He stood outside her door, listening. He knocked softly. Silence. He knocked again. He could sense her in there, frozen, like a little animal. He went on knocking for a while, until he forgot why he was doing it. He laid the TV remote outside her door, went downstairs and outside. He saw there were some weeds. He began pulling them out, kneeling on the concrete path, absorbed.

EIRLYS HUNTER

WhatSmartGirlsKnow

'MOLLY!'

Deb opened the door of the sleepout again. Nothing had changed. Molly was still an invisible lump under the duvet despite the heat, and the floor was still covered with a tangle of wet towels, clothes, books, magazines and used tissues.

'You haven't even opened the window.' Deb picked up a peach stone that was seething with ants and threw it outside.

'Because of the bloody mozzies. Look. They hate me.' An arm waved above the pillow. 'I hate this place.'

Deb didn't have time for a scene. 'Just get up. Please. Alejandra's bringing her stuff in here now so I can get the spare room ready for Janet.'

'Bloody great. I'm going home.'

But when Deb returned with Alejandra's bedding, Molly hadn't gone anywhere, just plugged her iPod into her ears and rolled to face the wall. Alejandra also had her ear-buds in as she trailed silently after Deb, carrying clothes on hangers. Deb pointed out a nail she could hang them from, and cleared Molly's backpack, dirty knickers and damp togs off the other divan bed. She opened one of the drawers underneath to show Alejandra where she could put the rest of her clothes and a drift of borer dust floated out.

On the way back to the house Deb picked some calendula for the spare room and put them into a jam jar, which she balanced on the windowsill because the top of the chest of drawers was still covered with Alejandra's toiletries. She'd never known anyone who carried so many potions and lotions around with her; there was a sponge bag and a makeup bag, but also cleanser, moisturiser, toner, depilatory cream, body spray and something called spritzer, as well as several jars and tubes with labels in Spanish. Deb loaded them all into the laundry basket, which she dumped on Alejandra's bed. Alejandra had lined the divan drawers with precisely folded sheets of newspaper, onto which she was arranging scraps of lacy red and orange underwear. She received her toiletries with a shrug.

No dressing table. Deb fetched the camping table from the shed, hosed it, dried it and fitted it under the sleepout window.

Alejandra nodded. 'Have you a mirror?'

Roland's deckchair was opened on the lowest notch. His ancient shorts were belted below his paunch, and his brown legs and torso were glistening with the factor three he always rubbed over his body hair. It was his credo that the risks of melanoma were exaggerated and the benefits of exposure to sun under-researched. A thesis — one of three he was supposed to have marked before Christmas — was on his lap, and his eyes were closed under his cricket hat.

Deb put a mug of coffee into his hand and sat in the other chair. 'You look comfortable.'

'I'm okay.'

'I could still ring Janet. Say sorry, maybe another time — suggest a B&B?'

'It's fine. You like having people.'

'She's your friend.' Deb sighed. 'But it'll be good. Anyone to dilute the girls.'

'Alejandra was not my idea.'

'No.' There was a cicada, the first of the year. And a skylark. A lawnmower down the road, and someone else's children in the distance. 'After Janet's been and gone, will you do something with Molly?'

Roland scratched his belly. 'Molly? What sort of something?'

That was the problem. What sort of something? Roland's day didn't include things he could do with his daughter, even on holiday. His walks never took longer than fifteen minutes. He didn't play games, or swim, or even go to the supermarket if he could help it. And his cooking was limited to bacon, which Molly wouldn't have anything to do with since she read about sow crates.

'There must be a movie on somewhere? I don't know. Talk to her about what she's reading? Or what you're reading?' She picked up the thesis. '*Woman as Muse in the Poetry of Dante Gabriel Rossetti.* Maybe not.'

Roland grunted. 'I said I'd take her out for driving practice.'

'When she gets her Learner's.'

'Up to her, isn't it?'

*

Molly was trying to read *Jane Eyre*. She was trying to read it because it was near the top of the list that Crazy Chloe had posted on the smartgirls 'what smart girls know' forum. Molly was working her way through as many lists as she could. The films were easy because the public library had lots of them on DVD (*Casablanca, All About Eve, Clueless . . .*). The list of what smart girls should know how to do was easy enough too: she'd followed the links and studied the diagrams and was fairly confident that she could now put up a shelf, do CPR, bump-start a car and catch and cook a fish — she'd probably even manage the scaling and gutting if she was starving on a desert island.

But getting through the smart girls' reading lists was giving Molly trouble. She agreed with all Crazy Chloe's opinions about Iraq, animal welfare and body image, so she was trying her list first. So far she'd ticked off *Alice in Wonderland, To Kill a Mocking Bird* and *Pride and Prejudice*, though strictly speaking that was the DVD not the book. The main trouble with *Jane Eyre* was that it was so long — though shorter than *War and Peace*, which was also on Crazy Chloe's list. Molly had stuck with it, not skipping much, and it had been okay until Jane met the Rivers family, when the whole thing became totally deadly. Why did anyone bother with all that religious stuff? Crazy Chloe could probably do speed reading or something.

Nina Simone finished and Aretha Franklin started up; the music lists were so much easier to get through. Molly chucked *Jane Eyre* on the floor and turned her attention to Alejandra, who had finished putting away her clothes. She had folded her towel in precise quarters, and now she was arranging an emery board, balls of cotton wool, clippers and a small red bottle on it.

Alejandra's lips moved but Molly couldn't hear whether she was saying something, or just singing along to her music.

*

Janet drove up in an old rise-and-fall Citroen. She was wearing an off-the-shoulder black top that showed off her tan and her cleavage; Deb realised she hadn't changed her T-shirt.

Janet held her arms out to the lemon tree, the overgrown macrocarpa hedge and the toetoe.

'What a wonderful place. A real old bach!'

Two young men clambered out of the car after her. 'You haven't met my boys, have you, Debbie? This is Liam, and this is Tom. Don't worry, they've got a tent.'

They smiled at Deb, shook hands. Said what a lovely spot, and how pleased they were to be here. Liam was nineteen, studying architecture, and Tom was twenty-one and was doing honours in politics. They were both tall and friendly. Nice-looking boys. Liam wore glasses with red frames (Liam — Glasses) and Tom had an armband tattoo (Tom — Tattoo). They looked Deb in the eye. They asked was there anything they could do? Their mother said why not be sweeties and unload the perishables?

'I'm afraid the fridge is rather small,' said Deb.

The boys followed her into the kitchen with a chilly-bin and an espresso machine.

'Janet takes it everywhere,' said Tom. 'I'll leave it on the porch for now.'

He looked inside the fridge and made room for a packet of mascarpone on top of the milk, then he lined up punnets of blueberries, strawberries and raspberries along the bench. Liam took a bottle of Pimm's from the chilly-bin, a bunch of mint and a cucumber. 'Do you — by any chance — have some ice and a jug?'

Alejandra must have seen them arrive, for when she appeared at the French doors her shiny brown hair was held back from her face by a clip with a scarlet nasturtium tucked into it, and her brake-light red toenails flashed out of shiny sandals. Deb understood, for the first time, why some people found toes erotic.

Alejandra gestured to the tray loaded with glasses and asked prettily, 'I will take for you?'

Tom and Liam stepped forward to be introduced and when Alejandra grinned up at them through her thoroughly mascara'd eyelashes, Deb was startled to discover that this girl, who had been living with them since September, had dimples.

They processed across the garden carrying tray, cushions and folding chairs, heading towards the sound of Roland's snorting laughter. Molly was sitting on the grass guarding her father and scowling — or perhaps just squinting into the sun. Janet was sitting in Deb's deckchair, leaning towards him, face shaded by the brim of a large straw hat.

'I'm just relaying some scurrilous departmental gossip. Which you're not to pass on to anyone, Molly!'

Molly didn't appear to be listening to Janet; she was staring at the boys.

Everyone sat with a glass of Pimm's, some in the sun, some under the shade of the sun umbrella that Tom managed to wedge so it actually stayed up.

Deb looked from one girl to the other. Both were nearly seventeen. Molly's unwashed hair was pulled back so tightly her face looked stretched. She was wearing jeans and a baggy T-shirt and sat with her knees up so her rounded shoulders made a cave for her chest. She was picking away at peeling skin on her feet with fingertips that were pink and puffy from being chewed, and she was still scowling even though she'd shifted into the shade.

No scowls from Alejandra. The critical, monosyllabic stranger had vanished, to be replaced by an attractive flirt. She was smiling, listening, answering questions about Chile, and gesturing with her immaculately manicured hands. Her English was surprisingly good.

The boys asked Deb if she minded where they pitched their tent. They asked in a way that gave her the opportunity to veto, or express an opinion, but absolved her of responsibility. If this was the new generation of men, then lucky Molly.

They settled on the patch behind the lemon tree. Alejandra made encouraging noises as they threaded the fibreglass poles into pockets. She told them she had never slept in a tent. Deb could hear their laughter but not what they said in reply.

When she went in to marinate the steaks, Molly followed her.

'Why are they here anyway?'

'Because we invited them. They're going to a family reunion up north. It's only two nights.'

'Did you know the boys were coming?'

'I wasn't sure who she'd have with her. Last time I saw Janet she was with someone. Vernon. But they appear to have split up.'

'Go Vernon,' said Molly.

Liam and Alejandra came back from the beach and said they'd decided against swimming as the waves were too big and there were red flags over the surf lifesaving club. Deb agreed that they were lucky the bach was in such a sheltered spot.

What would they do now?

'I know! You like volleyball?' said Alejandra. 'We play volleyball? I see a net in the garage!' It was the first suggestion she'd ever made in Deb's hearing.

The boys took charge of the preparations. First, they led an expedition to find a matching pair of driftwood poles. Liam and Alejandra — which the boys had shortened to Al — went ahead, but Tom insisted that Molly come too, and waited for her while she put on her Docs. They returned triumphant, two to a pole. The strings to hold the poles up were tangled in with the net, so they laid it out on the grass and Liam and Tom took a side each and had an untangling race, the girls shouting them on and laughing.

The garden had become a stage. Janet and Roland seemed to have cast themselves as sideline commentators, mostly talking to each other but sometimes calling out approving comments so that everyone would know they were paying attention. Janet had ventured into the kitchen for a bowl, and while she talked she was creating a fruit salad, Nigella-style, with her punnets of fruit.

Deb knew that the volleyball ball was soft, and she hadn't seen the needle that attached to the bicycle pump for at least a year, but she didn't want the performance to end prematurely so she took the ball and walked up the road, bare feet on the short grass of the berm. She talked to neighbours she'd never met before, all of whom were glad to be asked but sorry they couldn't help, until she got to the corner section where a man with peeling shoulders said yes indeed, and that he was delighted to be of service. His garage wall was lined with shelves full of labelled containers. When he'd pumped up the ball he offered her a beer and urged her to bring the whole family next time.

Meanwhile, the boys had fixed up the net and marked one back line with the extension cord from the sleepout and the other with the washing-line, which Tom promised Deb he would tie back afterwards. They cheered when they saw the ball.

Alejandra emerged from the bathroom wearing a bikini top that barely contained her breasts, and a bottom that was little more than a thong.

'Okay-dokay!' said Tom. 'Al's playing beach volleyball.'

'Can you please?' She held the sunblock out to him, though as it was after four o'clock she probably didn't need it. He rubbed it into her back as requested. Greedy girl, thought Deb. Greedy, greedy girl.

'Bloody hell!' Roland's eyebrows shot up when he noticed Alejandra. 'Poor boys.'

Janet laughed and pressed his arm. 'I expect they can't believe their luck.'

'It's as if the seventies never happened,' said Deb.

'It's choice, though, isn't it?' Janet smiled at Roland. 'The seventies were all about choice.'

They had pulled the two deckchairs to the side of the lawn, and Janet's plump brown feet were up on the apple-box table, next to Roland's. Deb stood.

'I'm not sure how much choice women can ever really have,' she said.

Janet smiled. 'Do you think it feels that way to you because you've never had much of a career? It must make a difference.'

Deb laughed. She was enjoying herself too much to be angry. 'No. I think it's because I have a daughter.'

Molly had taken her boots off again, but that meant her jeans trailed on the grass, and her toes got caught. Deb had offered, many times, to take them up for her. Now Molly appeared at her side with the kitchen scissors.

'Cut them off. There.' She gestured just above her knees.

'Can't you take them off first?'

'No. Hurry.'

Deb cut, and Molly stepped out of the bottoms of her jeans to reveal muscular calves, and knees so perfectly round and smooth that Deb had to stop herself from brushing her lips across them.

It was Liam and Al against Tom and Molly, to start with. They batted the ball to and fro across the net, but this was just the warm-up. It appeared that volleyball would be done wholeheartedly, like everything else the boys engaged in.

'First to eleven?' said Tom.

'I'll serve,' said Molly.

Over the net fast, and straight to the ground. One–nil.

'Wow!' said Janet. 'Impressive.'

'She plays for her school. It's her sport,' said Roland. 'Which Alejandra may have forgotten.'

Alejandra played well too, but Molly and Tom were the stronger team. They slapped hands and whooped whenever they gained a point. When Molly slipped and let the ball hit the ground Deb held her breath, but Molly jumped up laughing. When she hit the ball down just out of Liam's reach Tom cheered.

Molly was grinning all the time now.

When they'd won eleven–eight, they changed partners and Deb had a closer view of Alejandra, who could jump high but didn't have Molly's power or sideways reach. The sun had gone from that side of the lawn and Deb was pleased to see goosebumps on Alejandra's legs and stomach.

Molly and Liam won eleven–seven.

'Which makes Molly the champion,' said Tom, patting her back. Roland was telling Janet what he thought about the proposed 200-level theory paper, and didn't notice.

They had a break. Liam and Tom eagerly scoffed the remnants of the Christmas cake that Deb brought out.

'Brilliant cake, Deb!'

'Did you make it? Wow, delicious!'

Molly watched them, then cautiously put some cake crumbs into her mouth. For the last three Christmases she had rolled her eyes and said, 'Why do you even bother Mum? It's so stupid. You're the only one who likes it, you know.'

'Girls against boys now?' suggested Al. 'Okay, Molly?'

But Janet announced that she'd like to play. 'Come on, Roland! Three against three: Wilsons against Maxwells.'

He protested, but she held out her hand and he allowed himself to be hauled out of his chair. Everyone seemed to assume that the third Maxwell was Alejandra.

'Are you sure, Roland?' asked Deb.

'Me and the girls, eh?' Roland looked pleased and swung his arms around in a parody of stretching.

Liam pulled a chair to the side of the net and said, 'Deb can referee first. We can all take a turn.'

'It's probably time I got the barbecue going,' said Deb, but she sat in the designated chair, reluctant to miss a moment of this other Molly.

On the Maxwell side, Alejandra was up at the net and Molly at the back. Roland stood in the middle with his hands on his knees. Deb wondered if he knew the rules. She'd watched lots of Molly's games, but the only game he'd been to was last year's regional final, in which Molly's team had been narrowly beaten.

Alejandra returned Liam's serve. Tom went for it, but Janet went for it too, and knocked it to her feet.

'One–nil to team Maxwell,' said Deb.

Molly's serve. Alejandra was making signals with her fingers behind her back. Tom got under the ball and passed it to Janet, who missed, but Liam lunged for it and got it over the net where Alejandra was waiting to hit it straight down.

'Two–nil!'

Molly gave Alejandra the briefest of hugs. Roland retreated to the back corner.

The game went on. Janet seemed to think she had to get to every ball, which meant she was always in the boys' way; Roland stayed near the back line, and managed to knock the ball forward a couple of times. He also served when it was his turn. Liam showed Janet how to serve but she couldn't get it over the net, even though they allowed her to stand almost under the net and have several tries.

The score rose to nine–four. Molly and Alejandra were laughing together, doing high-fives and taunting the boys, who went on being endlessly kind and tolerant of their mother, although she was always where one of them was trying to go.

Then Molly passed the ball to Roland, a gentle hit, and called, 'Yours, Dad!' and everyone saw Roland shuffling backwards, grimacing.

Molly shrieked.

Deb reached him as he crumpled onto the grass.

He tried to speak but he was in too much pain. Perspiration was beading along the creases in his face, and his lips and the skin around his nose were blue and bloodless.

Molly ran for his pills. Deb put one under his tongue.

'He's had angina before. Not like this, though.'

'How far's the hospital?' said Janet. 'I'll drive.' Deb got on one side of Roland and Tom went to the other. Liam ran to open the car door.

'No!' said Molly. 'Call an ambulance.'

'One. Two three, up,' said Deb.

Molly stood over her. 'You'll kill him. He's got to go by ambulance. I know. Put him down.' Her voice was low and urgent; she knew. They laid him down again.

Tom had his phone. Molly told him the address, and that he'd get better reception out on the road.

Alejandra brought a rug out for Roland. She'd pulled on shorts and a sweatshirt.

Janet paced up and down, shrieking, 'This is ridiculous! We've got to drive him. We'd be halfway to the hospital by now!'

Liam put his arm around his mother's shoulders and propelled her into the house.

Deb was kneeling beside Roland, holding his hand.

'Pill's not working. So heavy. Squeezing me.'

'Come on, my love, my love, my love. Breathe in. Breathe out.'

*

Molly prowled between Roland, lying grey but just conscious on the grass, and the road, where Tom was waiting to direct the ambulance into the turning. Ten minutes. Fifteen minutes. The ambulance didn't come, and didn't come.

Then it was there, quietly, without a siren and only a discreetly flashing light. Molly ran ahead, leading the way to her father. There was a man and a woman in the ambulance; they fitted an oxygen mask to his face and took his blood pressure and his pulse. The woman put a needle in his vein. She got Deb to hold the bag of fluid that was connected to the needle by a tube, then she wired Roland's chest up to a machine and took a printout of his heart.

The sun had gone by the time Roland was strapped onto the stretcher with a red blanket around him. The stretcher's wheels dropped down and he was rolled into the ambulance, oxygen mask, drip and all. Deb climbed in with him, and the driver said he'd take her, but the rest would have to follow by car. Janet went to get her bag. The ambulance pulled away, and then, while Molly was in the sleepout scrabbling around for her hoodie and her phone, Janet drove off.

The boys were as appalled as Molly was. Janet must have thought that she was in the ambulance, they said. Could they drive her in her parents' car? But the keys weren't on the hook so Deb must have them — and she didn't have her phone: it was sitting on the charger in the kitchen.

'They'll ring you; they'll tell you,' said Liam.

'But they can't.' Molly couldn't stop shivering. 'They can't ring, because there's no reception, so how will I know?'

'I got two bars on the road,' said Tom, 'We could all wait out there.' So they walked up to the road. Tom rang Janet but only got a message.

They crossed over to the beach where there was still two-bar reception and also logs to sit on. Molly sat with her teeth clamped together and her phone clutched in both hands, and stared at the waves that just came and came.

'You're cold. Let's light a fire,' said Liam.

They piled up driftwood. It caught quickly and the wind blew the smoke and the sparks towards the sea. Someone fetched a sleeping bag for Molly, and she wriggled herself down in it, pulled the hood over her head and buried her nose in essence of boy. Then Alejandra went over to the house to get a jacket and came back with the potato salad and four forks. When they'd finished that they passed around Janet's fruit salad, and dripped scarlet juices in the firelight. They discussed the possibility of cooking the steaks; Tom said they'd need lots of hot coals, so they piled more wood on. The last light faded from the horizon.

It was Tom's phone that rang, in the end. Janet told him that Roland was being admitted to intensive care and that he was what the hospital called 'comfortable'. She said that Deb was talking to the doctors and would ring Molly soon.

Liam brought a steaming plunger of coffee over from the house. Molly had never drunk coffee before, but it smelled so sharp, so real, so like her father, that she gulped it down hot and black. So now she was a coffee drinker. She wondered what would be next.

She was warmer now, and pushed her head and arms free from the cocoon of the sleeping bag. The boys asked about school, and compared exam systems with Alejandra. Still Deb didn't ring.

The fire lit up faces and then disappeared them again. Alejandra told them that her youngest brother had been killed in a car accident, and her father injured. She mimed words she didn't know: her mouth turned down, her head hanging — always sad. Depressed. Her father was depressed.

Tom's voice came out of the dark and said that their father lived in Sydney, and that his new wife was pregnant.

Then Liam said they'd spent Christmas helping Janet sort out all the family junk, binning twenty years' worth of stuff, as they might have to sell their house. She'd only just finished buying their father's share of the house off him when Vernon announced he was leaving her. They'd been living together for three years and two weeks.

'And after three years of living together the law says that he owns half the property,' said Tom. 'In theory. Which may mean our house.'

'I was born there,' said Liam.

'Oh my God,' said Molly. 'That's so totally unfair.'

In Molly's whole life until now the most traumatic thing that had happened to her was when her cat got a tumour on its spine and had to be put down. But now everything was different. She'd been admitted to the group of people to whom big things had happened. Their talking got louder, and they started to laugh. Everything was funny, and Molly rolled off the log onto the damp sand. She hadn't had any alcohol — none of them had since the Pimm's in the afternoon — but she felt drunk with fear and happiness.

*

It was after one in the morning when Deb left Roland sleeping, surrounded by softly beating machines, and went out to the waiting area beyond the intensive care unit. Janet was holding *Love at Last for Jennifer?* on her lap, but her eyes were closed. Together they followed the red line to the exit. Janet offered Deb her phone, but Deb decided not to ring in case Molly was asleep and the phone gave her a fright. They'd be there in fifty minutes.

It should have been fifty minutes, but Janet drove so slowly, hunched forward, peering into the darkness. And she kept yawning, even though she said she'd had two cups of vending-machine coffee in desperation. The headlights lit the empty tarseal ahead; the engine hummed; there was no traffic for mile after mile.

The doctor had said that Roland was as good as could be expected. He would need blood tests; they'd know more tomorrow — today.

Janet began to tell the story of the heart attack that had killed her father but Deb shook her head. 'This isn't comforting,' she said. 'If it's supposed to be?'

After some miles of silence Janet spoke again. This time she told Deb about how she might have to sell the house that she'd lived in for over twenty years, and about Vernon.

'He may even have been a con-man from the beginning. I don't know.'

'And you'll have to give him half?'

'The boys are both flatting now but they still need a home, a base.'

'Your boys are terrific.'

'They cancelled everything. Said they'd come to the reunion with me and make a trip of it. They were always considerate, but I think this business with Vernon . . .' Her voice was cracking. 'They liked him.'

Deb handed Janet a tissue from the wad she'd taken from Roland's bedside.

'It may sound stupid, but I think they're being so nice to me because they feel responsible in some way.'

'Responsible for Vernon?'

'No, no.' Janet blew her nose again. 'For showing me, you know, that not all men are like that.'

*

There was a thermos in the bag, and apples, biscuits and sandwiches. Molly unwrapped one for her mother and one for herself.

'Don't know what's in them. The boys made them while you were in the shower.'

'Kind boys.' Deb's voice wobbled.

'Yes,' said Molly. Cheese, lettuce, avocado, tomato and mayonnaise. Delicious.

Her mother yawned. 'Keep talking to me, keep me awake. So it's not surprising Al didn't know which one to focus on?'

'Honestly, Mum!' Her mother was so transparent. So predictable. 'If either of them had come on to her she'd probably have run a mile.'

'Oh.' Deb slowed at an intersection, then accelerated again. 'So, do you like either of them?'

'They're a bit old for me. Anyway, Tom's got a girlfriend. And Al thinks Liam's gay.'

'You smell of wood smoke. Nice smell.'

Molly put her feet up on the glovebox. 'Is Dad really going to be all right? I mean, you can't get brain-damaged from having a heart attack, can you?'

'I don't think so. He's going to be okay. You saved his life.' Her mother's voice sounded awe-struck — as if she was speaking to a stranger. 'He wouldn't have survived if we'd taken him in the car.'

She'd repeated this several times now.

Molly smiled. She picked up Deb's hairbrush from between the seats and tried to balance it by the handle on one finger. 'I have my uses.'

'You insisted. How did you know?'

'I thought it was the sort of thing I ought to know, so I read it. On the internet.'

'The internet!' As if it was the book of magic.

Ahead, the hospital chimneys appeared in silhouette against the lightening grey of the eastern sky.

Molly pulled out her hair-tie and started brushing her hair. 'Poor old Janet.' She meant it. Poor old Janet.

'You heard about Vernon? Yes, poor Janet.'

'I reckon —' Molly tried to find the words for the realisation she'd had. 'I reckon that Janet and Al are the same, somehow. You know? If no one's admiring them it's like — it's like they're not sure they're really there, or something?'

They stopped in the vast and almost empty carpark and Molly unclipped her seatbelt. 'And if that's true, then it must suck to be them, don't you think?'

For a moment there was silence, apart from the ticking of the cooling engine, then Molly found herself crushed in a hug, her face pressed into her mother's shaking shoulder. And the muffled sound that she could hear through arms and hair and hoodie was her mother's hooting laugh.

WITI IHIMAERA

I've Been Thinking About You, Sister

1.

BRIAN RANG YESTERDAY TO ASK if I would send him a short story for an anthology he was planning to publish. The trouble was he wanted the kind of story I used to write thirty years ago.

'It should be easy for you,' he began. 'People love your comic stories about hockey games or sentimental ones about old ladies playing cards, not to mention the epic tales of girls who ride whales to save their iwi.'

'Brian,' I answered, 'I was just a young man when I wrote those stories and the world was a different place. I'm not that same person any more, not as innocent and my voice is not as lyrical. Nor is my work so essentialist any longer; it's more synthesised. And I'm a professor of English, into postcolonial discourse, Freire, Derrida and *The Empire Writes Back.*'

'I was afraid you'd say something like that,' Brian sighed, but he was not about to give up. 'Maybe you've got a story that you put in a bottom drawer years ago, something you wrote before you became, well, political? Something like the story you wrote about the wily Maori tohunga who puts a spell on a red-headed Irish woman? Readers just love that one! Can you take a look? And if you can't find a story, can you try to write one for me of the kind you wrote when you were younger? And keep politics out of it? Not that there's anything wrong with the stories you write now,' he added hastily, 'but they're, well, a bit more difficult for the gentle reader. You don't mind my saying that, do you?'

Irritated, I put the telephone down. I had worked so hard to become an indigenous writer of some critical distinction, somebody whom critics could admire for my polish and fearlessness in articulating the indigenous position. I had established myself as a writer who was not afraid to engage the complexities of race, identity and representation and examine the polarities that existed between majority and minority cultures. Despite this, while I now garnered hard-earned accolades from critics, the people who actually bought my books were always telling me that my earlier stories and novels were better. Some reviewers, when I started rewriting the earlier work, scolded me. 'Ah well', tutae happens.

Two days later, however, I began the following story, which happened to my mother in 1989. Being a fiction writer, I have altered some of the details and names of those involved in the story.

*

My mother was looking out the kitchen window of the house at Haig Street, Gisborne, when she saw her brother Rangiora sitting in the sunlight on the back lawn. She was baking scones for a kindergarten bring and buy and had just taken the last batch from the oven; she almost dropped them.

Mum was seventy at the time and although her impulse was to rush out the door and give Uncle Rangiora a hug, instead she first went to the bathroom to splash water on her face, run a comb through her hair and put some lipstick on. The bathroom window looked over the back lawn, so Mum was able to check that he was still there — he was. He was in his army uniform, wearing his khaki cap, and he didn't look a day older than when he had left for the war. She looked at her own reflection in the bathroom mirror. In comparison, with her grey hair and her dull skin, she looked so old. She was overwhelmed with self-pity and embarrassment.

Smoothing out her dress, Mum walked out the back door and toward Uncle Rangiora. As she approached, he stood up, took off his cap and smiled at her — it didn't seem to matter at all that he was still so young and she was so old.

'Hello, brother,' she said to him. 'Why have you come to see me?'

His eyes were twinkling as he gave a deep, grave bow. 'I've been thinking about you, sister,' he said. 'It's a long time since we had a waltz.'

He opened his arms in invitation and, with a laugh of pure joy, she stepped into them.

> When I grow too old to dream,
> I'll have you to remember,
> When I grow too old to dream,
> Your love will stay in my heart —

After the waltz, Uncle Rangiora bowed again and left my mother standing alone in the sunlight. As he did so, a brown bird flew past her, heading after him, and she watched it as it sped across the sky.

*

My father didn't know about Uncle Rangiora's visit until he returned from Waituhi; he had been shifting cattle from the hill paddock to the flat in preparation for the trucks that would come the next morning to take them to the saleyards. When he arrived home he found my mother speaking on the telephone. There was something different about her, something radiant.

When Mum hung up, Dad asked her, 'Who have you been talking to?'

'I've been making enquiries,' she answered. 'First of all I rang the Returned Servicemen's Association and then the army at Waiouru and the Maori Battalion Association in Wellington. I wanted to know when they were making their next visit to the Commonwealth war graves in Egypt and the Middle East.'

'What for?' Dad asked, puzzled. He could tell that Mum had a bee in her bonnet about something.

'I want to visit Rangiora's grave,' Mum answered. 'The Battalion aren't going until next year though, so it looks like you and I will have to make the trip by ourselves. I've just asked the travel agent to book our trip for us. He wants us to go into town to see him and to have our photos taken for our passports.'

My father was seventy-seven, and he was waiting to have a replacement hip operation. He didn't think Mum was serious but when she said, 'We're going and that's that,' he tried stonewalling. 'I better have my operation first,' he said.

Once Mum has made up her mind about something, however, nothing can stop her. She's always been strong-willed and even though she loves my dad there are moments when, if he gets in her way, he'd better watch out. 'In that case,' she said, 'Wikitoria can come with me,' referring to one of my sisters, 'and you can stay home.'

*

My mother wanted to go to Tunisia because Uncle Rangiora had been killed there on 26 March 1943, at Point 201, Tebaga Gap. He had been a member of C Company, part of the platoon led by Second Lieutenant Ngarimu as they tried to take the German-held position. Twenty-two Battalion soldiers, including Ngarimu and Uncle Rangiora, were killed that day.

Not only was Mum strong-willed but, when she made up her mind, she moved really fast. Once she'd had her discussion with Dad she rang Wikitoria and told her to meet her at the travel agent's the next morning. Satisfied that she was getting somewhere, she went to have a shower and prepare for bed. While she was in the shower, Dad rang me up in Wellington to try to get me to talk some sense into her.

'She's much too old to go travelling to the other side of the world,' Dad said. 'And how is Wikitoria going to get somebody to look after her fish and chip shop? Hoha, your mother, hoha.'

I knew that there was no way of stopping Mum. Once she had the bit between her teeth she was off and away. Uncle Rangiora had been her favourite brother. He was just two years older than her and, while they were growing up, he looked out for her; he loved taking her to swim down at the local river and together they would dive for beautiful white river stones. Even when he was a young man and had girlfriends, he and Mum were still as close as ever. Whenever church dances were held at Tokomaru Bay, Uncle Rangiora always saved the last waltz for her. There was a photograph of Mum and Uncle Rangiora taken just before he went to war — Mum always had it on her dressing table. In the photo, Uncle Rangiora was a handsome, laughing, cavalier boy; my mother was a slip of a girl in a pretty white dress, holding him as if she never wanted to let him go.

When Uncle Rangiora was killed, Mum was inconsolable. However, life goes on and, after the war ended, she moved to Gisborne to stay with her sister, Mattie, and worked as a shedhand in various shearing gangs. Dad was a shearer — that's how they met. But she never forgot Uncle Rangiora, who had been buried in the Commonwealth war cemetery at Sfax, Tunisia. For as long as I can remember, every year without fail, Mum has walked in to *The Gisborne Herald* office and placed the same notice in the In Memoriam column:

> *To my brother, Private Rangiora Wharepapa, killed in action in Tunisia, 1943. Sadly missed, never forgotten. Your sister, Aroha.*

Of course my sisters, brothers and I knew that Dad would never let Mum go to Tunisia without him. I was not surprised when Wikitoria telephoned to tell me, 'Well, as usual, there's no Judy without Punch.' Apparently, Dad had shown up at the travel agent's on his truck just when Wiki and Mum had almost completed the arrangements for the trip and were handing over a cheque for the deposit.

'You can go back to your fish and chip shop, Wikitoria,' Dad said to my sister. 'How will that husband of yours cope without you to boss him around?' He turned to the travel agent, a nice young boy named Donald. 'My name is Tom Mahana and I'm going to Tunisia with Mrs Mahana.'

Mum looked at Dad askance. 'With your bad hip you'll be a nuisance,' she told him. 'Look at you! You can't get around anywhere without a walking stick.'

'And look at *you*,' Dad retorted. 'You're an old woman, or have you forgotten? You've never been able to find your way around without my help, so how do you think you'll manage when you go overseas?'

'You'll slow me down,' Mum answered defensively. 'It's a long way to go with a lot of connections to catch. I don't want to miss the planes.'

'Your wife is right,' Donald said, pursing his lips. 'If you have hip trouble you'll have enormous difficulties.'

Dad was in no mood for an argument. Today was the cattle sales and he should have been there. 'We won't miss any planes,' he said. 'What do you think I am? I may have to use a walking stick but I'm not entirely hopeless.'

'And I'm not clever enough to get to Tunisia with Wikitoria, is that it?' Mum asked. She looked at Donald, who was really only the meat in the sandwich. 'You know,' she confided in him, 'when my husband asked me to marry him I didn't want to because he was so much older than me. But I thought, "Better to be an old man's darling than a young man's slave." I never realised, that when men get older it doesn't matter what their age is. They're all hopeless.'

Donald excused himself while Mum and Dad continued their argument, but eventually Dad got his way. After all, the money for the trip was coming from their joint account, so that was that.

*

Now I have to admit that the idea of the trip would have been much easier on the family's nerves if Mum and Dad had been flying on a, well, English-speaking airline. With an eye to economies, however, Mum had chosen to fly on Aerolineas Argentinas from Auckland to Buenos Aires to Barcelona to Paris, and thence to Tunisia by some airline that nobody had ever heard of.

'How are you going to communicate?' Wikitoria asked. 'How are you going to find your way around when you won't be able to read the signs?'

And, man oh man, the connections. When Mum sent me their itinerary I just about had a heart attack. 'How do you know whether those terminals have air bridges?' I said to her on the telephone. 'How's Dad going to get up and down all those stairs to and from the planes? And why does it look like the gates to your connecting flights are in other

terminals? I'd better get our cousin Watene to fly from New York to Paris
and go with you to Tunisia.'

'And spoil our great adventure?' she answered. 'Don't you dare!
Anyhow, your father's already in training.'

I'd heard all about Mum's training from neighbours in Gisborne.
'Oh, your poor father,' they told me. 'Your mother has been getting him
up at six in the morning for a run around the block. We hadn't realised
she was so fit. She takes off like a rocket and your father hobbles after her,
walking stick in hand. We can hear him complaining all the way about
the new trainers she has bought for him. He says they're too big and he
doesn't like the colour.' True, my father has always been proud of his
small feet and, well, aren't all trainers white? 'Does your mother listen to
him?' the neighbours asked. 'No, she just keeps on yelling at him, "If you
can't keep up, you can stay at home." By the time they finish their run
your dad is absolutely exhausted.'

Exhausted or not, Dad managed to pass Mum's fitness test. As
the time for departure approached, they bought backpacks, got their
passports and changed their money into pesos, francs and dinar. Mum
gave Dad a haircut to save him the trouble of getting one while they were
away. Three days before they were due to leave, she went up to Tolaga
Bay where she and Uncle Rangiora had lived. There, she headed for the
river where they had loved to swim.

What a nuisance. Mum had hoped to gather white stones from
the riverbank but the best ones were at the bottom of the river, and the
water was too deep to wade out to them. However, two Pakeha boys
who were playing truant from school were jumping off branches into the
water. She waved them over.

'Yes, lady?' they asked.

'See those white stones?' she said. 'I've come to get some.' She
explained that she wanted to take them to Tunisia to put on Uncle
Rangiora's grave.

The young boys nodded and were soon duckdiving to the
bottom of the river. Mum could see them, gliding like dreams through
the sparkling water. When the boys returned, gasping, to the surface, they
brought the white river stones to the bank. They soon had a good pile but
they sorted through them, throwing some away. 'They have to be perfect,'
they said to Mum, 'You can't take any old stones, can you, lady?'

'No,' Mum smiled. 'Only the best.'

The boys dived again. They were enjoying themselves. While
Mum waited for them she filled a small bottle with river water. Uncle
Rangiora would like that — he probably missed the cool of the water there in
the desert.

'Thank you, boys,' Mum said when the job had been done. She gave them a five-dollar note. 'Don't spend it all at once. I'm glad you played truant today.'

She left and gave them their river back.

*

At this point, my cousin Clarrie, her husband Chad and my Auntie Taina come into the picture. Somehow Clarrie found out about Mum and Dad going to Tunisia — probably from Wiki. Chad was American and, as it happened, they were planning with Auntie Taina to make one of their infrequent trips to catch up with his folks in Montana.

'Don't worry, cuz,' Clarrie said to me on the phone from Wanganui, 'We'll meet them in Auckland. We've changed our bookings and are now on the same flight as Auntie and Uncle as far as Buenos Aires. When we get there, we'll make sure they catch their connection to Barcelona.' There was a slight tone of disapproval in her voice that I was letting Mum and Dad wander around in a dangerous world where they could get mugged or murdered, the poor things.

'Thank you, Clarrie,' I answered, trying to sound suitably chastised.

*

The day came for Mum and Dad's departure. The terminal at Gisborne airport was crowded with my brothers and sisters, all trying to be brave. Mum sat stony-faced as they pleaded with her to change her mind; she was clutching her airline bag with its passport, money, river stones and bottle of river water, and turned a deaf ear to their words.

As for Dad, well, he was surrounded by his adoring grandchildren, all weeping and wailing and gnashing their teeth as if they would never see him again.

The departure call was given. 'Time to go,' Mum said. 'Come on, Dad.' She walked out to the plane without a backward glance. As for Dad, he was the last to board. He had to hobble really fast to get there before the door closed, his new white trainers flashing across the tarmac.

2.

I TOOK A BREAK FROM writing the story.

See what I mean about its essentialist nature? I recalled a meeting

I had with the great English-Caribbean writer V. S. Naipaul when he visited Wellington in the 1970s. The poor man had been taken out for 'a drive' and suffered an over-enthusiastic seven-hour odyssey to Palmerston North and back. That evening, I joined him at a local PEN dinner where Professor Beeby, a wonderful raconteur, prefaced every comment to him with phrases like, 'When I was in India . . .' or 'When I spoke to Nehru about the partition with Pakistan . . .' or 'When I spoke to Mrs Gandhi in Paris.' Attempting to pull me into the conversation, Professor Beeby said to Mr Naipaul, 'Of course we have a young Maori writer here whose work reminds me very much of your own first collection, *Miguel Street*.' Mr Naipaul's response was to give me a somewhat acidic look, sigh, and say, 'Oh, he'll have to do much better than that.'

I remembered with gloom how critics of my early work had pounced on its simplicity and pronounced that it was the literary equivalent of naïve paintings done by unsophisticated native artists: bold colours, representations of village life, but no subtlety — and where was the subtext? The critics seemed to be looking for somebody else; some Maori writer who was aware of literary theory, whose work they could fit into a more refined aesthetic and theoretical model — of cultural displacement, perhaps, directly concerned with the economic and political fabric of cultural existence, or with the racialised discourses of apartheid or colonialism — who would affirm the indigenous voice within the long-standing western European cultural anxieties to do with modernist texts. They wanted literature that operated on a more complex national, political, aesthetic, linguistic and cognitive level, contesting the language and discursive conventions that had historically been instruments ensuring that 'the Other' was kept subordinate.

Although I was Maori, I had the suspicion that ultimately the critics wanted that other writer to undo the discursive crime against Africa and to trace a genealogy through Foucault, Barthes and the later Blanchot to a reading — albeit from the South Pacific — of the upheavals in French literary culture precipitated by the anticolonial struggle in Algeria and by the events of May 1968.

Instead, they got me. That other writer must have got delayed when old lady Muse swung by in her Peugeot and mistakenly picked me up instead. Did she ever lose on the deal. She opened the door to sweet, stupid, lyrically voiced me, writing from the heart and not from the intellect, overabundant when I should have been minimalist, without any of those traits that critics wanted to see — particularly cynicism or pessimism.

You get what you get.

*

According to cousin Clarrie, the trip to Buenos Aires went very smoothly. She, Chad and Auntie Taina met Mum and Dad's flight in Auckland.

'Hello Uncle Tom,' Clarrie smiled at Dad. 'What flash white trainers you have. Auntie Aroha? Mum's just over there with the suitcases.' Mum was glad to have Auntie Taina's company; they had been close for all the years since they became sisters-in-law. They chatted on the bus to the international terminal about whanau, who had died, who had married, who had had children, their own hopeless kids and thank goodness for the compensation of lovely grandchildren. When the bus arrived, Dad was delighted to see that a group of strapping young rugby players were on the same flight. Just his chance to let them know how terrific he had been as a left winger.

Dad has always loved talking to strangers. He loves to tell them about his tribe, his big family of brothers and sisters, his girlfriends (when Mum isn't listening), his children, the farm, his exploits as a top shearer, how he almost became an All Black, how he could have been a world champion wrestler, and so on. Once he gets started he is difficult to stop — and on the flight he had a group of eager young boys who were trapped and couldn't escape. They were polite and kept nodding their heads at his stories — which only encouraged him.

Clarrie told me later, 'Don't be so critical of your father! He's just lovely! A real patriarch! Young boys love to hear your father telling about his life and giving them advice on what to do if the girl you like doesn't like you back — even if it's, well, somewhat old-fashioned and past its use-by date.'

'I know what you mean,' I said. 'The difference is, of course, that strangers have never heard Dad's stories before, whereas us kids have heard them again and again. And as for Dad's advice — well, if I listened to it, I would still be a virgin.'

But to strangers like the rugby boys, Dad's stories came out fresh, lively, splendid epics of trials that had been faced and triumphs accomplished against all odds. This was why people loved our father: he was such a terrific storyteller and a real spellbinder. By the time the plane landed in Buenos Aires, Dad had made many friends and received several invitations to come and visit.

'Thank you,' Mum said. 'We'll think about it.' This was her usual reply whenever Dad received such invitations. It was much better than saying yes or no. People liked to think there was the possibility of a maybe.

*

My mother had strict instructions to call home at each leg of the journey so that the family could rest easy, they had survived another day. Somewhat grumpily she telephoned from a hotel close to Buenos Aires airport.

'The eagles have landed,' Mum said, 'and, yes, your father is still hobbling along after me on his walking stick, so I haven't been able to give him the slip — pity.' I soon realised why she was grumpy when she gave me what-for. 'And I have a bone to pick with you, son! You have to get Clarrie, Chad and Taina off our case. They've made arrangements for your father and me to be met at the airport in Paris by one of Chad's old Vietnam veterans mates, who has plans to take us to dinner. But I've made bookings for us to see the Folies Bergère.'

I wasn't listening to her. I was more alarmed at what I could hear in the background: screams, yells, lots of laughter, motorbikes revving up . . . and then, over her words, were those gunshots? 'What the heck's all the commotion?' I asked.

'When I told Donald to book us into cheap accommodation,' Mum explained, 'I didn't expect he would put us somewhere we might get murdered in our beds. The taxi driver didn't even want to bring us here. But Clarrie and Chad have barricaded the door and rung the rugby boys we met on the plane. We are expecting the football cavalry to arrive any minute.'

Of course, that was the kind of news guaranteed to keep me awake all night worrying about my parents. But Clarrie rang me the next morning from the airport to tell me that they had just put Mum and Dad on the plane to Barcelona. Clarrie sounded tired and strained.

'What kind of hotel were you staying at?' I asked.

'Is that what it was?' Clarrie answered. 'You don't want to know, cuz. Do they have Mafia in South America? Whatever was going down, your poor mum and dad were in the middle of it. You owe me big time.'

However, my relief was shortlived when Mum failed to telephone in from Barcelona. And then I received a call from Charles de Gaulle International Airport in Paris, from Chad's friend, who introduced himself as Addison. 'Oh, hi ya,' he drawled. 'Say, I've been waiting for your folks at customs but we must have missed each other. Should I call the police?'

'No,' I sighed. 'I am sure they are okay.' Yeah, right. My mind was filled with visions of them being kidnapped by French thugs, robbed of their money and their bodies thrown into the River Seine.

Two hours later, Dad phoned. 'Your mother is getting all dressed up to take me out on the town,' he said.

'Why didn't you phone me from Barcelona?' I screamed. 'And why didn't you meet up with Addison at the airport?'

'Were we supposed to telephone you from Barcelona?' Dad

answered. 'And who's Addison?'

Mum took the telephone from Dad. 'We gave him the slip,' she said. 'As soon as I saw a man dressed like Rambo holding up a sign with our names on it, I took Dad off in the opposite direction. Otherwise we'd never be able to get to you-know-where.'

'How did you find your hotel?' I asked. Dad only had a smattering of French, learnt when he was a schoolboy in the 1920s, and I couldn't imagine how that would enable them to negotiate the horrors of the Metro, not to mention being prey to every pickpocket, pimp and prostitute as they trundled their bags through the streets — and any thief after Dad's white trainers.

'Oh, you know your father,' Mum answered. 'Talks to anybody. On the plane he got into a conversation with three boys who were backpacking through Europe and he ended up playing cards with them. Poker, the naughty man. How many matchsticks did you win, dear? Anyhow, they offered to escort us to this place; at least this one has locks on the door. But we can't stop, son, otherwise we'll be late for the show. I'll phone you when we get back.'

Two months later, I received a postcard from the three boys:

> DEAR MISTER MAHANA, MY FRIENDS AND I FELL
> IN LOVE WITH YOUR FATHER. BUT COULD YOU
> TELL US, DID HE AND YOUR MOTHER REACH THEIR
> DESTINATION AND THEN RETURN SAFELY TO NEW
> ZEALAND? WE ARE ANXIOUS TO KNOW. FELIX,
> MARTIN AND PLACIDO.

The three boys weren't the only ones to fall in love with Dad. When he and Mum arrived at the Folies Bergère, the maître d' was entranced by their formality and elegance. Dad was wearing his black suit. The jacket is a perfect fit, but it doesn't do to look too closely at his trousers, as he usually cuts the waistband to give some slack so that his stomach can fit in. Mum was wearing her blue sequined dress and lovely cape of kiwi feathers. They were seated at a table right at the front. The programme they brought home after their trip has the scrawled signatures of Lolo, Dodo, Jou-jou, Frou-frou, Clou-clou, Margot and Valencienne, so obviously Dad was a hit with the girls, too. Apparently he was so thrilled by the show that he got up at the end and did a haka.

'I wish your father would just clap like ordinary people,' Mum said on the telephone when she checked in with me. 'But your father became . . . well . . . somewhat excited. You'd think he'd never seen bare breasts before.'

'Or bare anything,' I heard Dad grumble in the background, referring to my mother's legendary modesty.

'Enough of that,' Mum reproved him. 'Our big day tomorrow, Dad. No funny business tonight.' Then she remembered I was still on the phone. 'You still there, son? I better hang up now. Dad and I have to get up very early to catch the plane to Tunisia. Don't worry about us. Love you.'

My mother was not going to leave anything to chance, particularly seeing her beloved brother who, many years ago, always kept the last waltz for her.

So kiss me again, and then let us part,
And when I grow too old to dream
Your kiss will stay in my heart —

The next morning Mum and Dad took a taxi, thank god, back to the airport to catch their first flight to Tunisia. Mum had organised with Donald that they would stay in Sfax for two days. This would give her and Dad plenty of time to visit Uncle Rangiora's grave. They would check into their hotel, go out to the Sfax War Cemetery, spend some time with Uncle Rangiora in the cemetery and return to Sfax in the late afternoon. They would stay at the hotel that evening, possibly go back to the grave for a second visit the next day to say goodbye to Uncle Rangiora, and catch the plane back to Paris.

The flight was smooth and uneventful. Dad was in an aisle seat and Mum was squeezed between him and an extremely well groomed gentleman sitting next to the window. The man wore a dark suit and a blue tie to match the blue handkerchief in his jacket pocket. But what Mum remembered most about him was that he had the shiniest shoes that she had ever seen. They were like mirrors.

I don't know who the man was, and Mum and Dad lost the card he gave them, but I can't write about him without giving him a name — so let us call him Monsieur Samaritan. Dad leaned across Mum and, as usual, began to speak to the man. Dad told him he was from New Zealand, and immediately Monsieur Samaritan's face lit up. 'Ah! Néo-zélandais! Go the All Blacks!' When Dad elaborated and said he and Mum were Maori, Monsieur Samaritan clapped his thighs and said, 'Ka mate, ka mate, ka ora, ka ora! Kia ora!'

Dad and Monsieur Samaritan shook hands, Dad exchanged seats with Mum, and very soon he and Monsieur Samaritan were talking as if they were old friends. Monsieur Samaritan told them that he was an official for the Tunisian government and had been on business in Paris, renegotiating landing rights for Air France in Tunisia; the negotiations had been somewhat exhausting and he was looking forward to getting home to his wife and children. He had never been to New Zealand, but he had met some New Zealand officials in his business — and he was a rugby fan.

'We're on our way to the Commonwealth graveyard at Sfax,' Dad said. He told him about Mum's river stones and bottle of river water, and Monsieur Samaritan was affected by Mum's simple gesture of love for her brother. He took his handkerchief out of his pocket and, dabbing at his eyes, waved to some other passengers across the aisle.

'C'est mon frère, le libérateur de la Tunisie —'

Well, that did it. Before too long, Dad was the centre of attention, and more cards and greetings were exchanged.

*

In this mood of general friendliness and bonhomie, Mum and Dad landed at Sfax. They farewelled their new friends, all native Tunisians, and exited the plane. Officials saluted Monsieur Samaritan at the gate, ready to take him through VIP customs to a government limousine that would whisk him into the city.

'Monsieur Tom,' Monsieur Samaritan said, clicking his shiny shoes together, 'I wish you a good visit to Sfax and a safe return to your homeland. Kia ora.'

Then he bowed to Mum — so you mustn't think that my father was the only one to impress strangers. Mum has her own quiet dignity and inner luminosity, and intrigues in her own way. She has never regarded herself as beautiful — her face is too angular and as a young woman she was built like a man with her wide shoulders and slim hips — but where other women lose their beauty as they grow older, Mum has come into hers. I'm not sure what gives Mum this look of having eternity in her, but I have seen it in other women who have lived life and, somehow, understood its ebb and flow.

Mum rummaged in her bag for some gifts to give to him, and pulled out a bone pendant and an All Blacks T-shirt. 'For your children,' she said. 'And if ever you come to New Zealand, Dad will put down a hangi for you.'

Now I have never been to Tunisia and I have no idea what the airline terminal in Sfax looks like. You will have to bear with me as I let my imagination take over.

I imagine Mum and Dad walking along the concourse — Dad just keeping up with Mum — and looking out the windows to a sky almost white with heat. I can hear the excitement in my mother's voice as she says to Dad, 'Come on, Tom, almost there!' The air conditioning in the airport would have cocooned them in coolness. The concourse would have been crowded with Arab nationals in the majority, and foreigners like Mum and Dad would elicit glances of curiosity. I can imagine Mum, as they approached the customs hall, getting impatient to be on her way to the Commonwealth graveyard and her rendezvous with her brother. And I can just see her hopeful face as they waited for the customs official to stamp their passports and let them go through.

The official frowned. 'Would you come this way, please?'

Mystified, Mum and Dad followed him. 'Is there anything wrong?' Mum asked. She was getting a terrible feeling about this.

The customs officer did not reply. His supervisor stepped up to look at the passports. 'Do you have baggage?' he asked.

'Yes,' Mum answered. They were escorted to the carousel to collect their suitcases and then taken to a small room where they were asked a number of questions and their bags were searched. The customs officer wanted to know about the river stones and the bottle of water, and he took a hammer to one of the stones to see if there was anything inside. A long consultation took place, and Mum and Dad were then advised of their predicament.

'I am very sorry to inform you,' the customs officer said, 'that you will not be able to enter Tunisia. You will be kept here in the airport and, when your flight leaves tomorrow, you will be put on it for return to Paris.'

At his words, my father looked at my mother. Tears were streaming down her face. Dad's love for Mum showed in his concern for her and, heart beating fast, he tried to intercede with the customs officer. 'Will you not give us just today so that my wife can go to pay her respects to her brother? Sir, we —'

He gasped for air. Then he gave a moan and would have crumpled to the floor had Mum not supported him.

'It's all right, Dad,' Mum consoled him. She looked at the customs officer. 'Do you have a chair for my husband?' she asked.

3.

I TOOK ANOTHER BREAK FROM the story. Once upon a time, I would not have questioned the directness or ingenuousness of my writing. But I know more postcolonial theory now, and not only do I write literature, I also teach postcolonial identity. Is any of this reflected in the story? No.

My problem was that I was, well, still indigenous. Unlike Derek Walcott, a poet of African, Dutch and West Indian descent, born in St Lucia and commuting between Boston and Trinidad, I was not a 'divided child who entered the house of literature as a houseboy' and who had become a paradigm of the polycultural order, making of English a polyglot literature. Nor, like Salman Rushdie, Booker Prize winner for his tumultuous, multiheaded myth of modern India, *Midnight's Children*, Kazuo Ishigura, Vikram Seth, Timothy Mo, Rohinton Mistry or Pico Iyer, was I a transcultural writer, the product not so much of colonial division as of the international culture that has grown up since the war, and addressing an audience as mixed up and eclectic and uprooted as themselves. Situated at a crossroads, they reflected on their hyphenated status in the new-world global village with a different kind of sophistication than mine as an indigenous writer.

And where was my sense of irony? To this day, my closest friends bemoan the fact that I don't have an ironic bone in my body. If I had, I might have been able to undercut the otherwise positive, sacralised and hopeful nature of my mythmaking. I would, instead, have highlighted the nihilistic despair of the victimised and oppressed and the need to continue to propose political and revolutionary solutions. Hybrid writers have often commented, as Edward Saïd did, that: 'The centre is full of tired scepticism, a kind of knowing irony. There's something very stale about it.' As for American literature, it had been sapped by such trends as minimalism. Bharati Mukherjee has written, 'The real energy of American fiction is coming from people who have lived 400 years within a generation. They've been through wars, orbited the world, had traumatic histories prior to coming, and they've got big, extraordinary stories to tell. In place of the generic account of divorce in Hampstead or Connecticut, the international writers offer magically new kinds of subject matter and electric ways of expressing it.'

Perhaps there is another way out. My postcolonial colleagues might honour me not for the more political novelising that has been the central poutokomanawa of my artistry — but, rather, for the activism that has been associated with it.

For instance, First Nations friends still talk about the time, over twenty-five years ago, when they came to see me at the Harborfront Festival, Toronto, where I was to read my work. They told me that no First Nations writer had ever been invited to read in Canada's most prestigious literary festival, and they asked me to represent them. I was so angry that when I came to read I instead let rip to the primarily white and unsuspecting audience, accusing them and Canada of racism of the worst kind: denial of the native existence and erasure of First Nations culture as a wilful exercise

of Canadian genocide. By the time I finished, there was a stony silence. Greg
Gatenby said to me as I walked off the stage, 'Well, that was interesting. I've
never seen a writer committing suicide in public before.'

I am an example of one of those writers who could never resist
the disastrous.

*

Ah well, to proceed.

To be frank, I do not know why my parents were detained at
the airport at Sfax. I imagine that there was some irregularity with their
passports. The most likely explanation is this:

'I am very sorry to tell you both,' the senior customs officer said,
'but you must have a visa to enter our country. Without it, I cannot permit
you to visit.'

But I am only guessing at the reason. There may have been
another: perhaps their passports looked too new and clean and therefore
suspiciously false. They may have needed different entry documents.
The names on their airline tickets might have been different from the
names on their passports — Mum and Dad had both Maori and Pakeha
surnames. Perhaps they had been mistaken for a couple of criminals on
Interpol's list.

'Therefore,' the senior customs officer advised them, 'I will retain
your passports and, as I have already told you, you will both be held in
custody at the airport. When your plane leaves tomorrow for Paris you
will be escorted onto it. At that time, your passports will be returned to
you.'

After a while, however, the senior customs officer relented
somewhat, and agreed to allow Mum and Dad to remain in the transit
area where at least there were dutyfree shops, food outlets and comfortable
seating. After all, how far would an old lady and an old man with a
walking stick have got if they decided to make a run for it? And without
passports?

Mum and Dad were just two old people, bewildered and unable
to get to their destination. But my father regained his strength. 'Sir,' he
tried once again, 'whatever the problem is, surely, as reasonable people,
we can find a solution? My wife and I are here in your country for only a
short time. What harm can we do in that time?' He showed the customs
officer photographs of Uncle Rangiora. 'All my wife wishes to do is to visit
her brother's grave, pay her respects, and then we will be on our way. Will
you not permit us to do that?'

No matter how much Dad tried to explain the situation and to apologise for any error they may have inadvertently made, he just couldn't get through to the senior customs officer, who was adamant.

What made it worse was that the incident really hurt my parents' sense of pride and personal honour. 'You are treating us as if we are criminals,' Dad said in a temper. 'I may have received the occasional parking ticket but my wife and I have never been before a judge or committed any crimes. To be treated like this is deeply shaming.'

The customs officer would not be swayed. He retained their passports, showed them the transit lounge, deposited their bags beside them and advised them that under no circumstances were they to leave. Of course, as soon as he had gone, Mum burst into tears. She's generally a strong woman but her tears were from embarrassment and humiliation. 'And now look at us, Dad,' she wept, 'we've become a bag lady and a bag man.' She was also aching because to come all this way with her river stones and not be able to put them on her brother's grave was a terrible heartbreak for her.

They sat, talked, waited, and slept. Every now and then Dad wandered off to get Mum a sandwich and a cup of chocolate. Mum talked about Uncle Rangiora and how they would waltz together. 'He was such a good brother to me,' she told Dad. 'He always saved the last waltz for me. I remember well when we danced together for the last time. It was on the platform of the railway station in 1941, just before all the East Coast boys got on the train to Wellington. I was still a teenager. Rangiora was looking so handsome in his soldier's cap and uniform; I had on my best white dress so that he would always remember me while he was fighting in the war. Rangiora had a girlfriend, a lovely girl from Te Araroa, but just before he got the order to fall in, he turned to me and asked, "Would you like to waltz, sister?" He opened his arms, I stepped into them, we both went onto our toes, and we began —

> *So kiss me again, and then let us part,*
> *And when we grow too old to dream,*
> *Your kiss will stay in my heart —'*

I mean no disrespect to my father, but Uncle Rangiora was the love of my mother's life. Dad knew it and we, her children, knew it. I suspect that when you lose someone you love when you are both young, the love for that person is heightened and romanticised in some way. The rest of us had to fit in and around that big love, realising that we had no chance of winning because, well, Mum knows our faults too well to let us get away with anything.

My parents continued to while away the day at the airport. They were distressed — but really, there was nothing that could be done about their situation. I imagine that some of the cafeteria workers, puzzled by Dad's constant visits for more hot chocolate and food, sympathised with their plight and offered words of comfort. When night came, I can imagine my parents sleeping sitting up, a crescent moon gliding overhead and shining on Dad's white trainers. I can see cleaners going by, hushing each other so as not to wake them. I know that Dad must have disengaged himself from Mum's arms a couple of times to go to the toilet, as his waterworks were not always reliable. But I know he would have hobbled back as fast as he could to make sure that Mum was not alone for too long. There have not been many nights when they have slept apart. No doubt Mum woke a couple of times to stare out into the dark velvet of the Tunisian sky, her face enigmatic and eternal.

The new day dawned. Mum went to wash her face, comb her hair and make herself respectable. When she came back, Dad did the same. She scolded him to put on a new white shirt and tie. 'That's better,' she said when he returned. 'Seven hours from now we'll be on the plane, Dad.' She tried to be light-hearted about it.

Mum's head nodded and she drifted into sleep. Then she felt someone shaking her awake. When she opened her eyes the first thing she saw was a pair of very shiny shoes. She would have recognised those shoes anywhere.

'Madam? Aroha? Did you enjoy your visit to Sfax?' It was Monsieur Samaritan, their companion on the plane from Paris.

Mum saw that Dad was still sleeping, his mouth wide open, and his trousers wide open too. She nudged him awake. Dad told Monsieur Samaritan what had happened. 'We have been in the airport all this time,' he said. 'Our passports were taken from us.'

Well, there's no other way to say it — Monsieur Samaritan went ballistic. 'Please come with me,' he said, tight-lipped. Mum and Dad had known he was a VIP but they had not realised that he was such a powerful government official. He stormed into the customs area and began to speak rapidly to every underling around, and then to the senior customs officer. I have no idea what he said but I can imagine that it was something like this:

'Don't you fools know that these two people have come all the way from New Zealand? Who was the imbecile who said they should not be allowed into our country? Do you realise that this lady's brother fought and died to enable our freedom? Why am I surrounded by such incompetent and stupid people? Do you think they are terrorists? Do they look like terrorists? Where are their passports? Give them back immediately!'

Monsieur Samaritan then looked at his watch. He mopped his brow and, calming down, bowed gravely to Mum and Dad. 'Please accept my apologies,' he said, 'but perhaps I can be of some service? Although you only have a short time left before your plane departs, it would be my great privilege to accompany you to the Commonwealth graves.'

He hastened them out of the terminal and into the heat to his car, and ordered the driver to put his foot down. 'Quick! Quick! As fast as you can!'

As I have said, I have never been to Tunisia, so I don't know what the roads are like from the airport to the Commonwealth war graves. My imagination conjures up heat and dust, roads crowded with traffic, the occasional camel, and the shimmering haze of a bright white day. Conscious of the restricted time, I can hear Monsieur Samaritan urging his driver to 'Go faster! Faster!', and the car, with its official pennant flying, speeding through a city of Arabic architecture, serrated walls and minarets.

At last, they arrived. But what was this? The gates were closed. Monsieur Samaritan commanded the driver to go and investigate.

'Alas, Monsieur Tom,' Monsieur Samaritan said, 'the cemetery is closed during the middle of the day.' Monsieur Samaritan instructed the driver to ring the bell at the gateway, and keep ringing until someone came. As luck would have it, a gatekeeper arrived and let them in.

'Thank you,' Mum said. She reached into her bag for one of her bone pendants to give the gravedigger, but the car was already moving swiftly through the gateway.

*

I'm told that the cemetery at Sfax is huge — rows and rows of white crosses — and Mum and Dad's time was ticking by. Even Monsieur Samaritan saw the hopelessness of the task. 'How will your wife be able to find her brother,' he said to Dad, 'among all these dead?'

The gatekeeper had pointed them in the general direction of the Australian and New Zealand section. Suddenly Mum yelled 'Stop!' She opened the door of the car and took off. 'I'll find him,' she said. All that training, running around the block in Te Hapara, was about to pay off.

'Aroha,' Dad called, reaching for his walking stick. 'Wait for me —'

But she was already far away, sprinting like a sixteen-year-old through all those rows of white crosses. She stopped at a rise in the graveyard. When Dad and Monsieur Samaritan reached her, they saw more crosses. Which one was Rangiora's?

'It really is impossible,' Monsieur Samaritan said.

Mum was standing with the sun shining full upon her face. Perspiration beaded her forehead and neck. Dad saw her face crumple and went to offer her solace. 'Keep your hands off me,' she screamed, frustrated.

Then she saw a little brown bird. It fluttered above her, cocked an eye and turned away. With a cry, Mum took off after it, following the bird as it dipped and sashayed around the white crosses, up, over and down a small hillock. When Dad and Monsieur Samaritan reached the top of the hillock, they saw Mum in the distance, kneeling beside a small cross, weeping. By the time they caught up with her again, she was putting her river stones on Uncle Rangiora's grave. She had already poured her river water out of its bottle and it was seeping into the sand. There was a radiant look on her face, as if something important had been completed.

Dad and Monsieur Samaritan waited in silence. Then, 'I will go back to the car and wait for you,' Monsieur Samaritan said. 'Please take as much time as you wish, but we should be returning to the airport shortly.'

Dad nodded at him. He watched Mum as she finished laying her river stones. She stood up, wiped her hands on her dress, smiled at Dad and put out her hands. 'I'm sorry I yelled at you. Will you dance a waltz with me, Dad?'

Gripping his walking stick in one hand and Mum in the other, Dad did his best.

When I grow too old to dream,
I'll have you to remember,
When I grow too old to dream,
Your love will stay in my heart —

Mum and Dad returned to the airport. Monsieur Samaritan escorted them through customs and saw them to their flight. 'I'm so sorry you didn't have more time with your brother,' he said to Mum.

'Sorry?' Mum answered. 'Please don't be. And thank you, Monsieur Samaritan.'

From Paris, my parents went on to New York. There's a photograph taken by a sidewalk photographer which captures the glow of Mum's happiness. She's with Dad, and he's balancing on his walking stick and wearing his white trainers. My cousin Watene took them to see *42nd Street* and *Cats*. Mum told Dad she didn't want to sleep for one minute, and dragged him up the Empire State Building and down to the ferry to see the Statue of Liberty.

Four days later, they boarded a bus for a tour across America all the way to the West Coast. Dad was looking forward to the trip and his eyes brightened when he saw all the other tourists boarding the bus. As I have mentioned before, he loves to talk to strangers about his family, his tribe, and his sporting exploits.

However, his face fell when he discovered that the other tourists on the bus were German-speaking and didn't understand English very well.

My parents survived the bus tour. They caught the plane from Los Angeles back to New Zealand, where they were welcomed with tears and much elation by a huge whanau that has never wanted them to go away overseas again — ever.

On their return home, Mum bought four huge scrapbooks and pasted every postcard, photograph and programme into it, including the souvenir programme from the Folies Bergère and the photograph taken in New York. Pride of place was reserved for a blow-up of a photograph of her and Dad standing at Uncle Rangiora's grave in the hot sun in Tunisia; with them is a gentleman dressed formally and wearing the shiniest shoes — Monsieur Samaritan. Dad had his hip operation, and put away his walking stick and his new white trainers.

If you go home to Te Hapara, you will see the map of Mum and Dad's travels on the wall in the living room.

*

Three months after the trip, Mum telephoned me in Wellington. She told me she was bothered about Rangiora being buried so far away from New Zealand. 'I want him to come back home,' she told me.

On her behalf I wrote to the Minister of Defence and the Minister of Maori Affairs. They both gave the same response: the Maori Battalion had made a collective agreement that all the boys who died on the battlefield should stay together in the country where they had fallen.

Dad is ninety-two this year. Mum is eighty-five. She still puts a memorial notice about Uncle Rangiora in *The Gisborne Herald* every year.

STEPHANIE JOHNSON

from *Manifest*

A novel in progress

YOU MAKE UP YOUR MIND. Either that or you lose it, in that instant, as you sit in your pyjamas at the kitchen table reading the morning paper. There's a thing about a new musical *Hair* showing at His Majesty's, a theatre you played in yourself a hundred times. It sounds appalling, you would never be able to sit through it, but you start to think, while you sieve tea through your teeth, jaw tight, of what you might do. At long last. There's forgiveness in the air, tolerance, compassion. Either that or the world is so morally degraded it's a fine thing you're as ancient as you are.

You take your tea and first cigarette of the day out onto the veranda and sit gingerly on Marjorie's new tubular-steel contraption, which always threatens to snap shut on your bony arse. The lawn runs along before you, across a long-gone circular rose bed, still mounded but grassed over, up a gentle incline before curling its lip into the tops of the trees that ring the cove below. Even if you screw your eyes up against the light you're still half blinded by the sea, flat and blue close in but choppy in the channel — enough wind to blow the pleasure yachts north. The only clouds are high, sparse and threadlike, like old hair. A perfect day for it, the dying of the summer, early autumn.

There have been lots of clues lately — hints that this is a possible course of action, a cause to be answered, a final statement, a coda, a deathbed confession. Some of them are so subliminal you are hardly aware of them, except as a softening in the air. A month or two ago there was that woman on television. Not very germane Germaine. No bra. She was earnest and healthy, in her early thirties, her nipples hard against her soft blouse, and you supposed she got a lot of sex. Most people did these days. There was an openness in her face that you envied; you didn't see a lot of that in your youth. You watched her talk about women and liberation and her forthcoming court case, and imagined her less cool and more animated.

Then there are the young men you see on the streets and beaches — long-haired, gentle-eyed, carrying guitars, smelling of flowers, like bloody girls: so lazy, soft and forgiving. There's a war on and none of them will fight it. They have an Arthurian aura of eternal youth; they seem to think they will never grow old as you have, they'll never die. There has been a paradigm shift, something to do with notions of abundance, responsibility, maturity, even immortality.

Not that you're dying yourself. Yet. And not that you are really a man who looks for clues, or believes in fate. You don't believe in anything, except maybe music. That's what's lasted. Every day is accidental. Otherwise how has Norman Martingale made it to the grand age of seventy-four, two years older than the century? No sensible and loving god would have intended it.

And the other clue — more solid. Yesterday's letter still unopened, hidden in a place your wife would never think to look for it. It can wait. Whatever is inside it has waited already for fifty years. You imagine Alphonse writing it in his narrow house high above the Mediterranean, perhaps in the same room as the dimly rendered photograph he showed you of himself playing the cello, on a morning like this one, the summer light bright behind long gauzy curtains billowing around him, in his lifetime embrace with 'the only woman in my life', as he used to say. There hasn't been a letter from him for decades but his hand in the address is recognisable — just as florid, the f's and s's as indistinguishable. It is perhaps a little less certain, the upstroke of the *M* for *Martingale* shaky. But Alphonse would be almost eighty now, five years your senior, and you suppose it's kind of a miracle he can hold a pen at all.

An hour later you're down the hall and out the front door in your hacking jacket with the purple cravat for colour, the letter over your heart. Your footsteps crunch along the white shell path under the trees, and you never give a single thought to Marjorie away over in her orchid house, the windows running with condensation and possibly heavy breathing. She has risen before you, as is the pattern, from where she's slept alone for years, in the musty maroon master bedroom. If you'd had a daughter she might come around to sort out some of the cupboards and cartons and boxes all stuffed with old linen and clothes, open the drapes and then the windows, air the place out. But there's no daughter.

Poor old Marjorie would have had her tea standing in her puce dressing gown at the kitchen bench, for fear of re-awakening her night-time lumbago if she sat down in the nook. There was a character in an Arnold Bennett novel who wore a puce dressing gown. Priam Farll in *Buried Alive*, the famous painter who takes on his dead valet's identity. It was one of your favourite books for years. In her puce dressing gown Marjorie in no way resembled him — she'd had no fame to run away from. Unlike yourself, who enjoyed a degree of it in business, sport and art. There could have been notoriety too, but you had avoided it. Until now, perhaps.

After her tea was drained to the last drop — Marjorie retained her depression mindset and never wasted anything — she would have limped out to her monstrous flowers that remind you always — against your will — of female genitalia. If ever you have the misfortune to be close to one, if you allow your eyes to alight briefly on the stipes, sepals and labellum, you try to see something else — a friendly face, a butterfly, a bee — but you never can. Sometimes, even now after all these years, to amuse and distract yourself, you like to imagine the woman that goes with the flower, yellow and red, green and orange, with striped or speckled eyes. But you don't have to look at them very often — Marjorie hardly ever brings them into the house, or sets them in pots around the garden. Since she fell in love with the species, orchids are the only bloom she has time for. The acres around the cliff-top house are flowerless — all lawn and trees, a masculine garden you suppose it is, so planted over with oaks and pines, a macrocarpa, a line of poplars — in parts a well-kept forest, what would qualify in England as a wood.

You pass under the magnolia trees on either side of the drive. Forty years since you planted them — tall, meeting overhead, the last of their creamy flowers like dying birds drooping their wings. Once, years ago now, you made the mistake of thinking the last flower of a season was a dead bird and you hurried from the house to see it fall.

Past the gate, the air smells cool and salty and your heart lifts with an almost painful elation, unfamiliar after all these years. How extraordinary it is to have finally made the decision and to be able to act on it so quickly. This morning, when you woke on the thin divan squab in the sunroom, your elderly aesthete's couch in the closed-in part of the veranda, you'd had no inkling that you'd be going off so soon and with such intent. It's your habit, to be certain, to get out each day, but usually you make sure you've at least said good morning to your wife before you leave. Sometimes you set off down to the beach, where you sit with a couple of other old codgers who would call themselves your friends on a wooden bench outside the sandcrete changing sheds, or sometimes you go to the shops and sometimes take the car across to the marina at Westhaven. If you weren't so taken with this plan you would go there now, down to the *Lady Rita* and take a walk around on her, enjoy the winter sun, give her brass bits a spit and polish, start up the engines and turn them over, dream about taking her out for a cruise, remember times with Lyn.

All the way down the steep right-of-way you hold tight to the too-wide white wooden railing that's seemingly designed to cut into your palms, hoping as you always do that a car doesn't come up, headed for the new houses built on your old, subdivided land. Your own garage is a converted boathouse under the cliff, with rotting concertina doors that no longer close properly, hanging off their hinges, the hinges themselves crumbly with salt black. You go through the usual motions, tugging and banging, slipping a little on the sand blown up from the beach and hoping you don't jam your finger or clout your bald head, as you've done countless times before, even when by your own reckoning you were still young. Then, at length, eventually, after graunching and to-ing and fro-ing, you reverse the old grey Rover out onto the road, find the reluctant first gear and drive carefully across the intersection. It's one of those new roundabouts and you figure that because the car is big and you are slow everybody has notice and time enough to get out of your way.

The phrase runs though your head as you turn the heavy wheel — *get out of my way, get out of my* — but some fool on your left toots at you, a long-haired, bearded git sitting up like Topsy in a Hillman Imp. He zips in front, giving you the victory sign and carries on ahead, a battered, sharp-cornered rusting box spinning ahead down Milford Road.

Get out of my way.

In your life you've done most of that. That's how it seems for you. Odd, because in every aspect you were not a man to whom acquiescence came easily, but that's what happened. Not on a day-to-day basis — you were ardent for Marjorie's domestic routine, mad for it, some said, a tyrant — it was more the big turns, the full spins of the wheel. In each instant — your career, marriage, childlessness — there had come a point when the most rational course of action was to step aside, not without grumbling or silent resentment, but you always came around in the end, and more often than not with the bitter conviction that you were cutting yourself short.

At the approach to the bridge you rummage in the rubble on the bench-seat for your cigarettes, light up at the tollgates and take the centre lane, with the best view of the upper harbour spreading silver in the morning sun. On the other side are the low cliffs of Herne Bay, yellow as old toenails, and the skinny old knob of Watchman Island, nibbled away to a shadow of its former self. When you were a lad you went on a Boy Scout picnic there, thirty of you and a couple of scraggy pines. Now it could barely hold half a pack. Away to the west the water darkens before Te Atatu, reflecting the black thunderheads rising above the ranges. There's a front coming. Maybe the day isn't as perfect as you'd anticipated. You drive on, across this bridge that spans a bifurcated city, divided geographically by water, if not more and more by class and race.

If you are to drive home again, an hour or two hence, this afternoon, it will be raining, and, judging by the heat of the sun striking your side windows, as far as your hand on the column shift, the roads will be steaming. You suppose the police will let you go.

1905

LYN COMFORT HAD LOVELY RED ears. They stuck out on either side of his head like red sails in the sunset. In one hand he held a preserving jar by a piece of string, which had an eel in it, a really big beggar — he must have had to roll it up from the tail to squeeze it in. Probably, it was dead. His legs were caked in mud, some of it thin and cracking like a second sunburnt skin, some in great greenish gouts sticking to his knees and his toes. His britches were wet and so was his shirt, a red flannel his brother had worn the year before and probably another brother before that, and now Lyn and maybe one day the new baby, which had come, and Lilias said it was a boy. Mrs Comfort was obviously quite good at babies — she had one a year; better than his own mother, who *perished in the attempt*. Norman smoothed the pintucks in his shirt and checked that his own knickerbockers sat neatly still, at the knees.

Was Lyn on his way home? He had come up onto the street, the long way around to Shelly Beach. It was quicker to go along the cliffs and drop down behind the wooden kiosk at the bottom. Norman walked up there on Sunday mornings, on Mrs Campbell's point, with his father, in all weathers, while the Comforts were at church.

Nervously, Norman looked towards the gate. His cousin would appear soon. She'd gone to get the gig without him, sending him out to wait on the street at the same moment she left the house to go around the back for the stable. It would take her an age to get the horse ready — she was hopeless at it on her own: she made sudden, frenetic movements that startled the poor fellow. Blackie wouldn't even come to her; usually he'd just hang his head, defeated, in the corner of his paddock until she took hold of him, and always too roughly. Norman was much better at it, on account of loving him.

'Stay clean,' Lilias had said, and cuffed him around the ears a little — hard enough to hurt so as to give him an idea of what might come later.

Lyn Comfort's ears glowed like they'd been boxed too, but it was more likely sunburn. He was gazing past Norman at the big white two-storey villa, his eyes on the high turret set into the gabled roof, which was also Norman's favourite part of the house. It was where Lilias let him practise his cello. He had a chair and a tuning fork and a music stand. Even when he wasn't practising he spent hours up there, at the edges of the octagonal room, pressing his face to each of the eight panes of glass in turn, round and round, the view shifting and intercepting in each frame. Four of the panes gave him consecutive views of their garden running down to the sea and the pinched waist of the harbour. On this fine busy morning he'd seen dinghies and yachts and steamships; to the east there were cutters and scows, passing through, blurring at the bevel, all the way from Stanley Point to the sugar works and on to Greenhithe. The town side was roofs and gardens, the close view of his own horse paddock and orchard, and up the hill to Jervois Road.

There was a fine view of the Comforts' house, which was interesting to watch for the number of times people appeared at the windows or went in and out of the doors, passing along the verandas upstairs and down and paths through the garden and out, over the hillside. At night they hardly ever pulled the curtains, not unless their mother sat up with them and she most often went to bed — *utterly utterly exhausted*, as cousin Lilias said, and lucky not to *have perished in the attempt*. The mother would ask for the curtains to be drawn while she lit the lamp, or she would draw them herself, at which point Norman would go downstairs.

Otherwise, he watched Innes and George out on the veranda with their cigarettes. He could see Lorna playing the piano inside, and Lyn with the other younger children singing and laughing. Sometimes they played cards. The father often sat in the same room, reading the paper. Sometimes he lowered the paper and said something to the children. Once or twice he'd stood angrily and yelled at them, waving his hands. If the mother hadn't pulled the curtains then Norman could have seen what she did. He used to hear her singing at night from his bedroom downstairs, but not since he was little. The new boy was her tenth, and Lilias hoped she'd *stop there*.

'Take me up to the tower.' Lyn put his jar down on the muddy pavement. 'You promised.' The jar wobbled, found its balance between a stone and a lump of macadam come loose from the road. The boys watched it steady itself, then Lyn returned his gaze to the turret. A gentle gust of wind lifted a lock of his hair, which fell in a dirty blond curl on his brow. His gap-tooth smile was a boat missing some boards.

What had become of his cousin? Norman strained his hearing for the horse, for the wheels. He shouldn't be talking to Lyn, even though Lilias seemed to think it perfectly fair to tell him every detail she heard about the Comforts. One more week until school went back and he could see Lyn every day. They'd be back to sharing their desk, running around together at play-lunch and down the hill to eat at noon. During the holidays Norman wasn't allowed to *add to Mrs Comfort's burden*. Lilias tried to keep him at home.

'Can you hear anything?' Norman asked. 'Lilias is trying to catch Blackie. We're going into town.' It stood to reason Lyn's ears would be better at hearing than his own, being bigger, standing further out from his head, wide enough even to catch the new Hertzian waves.

Suddenly, the jar at Lyn's feet gave a violent shudder and fell over. The eel slithered out and Norman saw that not only was it still alive, but it had turned into a snake that could move on land, which made him want to scream. He pushed his hands into his pockets, stood up very straight and pulled his feet closely together so tightly it made his backside ache.

Lyn Comfort was seven years old, like him, and he wasn't afraid, but that was because it was his own snake, which he was picking up behind the head and holding out towards him. It was all writhing black mud and slime, and horribly its skin had split on one side, showing grey-white flesh and slimy, so slimy he had to drop it. Mid-air the monster arched, stiffened and flew through the air to Norman, lying for an instant against his front like a whip, its smashed head thrashing and bashing on his cream cambric shirt, leaving a streak of snot and blood. Norman did scream then, his mouth open so wide his straw hat fell off the back of his head and he could feel the hot summer air on the root of his tongue. Then there were horse hooves and wheels ringing and running feet and Lilias's strong arms closing around him from behind and Lyn Comfort making a run for it, not home to his place but back down the hill towards the cliff path and the pines, his skinny legs pelting into the blue yonder.

Lilias turned Norman around and he looked up into her pretty young face, round and smooth, her eyelashes casting perfect spiny shadows like the fins of the eel on her white cheek. Her mouth was pursed and she was frowning and Norman quietened, drew breath to begin his explanation, but as he did she clocked him, hard, without asking for the story. He ran off, sobbing, towards the turret. When she called after him, just the once, he ignored her.

He stayed up there until tea-time, long enough to see his cousin return from town with a scowl on her face and so many parcels that the maid had to go in and out to carry them all in. He saw his father come down the hill on his way home from his tannery in Cox's Bay, pausing to stroke Mrs Campbell's cat, which was making a meal of the eel. He saw the glow of light up on the ridge, which meant the terminal lamp had been lit at the Barn at the top of Wallace Street, where the trams slept at night, their long green poles laid along their roofs. On the harbour side he saw fishing boats come in, the night fishermen go out; from his westernmost window he watched a light move about on a scow bringing logs, probably to Mr Comfort's mill, which was next door to Mr Martingale's tannery up Cox's Creek. He saw Lyn Comfort sneak home the back way with the next-brother-up, Walter; he saw the mother sitting on the upstairs paint-peeling verandah in the last of the sunset, holding the wrapped new baby in her arms. He saw one of the older girls come out of the kitchen door and go down to the vegetable beds to pick silverbeet; he saw Mr Comfort come to a downstairs window and look out at the golden evening. He heard a knock at the door. Some time ago. Why hadn't the maid come to get him for tea? Maybe Lilias had decided the eel was his fault and he wasn't to get any.

Norman's legs were aching and his forehead was numb in the middle, from where he'd pressed it against the glass, looking out onto the blue dusk. When he'd heard his father calling him he couldn't make his body climb down the narrow, steep stairs; he couldn't even make himself leave the room. His legs kept moving him to the next eye of the turret, and the next. Even when his father came right up into the little octagonal room he couldn't turn around. Instead he stepped sideways to the next window, which gave out down the gables and verandah roofs to the garden below, which was deserted. The heavy-headed white roses in the mounded bed at its centre cast faint, bobbing shadows. There were footprints in the sand and tar of the carriageway. Or were there? He couldn't see properly from here.

'Norman. Have you been practising?'

If his father looked around he would see that the cello wasn't here. It was downstairs in his bedroom. How could he practise if he didn't have his cello? He heard his father sigh.

'Norman. We have guests.'

Under the honeysuckle hedge was the Comforts' rugby ball, shared by all the brothers. Walter or one of the others must have kicked it over the fence again.

'Turn around, Norman.'

Norman did, enough to see that his father had his hand outstretched to take his. He took hold of it before he looked up into his father's face to see he was smiling, but it was a twisted smile on his wide mouth, as if one part of him wanted to be kind and the other didn't.

'Good boy,' was all he said. When they got to the bottom of the ladder he pushed him gently ahead and Norman led the way, dead centre down the red runner on the two wide, echoing wooden staircases and across the hall to the parlour, marching in step, with his father's warm hand on his shoulder.

Lyn Comfort stood snivelling in front of the fireplace and Mr Comfort stood there too, one arm resting on the mantelpiece, his fingertips on the base of the globe of kauri gum that Norman wasn't allowed to touch — though he lifted his arm and straightened as they came in. Above Mr Comfort's head hung the portrait, which had been painted by a visiting London artist a couple of months before Norman's mother died. Norman didn't like it, even though he was in it himself, a little boy of three leaning against her legs, all in lace. He thought she looked sad, as if she would like to step down from the picture and sit again in her fireside chair, which was a slightly smaller version of Father's. He hated looking at her beautiful face, her soft brown eyes, her piled shining hair. In one hand she held her violin, dangling it by its scroll as she would never have held it in life. Norman remembered it only under her chin, or held in her lap like a baby. It was false. What was true was the way her hand lay protectively against his back, that encompassing arm. If he looked long enough, when he came into the parlour on his own, he could smell the soap from her bath, the silk of her skirts, feel the soft skin of her cheek under his lips.

Quickly, before the tears came, he dropped his gaze to Lyn, who had tried to clean himself up but he hadn't gone the whole swag — his knees were possibly worse than before. He had on a different shirt but the same plus-fours, which gave off a smell of wet wool and worse. Mr Comfort was much older than his own father. He had steely grey hair and moustache and his teeth were yellow. Lilias said that before he took the pledge *he was a drinker and pulled himself back from the brink of hell.*

Lilias herself sat on the overstuffed ottoman under the window, bolt upright, flushed and as motionless as if the horsehair had somehow seeped up out of the furniture to fill her dress and skin. Her lips were pressed together and her hands clasped tightly at her breast as if she were about to burst into prayer. It was only last summer, when she was still fifteen and first came to live with them, that she ran one day with some of the girls, taking off down to the Salt Water Baths. She had to be fetched back to her duties by Father. What if she got up now and ran around madly? She could lift her long skirts and run around and around the room until she ran out of steam. She was bottled up. She'd come from a farm but she was bad with horses. She needed to let her spring run down. If she were a toy he would lose her key.

'Now, Lyn,' she said, before either of the fathers had a chance, 'you threw an eel at Norman and ruined his shirt.' And even though it was rude, she pointed at Norman and he found himself looking down at his front, just as everyone else was, and at the sight of the dried black eel blood and brown muck he felt his gorge rise. He hadn't looked all afternoon, though he had smelt the fishy stink of it rise between him and the glass. He swallowed again and again, felt a hard ball of air form in his stomach.

'It was dead!' Lyn lifted his face for the first time since they'd come into the room, and Norman saw that the snivelling had just been an act. 'Wouldn't have hurt him.'

'It was not!' Norman said, and the ball of air came achingly up his throat as a burp; he couldn't help it. 'It was alive and went stiff and flung itself at me.' The pressure on his shoulder increased. He'd forgotten his father's hand was still there.

'That's enough, Norman.'

The hand dropped away and Norman shivered suddenly, his father behind him radiating chill like a cold patch in the sea he had just swum through. Lyn gave him a look, which was probably to do with his burp. He felt like a stupid baby.

Mr Comfort took a step closer to his son. 'Lyn?' he said gently. 'Out with it.'

But Lyn said nothing. He just stared at Norman — *stare, stare, like a bear* — his eyes the same glinting blue as his father's.

'Hurry up, young Lyn,' said Lilias, leaning forward as far as her tight waist would allow. Lyn mumbled, and although Norman didn't hear it the fathers did, and that was enough.

'Now shake hands on it like gentlemen,' said Norman's father, 'and let's put this silly nonsense behind us.'

Lyn extended a grimy hand and maybe it was Norman's reluctance to grasp it that propelled him past it, to instead wrap Lyn in his arms in a fierce embrace. He felt his friend's breath gust against his ear; he pressed his warm cheek against Lyn's. Around them the grown-ups were silent and Norman kept his eyes shut tight, in order not to see their expressions. He held Lyn in his arms, everything that was Lyn — the smell of the sea, the wide grin, all the joy of him. At last, one of the fathers cleared his throat and Norman took it as his cue to step away. The men were smiling. Lilias, leaving her perch on the ottoman, was not.

'I don't think that quite serves as an apology —' but Norman's father quietened her with a look. He saw the visitors out to the front door, and in the short silence that followed, Norman, though he remained staring at his toes, was aware of Lilias glowering at him.

'Fancy coming downstairs still wearing that shirt,' she hissed scornfully. 'You silly, silly goose.'

Obediently, to put things right, Norman went out quietly into the hall and took the stairs to his room to change. At his back he heard his father's rapid stride up the hall. There were raised voices and he wondered if they were arguing about him, or the shopping his cousin had done, which pastime had got her into trouble before. She had a weakness for Smith and Caughey, for George Courts and a drapery at Three Lamps. Pausing on the first landing, he strained his ears and heard the name 'Lorna', and 'Queen Street', and the phrase 'cooked up', loudly, from his father. Back down the stairs he came, two treads, then three, close enough to hear Lilias explain Lorna's disregard for the seriousness of the crime, all because her brothers wore rags while she herself kept Norman so neat and it was *so difficult*. She began to cry. His father murmured, close and warm, soft words of solace that Norman couldn't make out but that filled him with an anguish he didn't recognise as jealousy. He wondered if his father had laid his hand on Lilias's shoulder, heavy and warm, as he had on Norman's as they'd descended the stairs.

Norman took off his shirt, rolled it up into a ball and tossed it over the polished balustrade, where it hung for a moment, unfurling a little before it began its shameful, grubby, floating descent: a skin he threw off into the well of the hall like a snake, like a peeled eel.

Tim Jones

Win a Day with Mikhail Gorbachev: A Melodrama in Four Parts

I: Off to Work

MIKHAIL GORBACHEV'S DAY BEGINS MUCH like that of any busy western executive. After a vigorous session of sexual intercourse, Mikhail and his wife, Raisa (a former student of philosophy at Moscow University who now drives a tractor in the Ukraine), enjoy a leisurely shower together before descending the central staircase of their modest Kremlin apartment to a hearty breakfast. Mikhail, trained as a lawyer, puts on the toast while Raisa brews up a stiff samovar of tea.

Over the breakfast table, Mick and Raisa chat about the news in the morning's *Pravda* and the hot gossip among their circle of friends — mostly the latest titillating details of Soviet Premier Nikolai Tikhonov's infatuation with a twenty-two-year-old Intourist guide — before sticking the dishes in the machine and heading off to work. For Raisa, it's now just a matter of setting the matter transmitter for the banks of the Dnieper and stepping through to the collective farm; for Mikhail, it's a brisk walk across the back yard to his regular job as General Secretary of the Central Committee of the Communist Party of the Soviet Union.

Wednesday the 15th of May is a comparatively light day for Mikhail, who arrives at the office at 9 am sharp, exchanging quips about the previous night's dismal performance by Moscow Dynamo (they lost 1–5 to Punta Arenas F.C.) with his guards as he pushes open the swing doors of the Central Committee's open-plan office and heads for his desk at the back. After taking a quick look at the morning's intelligence bulletins — it appears Ronald Reagan has fallen off his horse again — he welcomes in the man ultimately responsible for preparing them, KGB Chief Viktor Chebrikov.

Viktor, who wears a terrible line in spectacles, is an affable, balding secret police professional. Today he's looking more than usually pleased with himself, and the reason appears to be contained in a book he's carrying in his one good hand (the withering of the other is a legacy of the Sverdlovsk anthrax epidemic). The book, it transpires, is Arthur C. Clarke's *Expedition to Earth*.

II: Arthur C. Clarke

'ARTHUR C. CLARKE, EH, VIKTOR? How do you rate him in comparison with Asimov?' Mikhail, a subscriber to *Analog*, asks his security chief.

'Well, as an SF writer, I think Clarke's got the edge. He brings a real quality of transcendence to his best work, so that it attains a numinous quality that belies his claim to be a writer of hard SF. *Expedition to Earth* showcases this well, I feel — stories like "Second Dawn", "Encounter in the Dawn", and, particularly, the title story have a haunting, evocative quality that derives in large part from the revelation of powerful contemporary motifs in unfamiliar and often ironic settings. "The Sentinel" is of course of special interest as the progenitor of *2001: A Space Odyssey* — have you seen the film, Mikhail?'

'I have. Almost as good as *Solaris*.'

'If you make allowances for its crypto-bourgeois philosophy,' Viktor says severely. 'But as for comparing Clarke with Asimov — Clarke's a fine writer, but I can't go past the fact that Asimov was born here.'

'True, Viktor, although I don't think we should let national chauvinism influence our literary judgement.'

'If you say so, boss. Anyway, getting back to *Expedition to Earth*, there's one story in it that appears particularly relevant in the light of Academician Ivanenko's recent investigations. Called "Loophole", it's cast in epistolary form —'

'Letters, right?'

'Letters, yes. It starts with an exchange of missives between the ruler of Mars and his chief scientist. The Martians have just noticed the first atomic bomb test here on Earth, and — well, perhaps you'd like to read it for yourself, Mick?'

As Mikhail Gorbachev reads of the Martians' plans to dominate and eliminate humans by controlling interplanetary space, and of the loophole through which the humans strike first, Viktor Chebrikov's gaze strays to the window at the other end of the room. On the other side of that window the Lubyanka waits to receive its unwilling guests, three faceless bodies lie just beneath the melting snows of Gorky Park, and Arkady Renko and a small group of friends sit watching a smuggled videotape of *Hill Street Blues*.

In the snows east of Irkutsk, workers on the Baikal–Amur Mainline take care to prevent their skin freezing to the track, and in the Tunguska the trees are again laid flat. Nude bathers are causing a stir in certain Black Sea resorts, while in a dacha just outside Moscow, Nikolai Tikhonov gives his all in the arms of his beloved, as KGB cameras record the scene for posterity.

And more coffins return through the mountain passes from Afghanistan, and Vladimir Arsenyev roams through the taiga with his friend Dersu Uzala, and Stalin's daughter leaves and returns in pain, over and over, as the birches nod their heads in the breeze above the rich black Russian soil.

Mikhail Gorbachev finishes reading. 'Hmmm, matter transmitters, eh? What a bright spark that Arthur C. Clarke is. Well, Viktor, any other news? Can my doctors be trusted?'

'Not a disloyal thought in their heads, Mick. I think you're safe there. But I must be going. I have an ethnic minority to oppress.'

'Which one?'

'Why, the Russians, of course!'

'One of these days we'll have to stop laughing at that joke. Well, Viktor, show that story to our good friend the Marshal. Our team at Tyuratam may be able to make something of it.'

'Okay, boss, I'm away. See you at the Politburo meeting.'

Mikhail spends the rest of the morning going through his paperwork and reading his mail; there are five circulars, two chain letters, one misdirected subscription to *Krokodil* and no invitations to the Vatican. At lunchtime there's time for a brisk game of squash with Vitaly Vorotnikov before the 2 pm Politburo meeting.

III: The Politburo

THE POLITBURO HAD TRADITIONALLY MET in a sombre, marbled room, sitting six a side along a massive table. Mikhail felt that this arrangement was not conducive to increased productivity and efficiency, so did away with the heavy table and got everybody to sit in a circle on the ground, on cushions lovingly sewn in one of the more obscure Central Asian republics. The older Politburo members were not entirely happy about this arrangement, and still grumbled about it when they thought themselves unobserved. However, the younger men (for there were no female members of this most exclusive club) seemed to like the arrangement, and at the moment it was these men — Vorotnikov, Egor Ligachev, Nikolai Ryzhkov, Chebrikov, Eduard Shevardnadze, and Gorbachev himself — who called the shots.

Everyone is in their seats by 2 pm sharp, and Mikhail opens the meeting by pinning a big sheet of paper to the wall and asking for agenda items. Ligachev, who has charge of the minutes of the previous meeting, reminds everyone that the Geneva summit and the forthcoming grain harvest are matters that were not finalised at the last meeting. New agenda items include progress on the BAM rerouting, another increase in funds for technical intelligence, and the colour scheme for the Politburo's new Zil limousines.

The meeting opens with a sharing session, wherein each member lets the others know how they're feeling, so their private, personal problems won't fester unacknowledged beneath the surface of the meeting. Nikolai Tikhonov announces that he has never felt better; Chebrikov winks at Gorbachev. Andrei Gromyko, who has become slightly deaf, queries why anyone would want to feel butter. Shevardnadze, newly appointed Foreign Minister, reveals he's had an exciting day broadening his knowledge of geography, and now knows where Africa and Australia are. Someone whistles a derisory bar or two of "Georgia on My Mind". Generally, everyone is having a good day, although Vorotnikov claims that Gorbachev has obstructed him on a couple of key points — then must hasten to explain he is talking about the lunchtime squash game rather than matters of state.

The Geneva summit (where Mikhail plans to try for a propaganda coup by challenging Reagan to see who can stay on a horse the longest), BAM, a 25 per cent increase in funds for purchase of western microcomputers and microengineers, and the grain harvest (about which there was general agreement that having one would be a Good Idea) are all sorted out quite simply. As everyone fears, the big clash between Gorbachev's new guard and the remaining old-timers comes over the Zils' paintwork.

The matter had first surfaced under Gorbachev's predecessor, Konstantin Chernenko, and, in keeping with the dour Siberian's approach, the normal black colour scheme had been approved. However, Geidar Aliyev had felt even at the time that something more dynamic was called for, and was now proposing a trendy metallic red with racing stripes down the sides. A reliable source who did not wish to be named claimed that Aliyev had originally been planning to include mag wheels and furry dice in the package, but decided this might lessen Politburo members' dignity in the eyes of the Russian people.

After Aliyev has put his proposal, there is an uneasy silence in the room. When Gorbachev, who is facilitating the meeting, asks if there is any disagreement, President Andrei Gromyko rises to his feet.

'For twenty-five years I was the Foreign Minister of the Soviet Union. For all that time, Soviet representatives maintained the most punctilious dignity and reserve. The western imperialists seek to portray us as barbarians, but we have shown that we are the true standard-bearers of civilisation. Our sober black Zil limousines have long been an important part of our image as serious, responsible world leaders. I could never agree to such a proposal.'

'Does that means you'd be prepared to block consensus on it, Andrei?'

'Yes, Mikhail, I would.'

'Well, does anyone want to try to change Andrei's mind?'

Ligachev, who has a reputation for over-enthusiasm, rises to his feet.

'Listen, Andrei, we're living in the 1980s now, not the 1950s. We're talking marketing, we're talking positioning, we're talking selling ourselves in the marketplace. Today's Politburo needs to project a positive, upmarket image, inspiring confidence among our customers. Professor Lysenko over at the Soviet Institute of Psychodemographics tells me their latest survey indicates that more Great Russians in the 16–25 cohort know that Wham! recently played China than are aware that the Central Committee recently approved the latest five-year plan. Our collective name-recognition factor, with the understandable exception of Comrade Gorbachev, is less than that of Elton John's percussionist. The citizens of Ust-Kut have recently petitioned to have the name of their main street changed from Lenin Prospekt to Lennon Prospekt! When this sort of thing is happening in Ust-Kut, need I say more?'

(The citizens of Ust-Kut, a small but bustling city in the progressive Lake Baikal region, would doubtless have protested at this implied slur on their modernity, but as it has not until now been revealed, they went about their business in happy ignorance.)

'Egor, interesting as all this is, I don't see why it means we have to have red Zils with racing stripes down the sides.'

'Because they're new! They're modern! They're positive! They project the go-ahead image we need. Personally, I'd be prepared to compromise on the racing stripes but, after all, Comrade Gromyko, red is the colour of our Union's flag. Are you suggesting we should change that?'

Mikhail senses that tempers are rising. A good facilitator must be able to strike a balance between non-interference when a meeting is flowing smoothly and appropriate intervention when things are going off the rails. Now is a time for the latter.

'It's obvious we have considerable disagreement on this issue, and I don't think we can reach a consensus at this meeting. What I suggest is that a few people who have got strong feelings on the issue get together and see if they can work out a compromise proposal, or a new and better one, to present to the next meeting. I won't join that group myself, but, stepping outside my role as facilitator, I'd like to suggest a dual fleet, one in black for the more ceremonial occasions and one in red, with or without stripes, for trips to the movies and so forth. Are there any volunteers for the working party?'

Aliyev, Ligachev, Vorotnikov and, after some prompting, Gromyko agree to meet soon to come up with a solution that can be presented to the next Politburo meeting. The present meeting closes with an evaluation; everyone (even Gromyko) agrees it has gone well. Under Brezhnev and Chernenko, everyone would have headed off for a few vodkas at this point, but the fate of Grigory Romanov and other victims of Gorbachev's anti-alcoholism drive persuades them all to settle, in the public interim, for tea, coffee and Milo. After the last cup has been smashed in the fireplace, there's just enough time for Mikhail to pick up his dufflebag from the office before heading home to cook tea.

IV: Expedition to Earth

AFTER THE EVENING MEAL, RAISA and Mikhail would normally head out to the theatre or a movie, or invite a few friends round for a Pepsi. Tonight, however, they're off to Sheremetyevo Airport to greet the winner of the US–Soviet Friendship Society's 'Win a Day with Mikhail Gorbachev' competition. This competition attracted over 10,000 entries, despite unfavourable comment in the US media, and represents a significant propaganda victory for the Soviet Union. Contestants were required to write an essay on the subject 'US–Soviet Relations: Where to from here?', and as a tie-breaker had been asked to complete, in 25 words or fewer, the sentence: 'I would like to visit the Soviet Union because . . .'

The tie-breaker had not in fact been required, as the winner's essay stood head and shoulders above its competition, but his sentence read: 'I would like to visit the Soviet Union because I have in my possession complete design drawings of the prototype Strategic Defence Initiative antimissile laser system.' But this sentence contains 26 words and would, had the tie-breaker been required, undoubtedly have been disqualified.

The winner calls himself Jim Beam, and he arrives from Heathrow Airport by Aeroflot. He is met as he steps off the plane by senior officers of Soviet military intelligence, who relieve him of a folder of drawings he obligingly presents to them, and, after submitting to a final search, he is permitted to meet the Gorbachevs and the press. After exchanging pleasantries, the threesome return to the Kremlin for a private get-acquainted chat in Mikhail and Raisa's apartment. 'That means private,' Mikhail insists, shooing away the lurking Kremlin guards.

When the door has closed behind the last of the guards, it is Raisa who speaks. 'We have been awaiting this meeting for a long time, Anatar.

But why did you choose such a public method of arrival?'

The Ambassador to Earth of the Galactic Federation peels off his false head, legs and genitals, places them in a small attaché case, and squats before them in its true form. 'An old Earth custom, I believe — of hiding in plain sight. How could anyone so public as Mr Jim Beam be other than what he seemed? Well, we can dispense with Mr Beam now. How soon can you leave?'

'I've told my colleagues on the collective farm that I'm taking a week's holiday — I believe that will be sufficient,' said Raisa. 'I've packed my bags, and we recovered the atmosphere suit and other equipment from the Tunguska a week ago. The matter transmitter brought them in easily. I'm ready when you are, Anatar.'

'Very well. Mr Gorbachev, would you like to come with us to farewell your wife?'

'I certainly would. But there's one thing I don't understand, Anatar: why can't the matter transmitter take Raisa all the way to Galactic HQ?'

'I don't know, General Secretary. I'm a diplomat, not a scientist. But I've been told that both loci of the matter transmitter need to be on the same planetary body — something to do with frames of reference, I understand.'

'Science is a wonderful thing. I must introduce you to some of our more far-sighted writers on the subject.'

'Save the books for later, Mick,' says Raisa. 'It's time to go.'

The aliens' ship is waiting in a forest between Shar'ya and Kirov; their matter transmitter, of which an embarrassed Academician Ivanenko is still trying to provide a convincing explanation to the military, sends them through one at a time. The ship is the conventional saucer shape. A ramp extends to the ground, and between the pine trees small figures on trolleys are moving through the mist, collecting specimens. Before Raisa puts on her atmosphere suit and goes off to the headquarters of the Galactic Federation to present the case for Earth's admission, she and Mikhail say goodbye. They stand at the foot of the ramp, holding each other close.

'Keep everything ticking over while I'm away, won't you, Mick?'

'I don't expect any major problems. I'm sure we'll reach a compromise on the Zils without Andrei losing face. Nothing else should be too difficult — for me. You're the one who's got the hard work ahead.'

'Oh, I think I'll manage okay. It's a formality, really, isn't it? Well, Anatar is looking impatient probably. I have to go. I love you, darling. Take care.'

'I will. You take care too. I'll take a day off when you get back, eh?'

They hold hands as long as they can while Raisa seals herself into the suit. Then they separate, and she walks slowly up the ramp as the returning alien scientists whir past her. When they have all returned, the ramp is closed and the spaceship rises silently upwards. As Mikhail turns to return to Moscow, the sky fills with light and a peal of thunder echoes over the sleeping land.

Fiona Kidman

Heaven Freezes

SIMON AND HIS DAUGHTER RUTH are on their way to the supermarket when the sky changes from its ordinary cloud-strewn breezy Wellington look to a blue of such extraordinary radiance that for a moment he feels his heart freeze with the strange icy beauty of it.

This light has all the appearance of a blue rainbow. Beneath it, the surface of the harbour has become illuminated in such a way that a band of waves seems to lift from the ocean, as if moving towards them.

When the car is parked, father and daughter stand for some minutes absorbing what — it is clear now — is some optical illusion, a phenomenon of light, one they have never seen before. Around them in the carpark, others are also standing looking at it. Perfect strangers call out to one another, saying, 'D'you see that? What do you make of that?'

A woman laughs nervously. 'Perhaps it's a plane falling,' she says. There is a nervous twitch of shoulders. The supermarket is close to the flight path of planes. But there is no sign of things falling, no wreckage, no bangs.

'I reckon a space shuttle just flushed its toilet,' says a young man who has been collecting up trolleys, and everyone laughs, breaking the tension. But Simon cannot move, riveted to the warm asphalt. Ruth stands particularly close to his elbow, as if she might somehow protect him. She has a stocky build, more like that of her several aunts than her mother, who was tall and dark, with a rangy, loose-limbed figure. Ruth's sister, Janet, is like her, but she lives in Canada and Simon hasn't seen her in a long time. Soon, he hopes, he will visit her and hold his grandson. He sees him in little electronic moving pictures on his computer screen almost every day, but that is not the same. He sighs. So many of his decisions now depend on Stephanie's work. It may not suit her. She might feel offended if he goes off without her, but she may be too busy to go with him.

'We should start the shopping,' Ruth says gently. 'Remember, you have the boys to pick up at three, and we promised Stephanie we would make an early dinner so she can get away to her meeting.'

'She'll probably work through and we'll end up eating without her,' he says, and immediately regrets this seeming betrayal.

'We were going to start shopping for the lunch, too,' says Ruth, as if she hasn't heard.

On Sunday it will be his birthday — his sixty-second — and there is to be a lunch party. The guests will all be his friends. Although he has lived in Wellington with Stephanie for three years now, they have never had a party where the guests were not her friends. She is the director of the international section of a bank and knows a great many people with money. Because of her work, she entertains managing directors of insurance companies and property developers, investors from town and country, and she finds it very helpful that Simon is from what she terms the rural sector, because there is always someone for these out-of-town investors to talk to. She knows actors, a handful of writers and several film-makers. Not all of these people are rich, but knowing them appeals to those who are.

The suggestion for the gathering had been Ruth's. We should do something special, she emailed when she knew she would be visiting. She lives in Australia — not as far away as Janet, but still he doesn't see her very often. Ruth is a lawyer, independent and single. She has had some relationships but does not want to be committed to anyone, she says. Not until she meets the right person.

It grieves him that what she might really be saying is that even meeting the right person doesn't mean that love lasts for all time, or that you are certain to live happily ever after. That you may be abandoned when you least expect it.

Ruth knows too much for her own good, Simon has told himself, more than once. There are things he should discuss with her, but he puts it off. He promises himself that when he and the two girls are all next together he will, but he can't see when that might be.

'You should have some friends over,' Stephanie said, when the subject of the birthday came up, and he agreed that yes, it would be nice, provided his birthday was not announced. What he would have liked more than anything was for him and Stephanie and Ruth to go to a good restaurant, and let the day unfold around them. Except that Ruth and Stephanie cannot be relied on to get along, and then there are Stephanie's boys to consider, and so he let it go, falling in with the plan. Although drawing up a list of friends turned out more difficult than he expected. The truth is, he does not know many people well. His days stretch unpeopled before him, one after another, until he picks up his wife's children from school, and eventually she comes home to him.

When he first sees the strange blue rainbow he feels dizzy beneath the fragmented light, puts his hand on the bonnet of his silver Mercedes.

He feels as if something is passing through him — knowledge, perhaps. He hopes Ruth hasn't noticed, but he believes he has not faltered, that what has taken place has not occupied more than seconds.

Inside the cool interior of New World it is still possible to see the blue blaze of light through the tall windows, causing shoppers to look up as word travels. Ruth and Simon buy polystyrene containers of strong black coffee to sip as they move sturdily around the supermarket choosing good cheeses and wine. He notices how Ruth smiles at the checkout attendants and addresses them by the names on their lapel badges. As if they were in the country. As Aileen would have done. So, in this way, she is like her mother.

Matamata sits on Highway 27, between the Waikato and the Bay of Plenty. There is a long main street, with red brick banks on the corners, a huddle of grocery and drapery and hardware stores, as well as antique shops that sell very good silver. When you say Matamata these days most people think hobbits, and cameramen with rings in their ears, and girls with studs in their tongues bearing clapper-boards. Peter Jackson filmed parts of *The Lord of the Rings* there. In his wake, tourists have come to view the green rolling landscape searching for signs of magic. Simon and Aileen farmed five kilometres or so off the main highway, down a gravel road. Everyone knew everyone then when they came to town.

Simon wasn't meant to be the farmer. His brother Neil never wanted anything but the farm, and Simon only ever wanted to leave it. But Neil was a cocky sort of kid. He took the tractor down to the willow paddock one day when his father had told him the slope was too muddy. When it rolled, Neil went under and that was that.

There would be nobody, his father said, nobody to take the farm on. He said it over and over, until his wife begged him to stop. Then Simon said he would stay.

He never understood why he said this; he was due to begin an arts degree at the end of that summer. But Simon told his father this anyway, that he would stay, and when he did, it seemed like the right thing. He stopped reading so much, and went to dances at the hall, and drove his Vauxhall too fast on the long straight Waikato roads, drinking more than he should, and milking cows morning and night. Then Aileen arrived in town to take over as the dental nurse at the school, and he fell for her at one of the pipe band dances, which he always thought were a bit weird because some of the guys still turned up in their kilts, but they were a good place for a laugh.

Aileen had a special languid way of dancing, and ink-coloured hair that floated on her shoulders. Her family had a citrus orchard over near the Mount. They were plain, humorous folk, a little religious but not overly so. Simon thought he might die of happiness in her arms the first time she let him kiss her. His parents were ready to move into town by then, so the house was theirs for the taking. He knew he was Aileen's first when they got married.

You would expect Stephanie and Ruth to get on but they don't. They have Australia in common, because that is where Stephanie comes from. When Ruth stays she helps with Stephanie's boys, Terence and Jonathan. She plays Monopoly and Scrabble with them, though they are not very secretly bored by these attempts to distract them from computer games. Board games are what Ruth played with her Aunt Isabel when she was a child — that is the extent of her experience with children. Still she persists with her stepbrothers (not that she ever refers to their mother as her stepmother). Terence has under-eleven cricket practice after school, and Ruth picks him up and goes to watch him play. Last year when she visited she took the oranges for half-time to the soccer game on a Saturday morning. 'The boys' friends think I'm their grandfather,' Simon had told her. Perhaps she had seen how tired he was.

'I don't have to stay with you, you know,' she said to Simon more than once. Her visits were always connected with business, not just to see him. But on this point he was adamant. He wasn't having his daughter staying in a hotel in the same town as him. Country again, he knew that. This irritated Stephanie.

'Those girls rule your life,' she said during Ruth's last visit, and the whole thing blew up to a shouting match before he understood what was happening. Stephanie had come in from work very late, as she often did. She had a colleague called Phil who, she had explained from the outset, was not just competent but a good friend. True, he was a needy person — a man who had never married, with emotional uncertainties about his life — but she couldn't afford to lose him. She was so busy, always so busy at work, and he was really her right-hand man, so when he crashed she had to, you know, help him work through his problems, his relationships with his fellow workers. Besides, as she kept emphasising, he was a friend.

Simon had met Phil several times, mostly at gatherings of Stephanie's work friends. He understood right away that Phil was not in a sense a threat. He was one of those neutral middle-aged men, wearing a cravat with his shirt at the weekend, and well-cut slacks, Italian loafers (although Simon himself dresses rather like that these days, now that his wife has taken his clothes in hand). Watching Phil talk to Stephanie, Simon had no sense of chemistry between them. So it wasn't that. Only, friendship can be a worry. It occurs to him now and then that people might abandon love before friendship, that one might be a substitute for the other, at least in this ambivalent political city.

The evening his wife and daughter quarrelled, Stephanie had come in looking flushed, as if she had had a glass of wine, or perhaps two. She was wearing a brown coat like a cape and knee-high brown boots with heels. Stephanie is a small, fair woman, almost fragile in her appearance, and the way she was behaving was out of character, didn't suit her at all. Ruth and Simon had made dinner and, when the boys became fretful with hunger, fed them and sent them off to bed.

'Phil had another crisis,' Stephanie said, as if that explained everything. 'I hurried home to see the children. Now you've sent them packing.'

'No,' Ruth told her, 'their eyes were hanging out of their heads and Terence has a maths test in the morning.'

'You seem to know more about my children than I do. I like to see them in the evenings.'

'I'm sorry,' Simon said. 'They're still awake — why don't you go in while Ruth and I serve the dinner?'

But that didn't suit Stephanie either. She cast off her shoes, and let her bag fall on the floor as she dropped into a chair.

'It's all work, work, work,' she said. 'You don't understand what it's like. The pressure.' She put her hands up to her face.

'What can I do?' Simon said, kneeling beside her. 'Please, let me help.'

Ruth walked out of the room to the kitchen. Beyond the divider, they heard plates being pushed gently from one rack to another in the oven.

'We need to get out more. You and me.'

'Perhaps we do,' he said. 'Why don't we go out tomorrow while Ruth's still here? She could stay with the boys. What would you like to do?'

Stephanie decided they should see a movie. Someone had recommended *Little Fish* at the Rialto. When she named it, Ruth came out of the kitchen bearing a plate in each hand and put them on the table.

'No, Dad,' she said. 'No, you don't want to see that movie.'

'Why not?'

'Never mind why not. You just don't want to see it.'

'Have you?'

Ruth turned her face away. 'Just believe me.'

There was something dangerous in the air that he didn't

understand, some secret hanging between them. He wanted to make her tell him, demand not to be told what to do without an explanation here in his own home. Ruth's face closed and then Stephanie was shouting at them both, about how Ruth ought to mind her own business.

Later, after Ruth had gone, Stephanie said, 'So what was that all about?' putting the blame back squarely on Ruth.

'I don't know,' he said. 'I truly don't.' He could see, then, how it must have looked to Stephanie — that she was being excluded from something private between him and his daughter, perhaps something about her. When she understood that it wasn't like that, Stephanie had flowers delivered to Ruth in Melbourne. Please try again, Simon emailed. It will be all right.

After Aileen died, her sister Isabel came to live near Simon's farm so she could take care of the children. She was one of the plainer of Aileen's sisters, big-bosomed, with a right eye that wandered slightly inwards when she stared at you. Not that that should have made a difference, but there was something about her that announced her as less likely to marry than her sisters. At first she lived in the town and drove out every morning, but then a sharemilker's house came vacant at the farm along the road, when the owners switched to beef and sheep, so she moved in there; it was almost like having her living at the house. The only thing Simon and Isabel ever disagreed on in terms of how the girls were raised was about their going swimming. They were not allowed to go to the swimming hole at the river where Simon had swum with his brother and sister. Nor were they allowed to go on picnics with families who were going swimming. Isabel said it wasn't natural, he was denying them an ordinary enough pleasure. But when she saw that he was obstinate she said nothing more.

Even if she didn't seem the marrying kind, people began to expect that Isabel and Simon would marry, and for a while he thought they might too. It made perfect sense. The girls regarded her much as they would a mother, although Isabel never let the memory of Aileen disappear. But his life was changing. He had become a farmer who read, like he did when he was a boy at school. He joined the library committee, and became involved in local affairs. Someone said he would make a good mayor — a well-known and well-liked man, even if he kept his distance. They understood that, too. Many of the people in the town had Scots ancestry. Tragedy is tragedy but a man's own business. The local farmers asked him to join him in their advocacy with the Dairy Board, which he did for some years until the big corporations moved in and changed everything. These interests took him away from the town, to Auckland

and to Wellington.

In cities, he visited art galleries and saw movies and went to classical music concerts. He met women whom he could invite out to dinner and, when he had known them for a time, take them to bed. Each time it felt traitorous, although who he was betraying it was hard to say. Aileen's parents used to call sex 'nookie', and he and Aileen used to call it that, too, when they were being playful and silly. Let's have nookie, they said to each other. You want nookie? It was hard to get out of the habit of calling it that in his head. Nookie: he wanted it all the time.

He invited one of the women he met home for a weekend. There was no reason why he shouldn't, he told himself, driving guiltily past Isabel's house, half hoping she wouldn't find out, knowing perfectly well that the girls would tell her first thing on Monday. In the end he couldn't bring himself to ask the woman to his bed while his children were there.

A few weeks after this, Isabel told him she had accepted a proposal of marriage from a man who did bridge-building in the district. He would live with her in the sharemilker's house, and nothing about their arrangement would change. By this time, in fact, Janet was nearly through high school, and almost everything *was* changing. Soon the girls would be gone. He would begin to see less and less of Aileen and Isabel's family at the Mount. Isabel and her new husband would move away, and when they did he would rent the place for help on his own farm, because he didn't want to milk cows any more. After a while, he would switch to beef too.

He found himself settling to a routine of farming, reading, travelling to visit the girls wherever they happened to live, occasionally seeing women. After a time he seemed to need to do this less and less. The rituals of courting were uncertain and the publicity about STD's made him afraid; he was embarrassed to use condoms with women who were too old to have children, and frightened they wouldn't protect him with younger women who were hungrier and took it for granted that dinner meant sex. One day he was startled to realise that a whole quarter of a century had slipped by since Aileen died.

But just now and then he would hanker for live music and some company — something to break the dark circle of silence that enveloped the farmhouse in the dead of night. When the arts festival was on in Wellington that year, Simon found himself waiting for a concert to begin in the Michael Fowler Centre, and the appearance of the visiting conductor, a flamboyant Russian. Beside him sat a small blonde woman with a pert nose. The seat beside her was empty.

'My friend couldn't come,' she said, before the performance began, as if needing to explain why she was on her own. 'It seemed silly not to come when I already had the ticket.' She had a faint twang in her accent, so slight he couldn't immediately place it. I've been out of things for too long, he told himself. The woman's short hair curled at the nape of her neck. She was wearing a tight-fitting dark sweater with a scooped neckline and large amber beads with an antique design. When she looked up at him, her eyes seemed serious and steady.

As the musicians appeared on the stage Simon tried to find something to say before the hush for the performance began, but his voice came out cracked and raw. She leaned in towards him, her fingers to her lips. 'I'm Australian,' she whispered, as if that explained everything. She had a soft hot scent on her breath.

During her first visits to the farm, Stephanie tended his garden lovingly. She found shrubs that Aileen had planted long ago, covered by weeds on crumbling banks, but still going strong — misshapen camellias and rhododendrons, which she pruned and nursed, so that in the spring he saw them flowering again, and it was Stephanie he thought of, not Aileen. She planted a row of lavender along the front path, and wore big shady hats while she weeded them with her slim brown fingers. Usually she flew up to Hamilton and he met her at the airport. Occasionally she brought her sons, but back in Wellington she had a housekeeper who would stay over. Once, their father, who had gone back to Australia after his and Stephanie's divorce, came from Sydney and stayed with the boys. Simon didn't know if he was aware of where she was, or whether he cared.

In the big empty red brick house he was free to do whatever pleased them both. One night she whispered in his ear, 'I could have a baby with you.'

At first he was astonished by the idea, but from the way his cock lurched back into the fray he knew the idea pleased him. 'Would you?' he found himself saying later on, even though he knew he was near enough to being an old man. Stephanie herself was past forty.

She propped herself up on her elbow and looked down at him, her big rusty-coloured nipple brushing the side of his face. 'I'd do anything for you,' she said.

This didn't include coming to live in Matamata, as he soon discovered. 'I have my work in Wellington, and my friends,' she said. There would come a time, she went on, when they would need more than each other. That was the way of marriage. And didn't he love the city? There was so much for him to do there. Was it not, she asked him directly, time to move on?

Perhaps, he thought at the time, she had seen ghosts that he believed had disappeared with her presence in the house. The crooked shrubs. The old-fashioned kitchen. The bed with the same colonial-style headboard that had stood there since his marriage.

He does go to the movie at the Rialto, to a late-morning session. There are only two people in the theatre, himself and one other. At the counter, on an impulse, he buys a glass of wine, an odd thing to do at this time of day, but this whole secretive excursion feels strange.

The movie is about a beautiful reformed drug addict who had been a champion swimmer before she got hooked. When she is persuaded to get involved in one last deal that goes terribly wrong, and people die all around her, she goes to a beach and swims out to sea. Before she leaves on this last journey, she ducks under the water and waggles her hands jauntily above the waves, then swims out strongly and without a backward glance towards the open water.

The storyline is so bleak that once or twice Simon thinks about walking out. His glass of wine stands at his elbow untouched. He is still working out why Ruth had been so disturbed at the thought of him coming to the movie when the ending comes upon him unexpectedly. When it hits him, he drinks the wine straight down.

So, Ruth has known all along. He supposes that Janet must too, that they have talked about it over the years. That they may well have read the coroner's report, that people have talked to them. Isabel might have mentioned their mother's illness, assuming that at least they knew this. As indeed they should have, but if he told them that, then one thing would surely have led to another. Why had he let her go swimming alone? Hadn't he cared?

Does it matter how they know? They do. They know the story of the rolling surf carrying her away is a big fat lie.

Aileen didn't even wave.

About leaving. It's about leaving and being left, Simon thinks. The gap in between is so wide that you cannot see from one side to the other. Sometimes it is hard to remember what Aileen looked like. When she first had her dizzy spells she thought it was hormones. 'I've got another of these damn headaches,' she'd say, and take aspirin. It was the year of the Springbok tour riots and the start of the Roger Gascoigne wink on television, but she didn't watch anything — the light hurt her eyes. She decided she needed glasses. The optician in Hamilton was newly qualified and looked past the matter of her blurred vision. He thought she should see a specialist. This was how she came to learn that she had multiple sclerosis.

After the diagnosis he suggested they leave the farm. Already they were talking about ramps up to the house for when she needed a wheelchair. That was not what she wanted, Aileen said — the new pills she was taking would be sure to help. Yet she seemed to withdraw from him, as if she found him a stranger more often than not. This, the doctors explained, was part of the illness; mood and personality changes could be expected as parts of the brain began to close down.

But still there were times when the illness appeared to regress, and for a few days at a time she was the old Aileen, laughing, playing with the children, nuzzling him when she caught him unawares. During those times she would always suggest a visit to her parents at the Mount. The Mount was still the place she called home, even though it was built up with new houses and the drifting sandbanks had been tamed.

On one of these afternoons she said she wanted to go the beach for a little while, just her and Simon, and could her parents please mind the girls. In the car she sat quietly — not withdrawn, the way he was becoming used to, but seemingly content, as if just sitting there beside him was enough. It was a still, sunny day. She was wearing shorts and a halter-necked top, which pleased him because she wasn't disguising her body the way she mostly had since she got sick.

That was how she left him, before he understood what was happening, before he could catch up with her in the water, clothed as he was. She stumbled slightly as she got to the edge, but when she entered the water she launched herself in, her arms slicing cleanly through the waves. By the time he rushed in helplessly, then back to the sand to alert lifeguards that she was missing, she had swum beyond their reach.

Since then he has heard of other people doing it — young men and boys more often than girls. There was a boy who took off his clothes and folded them neatly in front of a waterside restaurant in Wellington, then swam past the windows, where a diner looking up from his Cajun fish and salad had seen him heading away beyond reach. He had disappeared long before the man could convince anyone of what was happening. How could it be? people said. But he knew it was easy. None of these incidents had ever been mentioned to him by the girls. He had no reason to think they would know.

When Simon had been married to Stephanie for two years, and not long after he had seen this movie, he said to her, 'Did you mean what you said about the baby?' Around that time he felt as if he was falling in love with her in a way that was deeper, stronger than before. Life might not be perfect, not just as he had imagined it, but he was fortunate and he thought he might not have given happiness the chance that he should

— he had held on to a past that should have been over. When he held her, he felt tender and virile and younger than he was.

It was a silly time to ask. They were stripping paint off the beautiful wooden doors of the house they were restoring in Kelburn. 'How could they have painted over this wood?' Stephanie said, grimacing. 'Oh my God, they've had varnish on them too.'

'Well, would you?' he said, knowing she had heard him.

'Darling,' she said in a half-mocking, vaguely amused voice, 'I work.'

'But you don't have to,' he said.

'I have children already.'

'I know, and they're great,' he began enthusiastically. But he couldn't go on with this.

After a moment of silence she put the paint stripper down carefully on a cloth. Her tone was unfriendly. 'Actually, I have to work tomorrow,' she said. 'In case you'd forgotten. I need to prepare.'

On the day of the lunch he has managed to assemble their kitchen designer, whom he has got to know quite well, and his wife who is a painter; also the son of one of his old Matamata farming friends, who is a graphic designer, and his girlfriend, an occupational therapist. Although the man is younger than Ruth at least they will know families in common, and the language of where they have come from. Then there is an older couple whom he met some years ago when fog closed the airport and they were stuck there together for hours. They are members of a chamber music society and have invited him to one or two concerts. The husband is a retired accountant and his wife teaches French. Altogether there are nine of them. He has sought to include some of Stephanie's friends but she has shrugged these suggestions aside. 'What about Phil?' he asks.

'I think he's tied up,' she says, as if Phil is a prisoner somewhere.

Stephanie has made a very large but also very light salad, and there is bread. Afterwards there will be dessert and cheeses. Simon feels that it is not enough, although this is the way well-to-do Wellington people eat at Sunday lunch. Light. He would have preferred a dinner but Stephanie thought lunch would be best. He thinks wistfully of the pot-luck dinners he and Aileen used to enjoy with their neighbours, remembers the dishes steaming in the frosty night air, the surprises inside (although everyone would have agreed in advance whether they were bringing mains or dessert). Nowadays he remembers Aileen more often, or at least their lives together. She is not the stranger to memory that she was. He tells himself this is healthy, that a sense of perspective has been achieved, that *Little Fish* and her wiggling fingers have freed him. Aileen would have said he'd 'stopped bottling things up'. These are private reflections but he is sure he is 'on the right track'.

The group talks in a desultory way, trying to establish links. Simon thinks the kitchen designer and the younger couple are wondering whether the salad is the first course. Stephanie attends to serving the guests, waving away offers of help, while Ruth talks to everyone in turn. She draws them in to talking about travel and places they have been, which takes quite a while. When that topic is exhausted, they move on — more guarded, because they don't know each other — to George Bush and the war in Iraq, and then the conversation drifts towards the weather, the odd cold summer they are experiencing, and that leads on to the blue blast of colour that lit up the sky earlier in the week. Everyone has a story about where they were and what they saw. The woman who is a painter is able to explain the phenomenon. It was, she says, a circumhorizontal arc, rare although not exceptional. The effect was created by light passing through wispy, high-altitude cirrus clouds that contain fine ice crystals. There is more to this, which the painter explains at some length. She is a middle-aged woman with heavy reddish-coloured hair that she pushes back behind her ears. Her fingernails have yellow and red paint beneath them. 'The arc is similar to a rainbow,' she says, 'but the ice crystals are shaped like thick plates with their faces parallel to the ground. When the light passes on the vertical side, it refracts from the bottom, and bends, like light through a prism.' Simon likes the warm, no-nonsense look of her, and the way she has stored up this knowledge.

It is at this stage that Stephanie gets up and leaves the table.

As soon as he is able, without seeming to be concerned, Simon follows her through to the kitchen. Her car keys are in one hand, her cellphone in the other.

'Where are you going?'

'I had a text message. Didn't you hear my phone? No, I suppose you wouldn't with all that talk. Congratulations, it seems to be going well.' She glances at the phone in her hand. 'Phil is having a crisis,' she says. 'He really needs me.'

'Phil? You're not at work now. Nothing can be that bad.'

'Life and death,' she says cryptically.

He doesn't say that she has gone. Ruth raises her eyebrows in inquiry and he shakes his head, in a way that only she can read.

'Ruth and I will do coffee,' he says during a break in the conversation. The guests drift into the sitting room. The designer and his girlfriend say they will have to go soon. Simon can tell from their faint tobacco smell that they are in need of a cigarette. Everyone else seems

content to talk and enjoy the view of the garden through the French
doors. Like the garden at Matamata, it is full of lavender, and a variety of
roses just finishing their spring flowering. Soon enough, the guests will
discover that there is no hostess to farewell.

He knows she will come back this time. And other times, until
there is a last time. She will not leave him for Phil. Or perhaps for anyone.
It's more likely she will leave and come back some day and tell him to
leave, and then she can get on with her work. She will be free of him
wrestling with things that happened long ago, even though he has never
told her exactly what they were.

He does not blame her, at least not yet, not while he is handing
around Turkish sweets with the coffee. It is not as if he didn't know. Just
the other day, when the light passed through the sky, he knew something
was up. That he had learned to read the signs of leaving. He has seen
them in himself.

Sue McCauley

My Friend Freddy

DISBELIEF WILL NOT CAUSE OFFENCE. I want that to be clear. Scepticism, at least at the outset, is a healthy response and I would expect no less. Even those prepared to accept that sheep might have emotions and a degree of intelligence are likely to have a problem with the practical question of how thoughts could transfer from my shapely head to the printed page. (In, what's more, coherent sentences, constructed, if I say so myself, with some feeling for the complexities of the English language.)

You no doubt accept, with no better understanding, that an image can be captured on a gadget the size of my ear and transmitted within seconds from one side of the planet to the other. Yet the idea of my thoughts taking shape on a screen, in a manuscript opened for the purpose of telling my story, will be dismissed as being beyond belief.

Blind disbelief is fine with me. I don't feel obliged, here, to provide a rational explanation for something even I find hard to grasp.

It's possible that I am a freak. Unique. A solitary glitch in the system. Yet, with 48 million sheep in this country alone, that does seem unlikely. Despite what's said about us sheep, 48 million surely offers some scope for individual variation.

At first I wasn't noticably different from the other 47,999,999. At least, I wasn't aware of being so. My earliest memory is of chill: the icy battering of a sleety south-west wind. Some fumble of instinct had me on my feet nudging for nourishment. My brother was there before me. Already the pattern was set. I probably tried to get food from him; I saw it happen often enough — the second-born latching hopefully onto an ear, or even down on wobbly knees tugging away at a brother's tiny scrotum.

My own brother was free of the membrane that still clung to most of my body. Presumably our mother had cleaned him, her first-born, and perhaps that took all her strength. Or maybe one baby was all she could get her woolly head around. We were her first lambs. Only a year before, she herself had been newborn. I know this now from putting together snippets of conversation, but at the time all I understood was the need to survive. Only gradually did I become aware of differences between me and my brother and feel envy, or at least a kind of cosmic sense of injustice.

In fact, the membrane that was left to dry on my body, though unsightly, gave me some small protection from the wind and rain and thus may have kept me alive. Which isn't to say my mother had reasoned this out. She wasn't one of those natural-born, fierce, foot-stamping mammas ready to fight or die for their babies. Those mothers made sure offspring would get the best shelter, the richest food. The biggest or greediest siblings would be kept in check.

My mother never pushed my brother aside. I'm not saying I starved, but I always had to wait my turn and make do with the little he'd left. My mother was not unaware of this. She saw my situation and, I believe, regretted it. In many ways I felt that I was her favourite. She liked underdogs — she was one herself.

On that icy day when we were born, other ewes — some with lambs at foot, others heavily pregnant — had crowded beneath the sheltering branches of the only tree in the paddock. Possibly our mother had considered her own privacy more important than our survival, but more likely she had been driven from the shelter by some tough ewe's show of aggression. Better to place our lives at risk than to stand up for us all.

Now — thanks to my epiphany — I realise that timidity is not a maternal crime but a simple and blameless matter of instinct and personality. This, I have to say, is an exclusively human rationale. A philosphical luxury. Brute strength, fitness, cunning: those are the qualities that count in sheep circles. Loyalty matters, too. Finding oneself alone is good reason for terror; the friendless sheep is a spectre almost too awful to imagine.

Our mother, though weak, was not unpopular. She belonged to a group of mild-mannered sheep. But friendship among the ewes did not, in my experience, extend to intervention. Besides, my plight was negligible compared to some. On perhaps my third day of life I watched a newborn lamb nuzzling for the teat of its dead mother. Later the poor creature must have staggered off to lie or die alone. Ewes went on grazing while a hawk crouched, pecking away at the lamb's eyes. Was it already dead? I still don't know.

I tried to be cunning, waiting until my brother had wandered off, but somehow he knew and would come charging back to knock me aside. The more my twin drank the bigger he grew, and the bigger he grew the more he drank. I would be left with an empty udder and my mother's worn-out patience. I learned to rely on grass. All us lambs nibbled at pasture in imitation of our mothers; for me it quickly became more than a game. Grass was my means of survival.

Unfortunately there was not a lot of it. Day after day the dirty clouds and harsh winds blew in from the south and the grass failed to grow. The ewes were hard pushed to find enough food to keep their babies in milk. The mean mammas would grab all the best spots, leaving my mother's crowd to forage beneath fences or snatch at forbidden dung grass when no one was watching. Lambs followed in their mothers' footsteps; it was like trying to feed on the tuft of a well-worn carpet.

Despite the cold, most evenings when the light changed into something brighter yet softer, my brother would join with other lambs in running and leaping games. A few times I tried to join in but couldn't keep up. Easier to pretend I was having such fun on my own that I hadn't even noticed their whirlwind scamperings.

There was another lamb, younger than me, who didn't join in. A black lamb, you would call her, though in fact she was a muddy brown. Her mother appeared devoted, but certain ewes, and some of the lambs, roughly pushed this lamb aside. At the time of those evening games she would sometimes stroll quite close to me and stand staring. I would pretend not to notice. My scrawny body and lack of energy already marked me out as a oddity; I did not need to be seen hanging out with a genuine freak.

Movement kept the cold away, but even the heartiest lambs could not keep moving all the time. There was a day here and there when the wind dropped and the clouds slid apart to taunt us with a taste of the heat we were missing out on, but mostly the weather got no better. At night we huddled against our mothers. The lucky ones slept under the tree but the nearest our mother, my brother and I got was just on the edge, at the fingertips of swooping branches.

One morning the farmer came with his shrill bike and silent, slinking dogs. I would guess I was not yet three weeks old. We were mustered up over the crest of the hill, then down to the flat land below. All I knew — all I was able to think of — was *staying in sight of mother.* If I failed to do this I was surely doomed. (To what? was a question I hadn't time or energy to ask, and certainly couldn't have answered.)

Amazingly, I managed to keep up. After the initial scattering panic the ewes pressed in together and slowed to a brisk walk interspersed with bursts of nervous speed. My mother and her friends were, of course, at the back. A couple of times I stumbled or paused to catch my breath and could sense a dog only inches behind me, but I wasn't the only straggling lamb and I didn't, like some, make wild escape bids back up the hill. And for once I wasn't cold.

When finally we got to stop moving it was in a small muddy

place, all of us crowded together, ewes having to literally rub up against other ewes they loathed or feared. The brown lamb was down in the mud, skewered by one adult sheep's foot and all but smothered by another toppled lamb. She was only a couple of sheep-lengths away from me but her head was wedged in the other direction. I listened for her to cry out but she made no sound.

Proximity kept us warm, despite the drizzling rain.

Eventually we were moved again — onto a truck. I know that now. This time I felt my mother's fear. I was crushed and shoved but managed to stay beside her. We reached a dark place but my brother was no longer with us. Our mother called for him, but so many lost or separated lambs were calling or being called for that her voice just merged into the terrible din. She continued to call and eventually we heard him call back — from somewhere above us, it seemed. In the meantime I'd drunk my mother dry; not quite a feast, for stress had taken its toll on her milk supply, but a deeply satisfying meal.

Moving again. More waiting in yards, but this time less mud. Other sheep — foreigners — staring in at us through the rails and human beings gawping down from above. Two other lambs tried to steal my mother's milk but she pushed them away and again I got to drink undisturbed. I fell asleep against the bottom rail of the fence and when I woke up we were moving again and my brother had joined us. I didn't expect to be pleased to see him but I was.

Another truck, but this time we were near an opening and, by propping myself on my brother's back, I could see grass. Green grass, lush with clover, but far below and racing past us.

This time my mother was careful about keeping us both in sight. She had no milk, but nor did other ewes — it was a long time since they'd last eaten. My brother was stunned and angry; he wasn't accustomed to hunger.

Despite the window gap, it was hot on this truck. Hot and stifling — a new kind of feeling. It was dark when we were unloaded. There was confusion as families and friends found each other, but the fear had gone. We were exhausted and hungry and way beyond fear. Our mother followed the leaders through a couple of open gates and finally there was grass beneath our feet. Real, clover-filled pasture. Now all you could hear was the tearing and munching of grass and, intermittently, a morepork's call. Our eating was frantic, feverish. The grass seemed too good to be true. It would run out, or we would be moved before we'd even made up for lost time. I was ripping away at that grass as fast as any fully grown sheep.

This was the beginning of a new and kinder life — at least for most of our flock. The brown lamb was no longer with us, so presumably had not survived. Another lamb, older and bigger than me, had a broken leg and hobbled about on three. But the days were now warmer, grass was plentiful, and our anxious bag-of-bone mothers began to fill out and grow placid. The udders of many became heavy and full. I couldn't help but notice, because this wasn't the case with our mother. Perhaps my brother's brief but involuntary fast had shocked him into a permanent state of greed for, no matter how determinedly she grazed, our mother could barely sate his appetite.

Grass was now plentiful. Our flock flourished and my brother grew bigger and rougher. I grew taller, but also thinner and weaker. It happened slowly and possibly no one noticed. I was sleeping much of the day and yet constantly tired. It had become an effort to co-ordinate my lengthening legs and get to my feet.

I would like to claim that, faced with death, I fought to stay alive. In fact sleep brought such relief I would gladly have gone to sleep forever. Yet herd instinct runs deep and when the man and woman came with a large, barking dog to move us on — for what purpose I still don't know — I managed to get to my feet and totter some small distance behind my brother before collapsing.

Human hands slid beneath me and raised me until my feet just reached the ground. Obligingly and in terror I staggered a few steps. All my instincts told me that this was a situation I should have at all costs avoided. But my knees buckled and I was again raised up, this time higher than my mother's back, and nothing but space between me and the sloping ground.

So there I was hanging, bent like the moon, but not in discomfort. Her hands were around me and, oddly, I no longer felt fear. There had been a strange surge in my stomach as I was lifted, but now all I felt was my customary urge to sleep.

I was carried some distance then laid down, and again my stomach felt strange, as if it couldn't keep up with the speed of descent. I was set down beside a sheltering wall and the grass that brushed at my face was lushly tempting. I lay there waiting for my jaws to agree to move. I could hear my mother calling not too far away and I called back to her. Or possibly I dreamt I called back because just after that the woman woke me by picking me up again. This time I was carried less carefully — a hand under my ribs, legs swinging in time with her gumboot steps.

Again she tried to stand me up. Again I tried to stand, but my legs were like water. She took me inside, then, out of the weather, and made me a nest with sides to hold me in. Now I panicked; my mother, my brother, how would they find me? But I hadn't the strength to move or struggle.

She was poking something at my face and making sounds. Over and over — the sounds, the poking with something shiny and swollen. She got rough and pushed her finger into my mouth, forcing my jaws apart, pushing the shiny thing inside where it lay like another tongue on mine. She took charge of me, holding my head, stroking my neck, moving the thing on my tongue so that drops of something almost familiar trickled down into my throat. And all the while she made little sounds that ran on and on like a fence.

The next time I woke I thought my mother was there, warm beside me. But the smell was all wrong, so was the weight. It was only a sack. And there was no sky and no wind. Then I remembered I was in some place like a very big rabbit hole. She kept coming to make me drink. No longer with the shiny tongue; she'd given up on that and settled for simply trickling the stuff down my throat, a little each time.

I don't know how many hours or days I lay there, or how many times she came with the bottle and forced a few drips of liquid on its way to my indifferent stomach. I do know I missed my mother and longed for her to step into sight. I could, with some difficulty, still raise my head and stare at the daylight space I thought of as the entrance to my tunnel, but I never so much as glimpsed a sheep.

There must have been a point, a moment, at which the process of dying halted and went into reverse. Why or when, I have no way of knowing, but I do know I got very close to death. And I know that when I began to revive I was no longer just a lamb. I was a lamb with human memory.

Well, yes. I too had trouble believing — but the realisation came slowly. At first there were just glimpses: bewildering flashes of places, events, human perception. They came upon me like a secret assailant, and left me staggering (metaphorically, of course, for I was still unable to stand on my own four feet).

Perhaps these flashes of memory also gave me the will to live — if only to make sense of the remarkable creature I seemed to have become. Had my physical shape changed? It was hard to tell: most of me was covered by hessian blanket, but my legs felt the same as they had before, and the smell that wafted from the straw beneath me had grown no sweeter.

When the woman next went to prise my teeth apart I startled her (and myself) by taking the teat and sucking. *Suckling*, in fact, as if the skill of my early infancy had returned. And *I knew the words*. I knew the difference between *sucking* and *suckling*, and I knew that the fusion between me and that make-believe nipple was due to *suction*.

All this information — not always clear or complete, or even necessary, but there inside me like something buried and now being uncovered bit by bit. Something possibly immense.

I drank until the bottle was empty, and she was so pleased. She pushed her face against mine. 'You are so clever,' she said. 'A clever, clever boy.'

I wanted to laugh. This was bizarre. I wanted to laugh at the thought that sucking equated cleverness. But lambs cannot laugh. Sheep don't do funny. Or cruel. Or phoney. Or ironic.

I wanted to laugh and I had a memory of laughter so intense it was painful. I was in a theatre, sitting in the front row, and a woman was on stage talking about the erotic charms of stupidity. And it was no doubt cruel but very funny. Also I fancied the woman on stage. But my laughter felt real and not just for her benefit.

After a tentative beginning I was deluged by such memories. They were like jigsaw pieces and I imagined that some day I would sort through them and connect them all up.

The clever boy continued to suck and as a result to foul himself, so me and my cardboard box and I were both banished to the orchard. But the weather was kindly and I was now sitting up and taking an interest in all that was around me, which made the woman ridiculously happy. Soon I was able, if lifted, to totter about on my wobbly legs.

Once in a while the man would come and look at me and shake his head. He was a tall, skinny fellow, old enough to be her father. Which was what I supposed him to be until I saw the way he would wrap his big hand around her little one, and the goofy smile that would slide onto his face. I decided she was a quite recent wife. Perhaps not his first, but one he hadn't expected to acquire and was enormously grateful for.

He would look down at me and shake his head, and if she was with him he'd grumble about the cost of feeding me, which was, he said, at least twice the amount I would fetch AT THE WORKS. He'd say those last words loud and with the trace of a grin. Winding her up was evidently his idea of flirtation.

'Never,' she'd say. 'Not Norman.' That was the name she had given me, for no reason that I was aware of.

'You'd so regret it,' she'd tell him, looking small but fierce. And the man would gaze down at her and grin as if she was a very cute puppy nipping away at his shins.

So now I was a lamb with a healthy appetite, legs I could manoeuvre unaided and a vocabulary greater than that of the woman who had saved me. No way of voicing that vocabulary, but did I really want to? I had a suspicion that in my previous life I'd done rather too much speaking. Silence may or may not be a virtue but it could certainly be a relief.

She was so kind, the small and recent wife. She coddled me as she would her own child, applauded my progress, told me I was very, VERY special.

'You can laugh,' she told the man, 'but this is no ordinary lamb.'

The man didn't quite laugh but his smile was huge. 'Well,' he said, 'you're not doing him much of a favour. One lamb is a sad thing.'

'So find him a friend,' she ordered. 'A little sister or brother.'

No, no, no, I wanted to shout. Not a brother, please not a brother. A terrible and human jealousy burned in my chest at the thought.

A few days later they brought me Freddy. He was tiny, ugly and rank. His face and body seemed to have been smeared with some kind of unguent that had dried, trapping his baby fleece into hard little furrows. His ugliness was such a relief that I warmed to him a fraction.

'He looks,' she said unhappily, 'like Freddy Krueger.'

'Who's he?'

'He's . . .' She stared at the husband for a moment. 'Never mind. Just . . . we'll call him Freddy.'

I tried to catch her eye. I badly wanted to let her know that *I* knew where the name came from and why.

The husband shouldered the blame for Freddy's unappealing smell and appearance. The poor little fulla had been abandoned at birth. In an effort to make him appealing to a ewe with a stillborn lamb the man had smeared Freddy with the dead lamb's moist and membrane-covered fleece. Unfortunately (understandably, in my opinion) the ewe had not been fooled into thinking her lamb had returned to life. Beneath the stench she recognised an impostor.

Freddy's IQ was not high, even for a sheep. To think he could be a proper companion to me was, frankly, an insult. Despite a weak chest, Freddy could suck like a vacuum cleaner, and at first his only interest in life was the bottle. But soon he extended his interest to me, and followed me everywhere. The bottle and me were the only things in Freddy's life.

He felt the cold and would be torn between staying outdoors with me or taking shelter in the woodshed. She had made me a bed of hay in the shed and I was in the habit of sleeping there at night, but Freddy would want to hang out there during the day. We would be grazing — he would be clumsily copying me — and he would silently disappear. I would call out, summoning him, but he would seem not to hear. I worried about glue ear — at least its agricultural equivilent. He was a straightforward little chap and his innocence invited concern. Sometimes, on hearing me call, the woman would come and coax Freddy out of the woodshed.

'You're upsetting Norman,' she'd tell him sternly.

She made him a coat from a fabric softer than fleece: a silly little jacket she stuck his legs through and did up with velcro. I wasn't jealous; he looked ridiculous. It kept him out of the woodshed during the day but I cringed at the thought of us being seen together.

Mind you, I had more pressing concerns. My wool appeared to be falling out and I was constantly itchy. She noticed.

'Norman, love, you seem to be moulting. Don't tell me you're lousy?'

By now my wool was coming out in chunks. When I looked down between my front legs I could see my skin, as pink and bald as a freshly hatched sparrow. At the same time the southerly delivered a last winterly lash and now it was me who waited it out in the shed, while Freddy chomped happily at spring grass, wearing his stupid coat.

She brought the man to look at me. They stood in the rain, peering into the woodshed.

'Wool break,' he said. 'Fever or bad illness weakens the fibre. Takes a while to show. Gotta say, young Norman, your timing's bloody awful. They reckon this cold snap's gonna set in, and you're heading to be a skinned rat.'

She cut up two pairs of leggings (she told me that's what they were) and forced me into them. Holes for legs, head, pizzle and tail. The idea was to stop my severed wool from leaving my body until the weather had eased up or regrowth was established. Resistance was futile but, believe me, I tried.

Freddy's little eyes lit up when he saw me. Now we even looked like brothers. I took my anger and humiliation out on the grass. I was a mowing machine, tearing the stuff, mashing it up in my jaws. Never again would I deign to drink from her stupid bottle. I did not need her. She had no place in my life.

The cold snap still hadn't moved on when the man and his dogs brought my old flock into the paddock next to the orchard. I thought I might be mistaken until my brother ran up to the fence and, on seeing me, stopped dead. He stood there staring. It was him, no question. And he recognised me, I was almost certain. He looked at me for a long time, then he turned and ran off.

I thought he'd gone to find our mother and bring her to see me. For the rest of that day I hovered near the fence and sometimes called out, but the replies were mocking ones from lambs I no longer remembered, all much bigger than me. Freddy hung about watching me in a worried, bewildered way.

The next day was calm and fine, so the woman removed Freddy's coat and, as she remarked, the Krueger connection had gone. The furrowed fleece had fluffed out and the little lad now had an appealing soft-toy look. She opened the orchard gate and propped it wide, inviting me, surely, to join my family. But I wasn't going to oblige. Let them find me, I thought.

I waited all that day and most of the next with increasing agitation. I told myself it didn't matter, I didn't care, I was better off without a mother, and Freddy was a better brother than my selfish twin had ever been. But on the evening of the second day I sneaked away from Freddy and out through the gate. I sauntered about in a casual way as if simply out for a stroll. I pretended not to be looking for anyone in particular, but there were faces I recognised and this felt so exciting I would hurry towards them. Each time the lamb or ewe in question would back away or just turn and run. Because they didn't know me or because they did? I was far too agitated to think clearly. A pariah among one's own flock — who would have imagined it could be so devastating?

Eventually I sat down to rest in the clearing that my presence had created. I could hear Freddy calling in his sad little gravelly voice, but I stayed where I was.

When I woke in the morning I had a circle of spectators carefully keeping their distance. My mother was among them. My heart leapt — I felt it leaping. I jumped to my feet and ran towards her, but as soon as I moved she was off charging across the paddock, her udder swinging like some taunting semaphore signal.

The rest of the circle had run with her. I was behind them, and they would not, did not, slow down. Running from me as if I was some mean-eyed dog, though I was calling out as I ran. Had she even forgotten my voice?

So I stopped running, but I didn't go home to the orchard and Freddy. For the rest of that day I sulked around in the paddock waiting for my mother, my brother or anyone in that flock to have a change of heart.

By mid-morning Freddy gave up calling me. In the late afternoon the woman came. She walked down the hill towards me, smiling and shaking her head.

'Poor Norman,' she said. 'They must think you're from Mars.'

I looked down at my chest. Of course — my body was wrapped like a garish sausage. I had got used to it and forgotten.

'But if we take it off you could get pleurisy. And you'll still look like a freak to them and scare them away.'

I wouldn't let her catch me but, pretending reluctance, I followed her back to the orchard, where she chased out a ewe and her twin lambs before shutting the gate behind her and me.

'I'm so sorry, Norman,' she said. 'But at least you've got Freddy. If you'd seen what a sad little fellow he was, all on his own.'

Freddy watched us approach but didn't come running. I had abandoned him; he was angry at me and feigning indifference. I understood — I'd been down that same road. But my friend, simple soul that he was, could only sustain pretence for a couple of minutes and soon came bounding to greet me.

Next day — perhaps at his wife's request? — the man and his dogs moved my flock from the paddock next door and life went back to normal.

Beneath the ridiculous garments and the dead wool they trapped inside, I had grown a tight new fleece. The husband came to watch the unveiling and resurrected discussion about my fate. He'd already let her persuade him that I should remain a ram on account of my 'special qualities'. I could go into service on the farm and thus be saved from the slaughterhouse.

But ram lambs grew bigger than neutered wethers and thus fetched higher prices. Retaining one's nuts was no guarantee of survival. Freddy was also still a ram and no one pretended that he might shape up as a desirable sire. The freezing works, alas, were not yet out of the question. And, this day, as she sliced away at her leggings, the husband grew playful over my 'specialness' and demanded details. She sighed over his lack of perception, and gazed steadily into my eyes as if they would give her the perfect answer. Finally she told him I had a spiritual quality.

'Spiritual?' He grinned, then looked at me in my freshly legging-free state. 'Okay, Norm lad, gimme a sign. Which of those trees behind you do you reckon is an apple tree?'

'Oh,' she said, 'that's ridiculous.'

I took my time. Best, I figured, to make it appear within the bounds of coincidence. I ambled apparently purposelessly in the general direction, checked that they were still watching, then wandered off under the apple tree. I stood there staring straight at the man. His tiny wife was hopping about, crowing and clapping.

'Wow! Way to go, Norman.'

'Test number two,' he said.

'Nah,' she said. 'Unfair. You can't do that.'

He stood there enjoying her rage.

'The little fulla,' he said. 'Young Freddy.'

'I've never said Freddy's anything out of the —'

'So, the next draft?'

'No.'

'But he's fattened up nicely. You've done a good job. I'm running a business here, and I've got to recoup some of our losses.'

'He's Norman's friend.'

'His milk powder's cost us a fortune. That right, Freddy?'

Freddy looked up, knowing his name.

'So you're Norman's friend. Okay — go give your mate Norman a kiss.'

'You're sick,' she said.

'I'm waiting, little buddy,' he told Freddy.

I could have made it happen. If I had caught Freddy's eye and raised my head in a certain way he would have come at a trot, then I could have reached out to sniff his nostrils. Close enough to a kiss.

I could have, but I didn't.

'Sorry, Freddy, old chap,' he said.

'You mean it,' she whispered, barely believing.

'There'll be pet lambs every year. You're gonna have to get used to it.'

He put his arms around her.

A few days later they took him. She called his name and off he went on his sturdy legs, out through the gate and down towards the yards. He went off without a second thought, full of trust. He went, as they say, *like a lamb*.

It wasn't my doing.

Okay, in a way it was.

Why didn't I save him?

I've thought about that. I've told myself it was by way of a favour: Freddy might come back as something more exciting than a cog in the food chain.

And I've told myself I was flustered and didn't have time to consider.

But the truth is I didn't want her, or even the husband, to think that Freddy was the same as me. I wanted them to know that he was only a lamb, while I possessed human sensibilities. *Look at me*, I was saying to them. *I'm one of you.* Clever, complex, sensitive, better.

PAULA MORRIS

Red Christmas

THE EVENING BEFORE THE INORGANIC rubbish collection, the three McGregor kids walked to Uncle Suli's and asked to borrow his van.

Ani didn't like asking Uncle Suli for things. It seemed like they were always there, crowded onto his peeling doorstep, waiting for the familiar dark shape to appear behind the frosted glass of the front door. He never said no to anything, not to requests for a loan of a sleeping bag when Tama had school camp, or to half a loaf of bread when they'd run out of everything at home except tomato sauce and there was no money left in the tin under the sink. He'd signed school reports for them, and handed over creased copies of Saturday's *Herald*. Sometimes there'd be something extra, unasked for — a calendar he'd got free at work, the occasional dollar coin for Henry. Once he offered up a hapuku wrapped in damp newspaper: their mother had boiled it into soupy white chunks that made the house stink for days. They always arrived with nothing and left with something. It was embarrassing.

'Getting late for the kiddies to be out,' said Uncle Suli, scrabbling for the keys in his back pocket. He wore his usual summer weekend outfit: loose canvas shorts and a polo shirt striped like a deckchair.

'We won't be long,' said Ani, the only one of the McGregor kids old enough to drive.

He told them to try the streets on the harbour side of Te Atatu Road: they'd find a better class of rubbish there, though they were leaving it late, in his opinion.

'The Islanders start cruising before lunch,' he said. 'Soon as church's over. They'll have picked through the lot by now.'

'I don't like going in daylight,' said Ani, staring down at Uncle Suli's feet: his toenails looked like pickled onions. 'It's embarrassing, going through other people's stuff.'

'They don't want it, do they?' said Uncle Suli. 'Nothing to them.'

'I guess.' Ani gripped the keyring tight, its feathery fuzz tickling her palm.

'Everything all right at home?'

She shrugged.

'Well, take care.' He nodded towards the driveway and the dusty green van, the two boys smudged against its scuffed flank. Tama's eyes were closed, and Henry was rolling his tongue around inside of his mouth. 'Don't want another accident.'

'I don't have accidents.'

'You don't have a licence. Here.' Uncle Suli leaned towards her, pressing something crisp and papery into her hand: she glimpsed the blue corner of a $10 note. 'Buy yourselves something to eat. And if you see anything like a toilet seat or a sink, chuck it in the back. I'm after a new bathroom.'

'Thanks, Uncle Suli,' said Ani, signalling the boys into the van with a jingle of the keys. They clambered into the passenger side, Tama hoisting Henry up by the shorts. Ani leaned against their door to close it. Uncle Suli stood in the doorway, gazing up at the streaky sky.

'Don't forget my Christmas present!' he called.

'Did he give you some money?' asked Tama, struggling with his seatbelt.

'Maybe.' Ani shoved the gearstick into reverse and backed out of the driveway in rapid jerks.

'Look,' said Henry, who sat squashed in the middle, one scrawny leg pressed against the gearstick, jandals sliding off his feet. Uncle Suli was staggering towards the stumpy bushes of the front garden, miming a heart attack.

'He was the one who taught me how to drive,' said Ani. She rammed the gearstick into first and drove away up the hill, eyes narrowed against the glare of the dipping sun.

Almost every house had a stack of rubbish, but Uncle Suli was right: most of it looked picked through, pieces of wood and machine parts and broken toasters separated from their original tidy piles and scattered across the mown grass verges. He was right, too, about the class of rubbish. The inorganic rubbish collection in their own neighbourhood, two weeks ago, had been a waste of time; much of the debris still leaned against letterboxes, unacceptable to the council's rubbish trucks, unwanted by anyone else. Next door to the McGregors' house, a hunk of concrete base from an uprooted washing line still lay on the verge, and a car door from an old Holden, rusty and dented, remained propped against the leaning letterbox.

On the quiet streets on the far side of Te Atatu Road the stacks were higher and looked more inviting. People threw away whole appliances, not just broken parts; they carried corrugated iron and decking planks into the street, pushed out lawnmowers and old wheelbarrows. They dumped all sorts of useful things, like wire coat-hangers and galvanised buckets and pieces of carpet. Last year someone Tama knew at school had found a black bin bag filled with rolled-up socks, every pair perfect.

On a long curving street where the back gardens tumbled down to the mangroves of the creek, the McGregor kids passed another van, an elderly Asian man sitting behind the wheel. Two younger men were angling a washing machine through the rear doors.

'Lucky,' said Tama.

'It's probably broken,' said Ani. 'Seen anything, Eagle Eyes?'

Henry knelt on the seat, one hand on Ani's shoulder, peering around her towards the footpath. He was the best at spotting useful objects obscured by tumbles of plastic and metal. So far this evening he'd found them a rake with only one broken tine, a director's chair and a bag of knitting needles.

Last December, he'd uncovered a ripped footstool and a box containing eighteen green glazed tiles. When they got home their mother sat at the kitchen table fingering each tile as though it were a sea shell, arranging them into a perilous tower. They were too beautiful to use, she decided; she loved green, but they were too green. They reminded her of mussel shells, and of the sea at a place on the coast she visited as a child. They made her sad, she said, and Ani had to pack the tiles away and hide them in the carport.

'There's a lot of stuff there,' Henry said, pointing down the street.

'Quick,' said Tama. He looked over his shoulder, craning to see the other van. 'Before they catch up.'

Ani pulled up outside a dark brick house, its garden and driveway secured behind black wrought-iron gates, a dog yelping from somewhere inside the house. Tama tore the pile apart, but careful Henry crouched with his back to the van, picking through the contents of a cardboard box. The house's cobbled driveway led to a grey garage door, a striped basketball hoop fixed on the wall above. It looked like the kind of house that might have good rubbish, but you could never tell: often the shabbiest houses threw away the most. The poor were too lazy to fix things, according to Uncle Suli; that's why they were poor.

Henry raced up, panting with excitement.

'Here,' he said, shoving things at Ani through the open window. He'd found a power strip and a small metal box, the kind they used for money and raffle tickets at the school gala. Ani wriggled around in her seat to dump them in the back.

'Ani!' Tama slapped the side of the van. 'Open up the big doors.'

He sprang away, thudding off along the footpath to a house three doors down. By the time Ani swung the back doors open, Tama was weaving towards her like a drunkard to make her laugh, balancing a wooden step-ladder on his head.

'I saw it,' Henry told her.

'Shut up,' said Tama. He slid the step-ladder into the back of the van and pulled something out of his pocket. 'Look at this.'

Cradled in his hands was a bud vase, its narrow flute a mosaic of green glass.

'No chips or anything,' he said. 'Mum might like it.'

Their mother might be up when they got home, staring out the back window and dripping cigarette ash into the kitchen sink, or she might still be in bed, her face turned to the wall, one fingernail picking at a spot in the wallpaper where she said the pattern made an ugly face.

'Shut the doors.' Ani pulled herself up into the driver's seat.

'Move,' said Tama, pushing Henry over. The van crawled away again, and he cradled the vase in his puddled sweatshirt on the floor.

'I'm surprised they threw it away,' said Ani. 'Maybe they'll change their minds.'

'Too late.'

'Feels a bit bad, though, stealing it.'

'It's not stealing.' Tama lifted his feet onto the dashboard. 'And if we don't take it, the Chinks will.'

'I guess,' said Ani, slowing the van as they reached another half-toppled pile, pausing to see if Henry could make anything out in the mess.

The evening sky turned inky blue, splotched with stars. Ani drove the van down a long looping road, looking for the house they'd noticed last year. The rubbish wasn't great, but the boys liked looking at the front garden.

The house itself was small and expressionless, the kind of plain-faced brick house that looked like the owners were always away on holiday. Flowerbeds busy with marigolds edged a path twisting towards the terrace; a bridge humped over a tiny pond rosy with orange fish. A plaster gnome was seated, fishing line dangling, at the water's edge. In their street, the gnome wouldn't have lasted a week.

Any rubbish left out had already disappeared. The boys stood a footstep shy of the wall, surveying the garden as though they were prospective buyers. Tama planted his feet far apart: they seemed too big for his body. He was nearly as tall as Ani already, built on a larger scale.

His father had lived with them for almost a year, off and on; he was the kind of man who filled a room, their mother said, and that's how Ani remembered him — bulky and towering, wide as a doorway. He was nothing like her own father, who appeared slight, almost ill, in the one photograph she'd seen.

Henry looked more like her in some ways, lean and small for his age. Ani wasn't sure about Henry's father: Uncle Suli referred to him once as a nasty piece of work, but that could have been any number of her mother's friends. Henry's skin was the darkest and Ani's was the lightest. She looked jaundiced, her mother said, like she'd been dipped in cat's piss. There was something of their mother in each of them, something around the eyes or the mouth that told strangers they were a family.

Behind the house, the harbour glinted beyond the dense mass of mangroves. The motorway was a string of lights, stretching across the water like a washing line leading to the city. Ani hadn't been to town in months, not since a school trip to the art gallery. Every trip she took was local — a bus to the mall, a walk to the dairy. Even these suburban streets in Te Atatu South, only minutes away from home in the van, felt like a foreign country.

If she drove away now, she could be downtown in fifteen minutes. Ani had never seen the open-air cafés of the Viaduct at night: there'd be candles on every table, wine glasses, white plates. Downtown was like television: brash and glamorous, humming with conversation and music. And beyond that was the rest of the country, a blur of green in her mind, indistinct and unknown. She could follow the snaking line of the southern motorway to where the city dissolved into the Bombay Hills.

She'd have to leave the boys, of course — leave them right here, staring at the pond and the fishing gnome. Perhaps the old people who lived here would take them in. Tama was a hard worker: he could weed the garden and fix things around the house, and they could send Henry out at night to crush snails, his favourite after-dinner activity.

But nobody would take them in; she knew that. The people who lived here wouldn't even invite them in for a mug of Milo; more likely they'd be calling the police to report two Maori kids messing up their neat front garden, trespassing on their front step. The boys wouldn't stick around, either. They'd chase the van up the street, calling her name; they wouldn't understand that they'd all be happier living somewhere else with new parents, a new school, a different name. They'd find their way back eventually to the scruffy blue house where the cracks in the driveway spewed weeds, where everything needed picking up or putting right, where their mother would be waiting.

And there was Uncle Suli's van, of course. He needed it because the buses, he said, were overpriced these days and, even worse, they were full of students, layabouts and foreigners.

Tama rapped on the glass and Ani wound down the window.

'Turn the van around quick,' he said. 'The big house back there, see? They're still putting stuff out.'

Ani jammed the van into reverse: it surged like an old sewing machine up to a big brick house they'd passed earlier. The boys ran alongside, Henry tripping out of his jandals, Tama racing ahead. They'd never got their hands on fresh rubbish before.

From the open garage a grey-haired man in sweatpants and a young woman dragged rattling boxes onto the sloping driveway. A teenage boy, jeans sliding off his backside, climbed out of a silver Pajero parked on the front lawn. It was hard to believe such a big car would ever fit in such a cluttered space. Some people had more possessions crammed into their garage than the McGregor kids had in their whole house.

Tama and Henry lingered in the shadow of the van, waiting to pounce. The woman struggled up the driveway with a rusty pair of shears and a garden hose, its tail dragging along the concrete.

'Damian, you carry the particleboard,' she called back to the boy. 'It's too heavy for Dad.'

Her father dumped a box full of jangling parts on the verge. Tama and Henry conferred; Henry shook his head. Damian loped up with an armful of cork tiles, glancing up at the parked van and the huddling boys, flashing them a grin. Ani wound down her window.

'Get them,' she hissed to Tama, and he dashed to the verge, scooping up the tiles. Damian returned with a giant square of particleboard, leaning it against the front wall and hitching up his jeans.

'It's too big,' Tama told her. 'We'll never get it through the doors.'

The boys made a few more quick raids, picking up a paint roller and tray, a tartan flask and a sagging shoebox packed with nuts and bolts. A car with a trailer had pulled up behind them and a man scuttled out, making for some lino off-cuts and the particleboard. Tama scowled at him.

Damian lurched towards the verge, lowering a long folded screen with glass panels onto the ground.

'This is the last of it,' he said, to nobody in particular, and loped back down the driveway.

Henry sprang forward and dropped on top of the screen, his arms spread wide, guarding it with his entire body. The man jamming the particleboard onto his trailer looked over, suspicious.

'The doors,' Tama told Ani. 'Quick.'

Ani slid from her seat and scampered to the back of the van, flinging the back doors wide open. Tama lugged the screen towards the van, Henry darting around him, protecting the flank. One of the panels swung free, revealing a brown plastic handle. It was a folding shower door.

'Well done,' whispered Ani, helping Tama to slide the shower door in. She leaned over to unfold it: each section was perfect, ridged brown plastic with slender panels of knobbled amber glass.

'Sure you want that?' asked the man with the trailer, pointing an accusing finger towards the dusty back window.

'Bugger off,' said Tama, and they all scrambled back into the van.

'We got Uncle Suli's Christmas present,' said Henry, drumming his heels against the bottom of the seat. Ani drove away from the big house and its shining garage.

'It doesn't even look broken,' said Tama. The previous winter he'd borrowed Uncle Suli's saw and cut down a broken desk the Tongans across the street were throwing away: now they had a coffee table. Ani had thought about re-covering last year's plush stool, but a month ago her mother got upset with Henry walking in front of the television when *Shortland Street* was on, and the stool had been slung through a window. One of the legs snapped when it hit the window frame. Henry got five stitches that night: Ani hurried him up to the emergency clinic on Lincoln Road, a pyjama jacket wrapped tight around his punctures. When Uncle Suli knocked on the door later that week, wanting to know about the shattered window and Henry's bandaged arm, she told him that Tama had been mucking about with a cricket ball.

'Anyone hungry?' Ani asked. 'Who feels like pineapple fritters?'

She turned left onto Te Atatu Road, driving faster now, in a hurry to get to the fish and chip shop before it closed.

Uncle Suli's $10 note bought two pineapple fritters, one for each of the boys, and a bag of chips to share, with money left over for some milk and a loaf of bread from the dairy.

'I'd rather have another bag of chips,' said Henry, standing over the rubbish bin outside the dairy, nibbling the golden rim of his fritter.

'Where's everyone going?' asked Tama, his mouth full. The people in the cars parked either side of the van were hurrying off down Roberts Road.

'Maybe they've got good rubbish there,' said Ani. She locked the van door and walked to the corner. Roberts Road was packed as a carpark, groups of people strolling down the street towards a house burning with white lights, lit up like a stadium.

'I know what this is,' said Henry, scampering ahead. 'It's the Christmas house.'

He danced a few steps away and then zigzagged back to slam against Tama.

'Don't muck about,' said Ani. She pushed them both past stopped cars towards an empty patch of fence.

The house glimmered as though it were studded with diamonds, each architectural feature picked out with a sparkling string of white lights. A gaudy giant Santa perched on the garage roof, his sleigh hanging off the guttering, the reindeers' antlers blinking candy stripes of red and white. Icing-sugar frost sprinkled the grass. The tiny front garden was cluttered with displays — an illuminated snowman, a waving penguin, a model train zipping around an ornamental pond. Even the Norfolk pine was festooned with giant red baubles and drooping lines of lights.

Ani had never seen a house covered in lights, or a street so busy at night. She'd thought that only shops got decorations, holly and snowflakes spray-painted on their windows, artificial greenery swagged across their counters. The rest of the year, this place probably looked like any other suburban house — parched weatherboards and sandy tile roof, tight-lipped venetians closed against the sun. But dressed up for Christmas, it was an illuminated palace.

'Wait till we tell Uncle Suli about this,' said Henry.

'They must be made of money,' growled Tama in Uncle Suli's voice, and they all laughed.

Some people were brazen, opening the gate and walking into the front garden to admire the decorations close up, shuffling around the displays as though they were visiting the zoo. A man carrying a pug dog was leaning over the terrace railing to shake someone's hand. The McGregor kids stayed on the other side of the fence, eating the last of the chips. A loudspeaker rigged to the garage door broadcast a tinny-sounding 'White Christmas'.

'In Iceland,' Ani told the boys, 'when it doesn't snow, they call it Red Christmas.'

'Why?' Henry's mouth glistened with fritter grease.

'Not sure,' she said. It was something she'd heard at school, from a geography teacher. He'd been to Iceland to look at their volcanoes and glaciers, because they were different, in some way, from the volcanoes and glaciers here. Ani knew what volcanoes looked like: ordinary green lumps, neutered and serene, lay all over the city. But she'd never seen a glacier. They were all far away, somewhere south of the Bombay Hills.

'Red Christmas,' said Tama. 'We have one of those every year. We don't need to go to Iceland.'

'Come on,' said Ani. She reached out a hand to stroke Tama's hair, but let it fall on his shoulder. 'It's almost ten. We better be getting the van back.'

Tama nodded, but he didn't adjust his grip on the fence or on the ripped piece of newsprint, spotted with grease from the chips, still pinched between his fingers. His gaze followed the miniature train chugging along the circular track around the fish pond, its caboose painted a cheery yellow, a wisp of silver tinsel poking from the funnel.

'Can we stay a bit longer?' asked Henry.

'Two more minutes,' said Ani.

Although Uncle Suli wouldn't be annoyed however late they arrived, she was suddenly eager to go, to pull the van into his driveway, to see the look on his face when they unloaded the shower door. And when they got back to their house, if they were lucky, their mother would be asleep. They could stow everything in the carport until morning. If she was asleep, it wouldn't be like the time they brought home the glass bowl. She wouldn't have the chance to smash it to pieces; she wouldn't slice Henry's fingers, or half-scalp Tama, or slash Ani's clothes — with Ani still in them, thin ribbons of blood lacing her like a corset. The vase could be hidden, maybe even till Christmas. None of the kids would breathe a word. They were good at keeping secrets.

CARL NIXON

The Last Good Day of Autumn

AT THE TIME OF MY uncle's heart attack I was working in a souvenir shop on Colombo Street. I remember that it was autumn and that the weather was unpredictable; people carried umbrellas on even the finest days. They craned their necks in the streets, scanning the sky in the expectation of better or worse to come. On certain days the wind funnelled down between the tall inner-city buildings, knocking over the triangular wooden sign that stood on the footpath in front of the shop. Part of my job was to retrieve the sign, which advertised souvenirs in five languages. I propped it up on its feet again, ready for the next gust.

Tim and I placed small bets on how long the sign would take to blow over again. I cannot remember Tim's last name now, but he had worked at the shop virtually forever — for five years at least. As we stood, watching the sign through the window, he talked about moving to the Sunshine Coast and buying a house near the beach. He could talk for hours about the growth rates of tropical vegetation or the quality of the surf. He was an authority on the floating design of Queensland homes.

The sign fell with a clatter.

As is often the case with people who get paid regardless of performance, no one bothered suggesting modifications or alternatives to the system. The sign blew over. I picked it up. We placed our bets.

I had finished university three years earlier, graduating with a BA with honours in English and Religious Studies. As I didn't want to go teaching, I had no real career prospects, so right after graduation I travelled overseas.

I did temp work for two years in London, where I lived in a big old house in Earls Court that had such long, dark corridors that going inside was sometimes like venturing into a series of mine shafts. Most of my conversations with the other people in the house took place while we queued in the hall outside one of the two shared bathrooms. The other residents normally turned out to be Kiwis or Australians who, like me, had heard about the house through word of mouth.

In London I mostly worked in administration, filling in for people on leave. I checked application forms at a large insurance company for three months. My longest stint was at an office supply company called Harbidge's. At first I liked the variety of temping but by the end I had grown sick of it.

People were always coming and going from the big house where I lived, and temp work meant I was always meeting new people at work as well. The faces and the stories all began to blur. People talk about how easy it is to travel to Europe from London, but I always seemed to be short of cash. During the whole time I was there I only went to the continent twice: once to Paris for a week, where it rained the whole time, and once to the Greek Islands. On Santorini I fell in love with a German girl but she never travelled to visit me in Earls Court, as we had arranged, and she stopped writing six weeks after I got back to London.

It was shortly after that that I flew home to Christchurch and got the job in the souvenir shop. It was supposed to be temporary, until I could find something more suitable, but by the time my uncle was admitted to hospital I had been there almost a year.

To this day I do not know the exact details of the morning when my uncle's heart hesitated, stuttered, and then fell into the ill-kept rhythm of a lousy dancer. I have never asked and my mother has never volunteered the information. Watched by paua-shell eyes, I killed time at work by imagining him clutching his chest, with a look of round-mouthed surprise, a buttered and marmaladed piece of toast landing messy side down on the lino. But that was idle speculation. All I knew for sure was what my mother had told me: that a neighbour had spotted him crawling down the garden path with scraped knees and his pyjama top flapping open in the wind.

The hospital was only ten minutes' walk from where I worked, on the edge of Hagley Park, but almost two weeks had passed since my uncle was admitted. My mother took to ringing me every day asking if I had visited yet.

'It's been flat out,' I said. 'I'll see if I can call in tomorrow.'

'You should go. He's your uncle.'

'I know. I'll try. Sorry, gotta hang up now, there's a queue at the till.'

'Mark. He's your uncle.'

It's not that I didn't like him — I did, but the simple truth was that he was a Christmas relative. I had no context for my uncle outside of him sitting at the table in my parents' lounge, ladling minted potatoes and turkey onto one of the bone-china plates. He was my mother's older brother and, since his marriage had broken up, he came to our house every Christmas day for lunch. Once he brought a woman with a ledge of hair over her forehead like an ice-shelf, but the following year arrived alone as usual. He always smelt of whisky and mints that were never strong enough to do the job he intended.

I went to the hospital during my lunch-hour that Friday, armed with the excuse that I needed to be back by one o'clock. Ward 16 contained six beds and his was in the middle, on the right-hand side. A nurse was arranging his pillows with short chops of her hands when I arrived. I noticed that she had nice legs, although they were very pale, but her hands were large like a man's. Her hands chop-chopped into the pillows, bullying them into a shape she was happy with.

My uncle had to lean forward while the nurse worked. The business with his heart had made him lose weight, uncovering the bones around his eyes and the tendons in his neck like river stones in a time of drought.

'There you are, Mr Roberts.'

'Thank you.' As the nurse left the room my uncle leant back on his pillows and saw me. He grinned so that his eyes folded up into nothing. We shook hands and I gave him the bag with the three oranges I'd bought on the way over, from a dairy smelling of curry and incense. When I had chosen the oranges they had seemed festive and generous, but under hospital lights I saw that they were slightly mottled and that there were only three after all.

My uncle put the oranges on the bedside table, next to a single card with a watercolour picture of roses. I thought it might be from his son, who had moved to London years ago and who was in banking or accountancy, something like that. Apart from the card there were no other flowers.

'Aw, can't complain,' he said when I asked how he was.

We talked for a bit about the price of fruit, and agreed that it was too high and that cheap imports were killing the local product. We also talked about the hospital food, and he said he had no complaints. He said that feeding so many people three times a day must be a hell of a job. 'Rather them than me, especially considering all the special diets and such. What's it like out?' He turned towards the window but the only view was of the side of another wing of the hospital. I told him that the sun was shining but the wind was cold.

'Better than in here, anyway. The air doesn't smell good.' I noticed that he kept a can of lavender air-freshener next to the bed. 'Would you mind taking me out for a bit? There's a wheelchair.'

'I've got to be back at the shop by one.'

'We'll tell one of the nurses. They can come and get me when you've got to head away.'

I found the nurse I had seen earlier. She was passing in the corridor and I stopped her and asked her if it would be all right to take my uncle out. 'We've been having a few problems with Mr Roberts,' she said. Her forearms were slim, like her legs, and added to the illusion that her hands had been grafted from a different body. The skin of her neck was almost as pale as her uniform, and there were large freckles across the narrow bridge of her nose like ladybirds entombed beneath her makeup.

'Oh, what type of problems?'

'He insists on listening to talkback radio in the middle of the night. Some of the other men in his room have complained. It disturbs their sleep.'

I guessed that she was a few years older than me and I was surprised to find that I was attracted to her. I watched her lips move as she talked and imagined myself brushing the ladybirds away from her skin.

'I'll mention it to him if you like.'

'That would be good. Thank you.'

She half smiled and told me that someone would come down to bring my uncle back close to one o'clock. I thanked her. I wanted to talk for longer but had no topic ready to pull out of my sleeve. As she walked away I contemplated what it would be like to ask her out, perhaps to dinner or a foreign movie, but I was resigned to the fact that I was a coward, that I would never have the courage for something so momentous. She walked away up the corridor and all I could manage was to look at her legs again. When I turned I saw my uncle watching me through the doorway but he did not say anything.

I pushed the wheelchair along the bank of the Avon River, which runs past the back of the hospital. There was a path of crushed stones that crunched like glass beneath the wheels, and the sky was the blue of thrush eggs. In the Botanic Gardens, on the other bank, a man was herding leaves into deep drifts with a blower.

The top of my uncle's head had a wispy layer of reddish hair, and there were brown spots that formed a pattern like Rorschach's ink. I didn't find the marks as disturbing as I might have if I'd only heard them described. They were nothing like the watermarks on the bedroom ceiling of my flat, swelling in the heavy rain.

'A little further,' he said.

I looked at my watch. Still twenty minutes before I had to start back so I pushed him past the place where several patients were gathered in the sun. Further downstream there was a footbridge but we stuck to our own side of the river. We talked about nothing in particular but I was suddenly glad that we had come outside. I enjoyed the casual pace and the sound of the wheels on the crushed stones.

We came to a spot where we could look across the river at a boatshed painted in green and white stripes. People could rent canoes or rowboats or paddle-boats with steamer wheels at the back. 'This will be fine,' my uncle said. I stopped next to a park bench where I could sit, and locked the brakes of the wheelchair with my foot. The sun was out and the water-weed and the mud made patterns on the bottom of the river. Slightly downstream from us was a small weir. The river passed over a lip and scattered down across concrete into a deep pool. We could hear the white noise of the water.

We sat looking across at the boatshed, where a group of four people — I guessed they were from India — were renting canoes. A man and three women. The man was about my age and had on a suit and shiny black shoes. His face was the colour of teak. The women wore saris that draped over the top of their heads. They had bright red dots smudged on their brows, and they moved awkwardly over the sloping wooden slats of the decking.

'Your mother says you're pretty busy at work.'

I told him the shop was okay but it was just a job, something to tide me over until I found what I really wanted to do. I confided in him about the betting on the sign and he laughed and told me a funny story about a bloke at his work who used to sleep in the storeroom during the afternoons. I was feeling good so I said I had some ideas for developing a business of my own. I had a friend who travelled to Asia regularly and could send back statues and baskets, furniture and rugs — anything, really, all purchased for a song. My uncle expressed his enthusiasm. He implied that if I was looking for a business partner then he could be interested. I tried to remember what it was that he had done for the past thirty years. I had a feeling it was something to do with supermarkets, but I couldn't be sure and I didn't want to offend him by asking.

The Indians had succeeded in renting two canoes. The boatman tipped over the fibreglass pods to empty them of rainwater, then placed them in the river. The teak-faced man sat in the front of one and a woman got in behind him. He began to paddle up the river and we watched them until they passed into the shadow of the bridge.

The other two women took longer. They wobbled and squealed as they were helped into their canoe. One was wearing yellow and blue; the other was all in shades of green with white at her throat and wrists. When they were seated, the boatman passed them the paddles and pushed them off gently out into the river with his foot. They did not lift their paddles but simply sat in the sliding canoe looking around as though they could not understand where they were or how they had come to be there. They were side on to the current and it caught them and began to carry them down the river at the slow pace of the brown leaves that also drifted along.

'The nurse said that you listen to the radio at night.'

My uncle swivelled his head to look at me. 'I bet she did. That one's a real bitch.'

I was surprised by his vehemence. 'Why's that?'

'Took a real dislike to me straight away. I don't know why. When she's changing the bed she's too rough.'

I remembered her hands chopping into the pillows. 'She says your radio keeps the other patients awake.'

'I only have it on for company.' He stopped talking and all the anger seemed to flow out of him and evaporate. The wind moved over the water, hiding the patterns on the bottom. Then he said, 'At night it sometimes feels like I'm the only person left alive.'

I didn't know what to say to that so I looked back at the river, where the two women had begun to dip their paddles. They seemed to have no understanding of how to turn the canoe. The woman in the green sari was sitting in the front. She poked at the water, slicing through it with the edge of her paddle. The canoe wobbled as she moved and the other one said something in a thin voice. As the woman in front struggled with her paddle her sari slipped from her head. Her face was puffy, not pretty as I had expected. Her hair was very black and pulled flat across her head and the part was powdered the same red as the dot on her forehead.

There was no real danger. At any point either of them could have slipped out of the canoe and the water would only have been up to their thighs. The weir, towards which they were drifting inevitably, was not high. Even so, they cried out. First to each other and then to their friends, who had paddled up the river and under the bridge and were now out of sight. All the two women had to do was dig their oars into the water to turn the canoe but this seemed hopelessly beyond them.

My uncle and I did not comment. We sat and watched. A few people stopped and gathered on the bridge.

Inevitably, the canoe struck the concrete lip of the weir. It made a hollow fibreglass *thunk* like a dropped drum. The women cried out in their own language, thin and piercing. They were still side on to the current and I expected the canoe to roll or tip sideways, but it did not tip or ride dramatically over the weir. It simply stuck on the lip, leaning slightly towards the bridge, as though offering up its contents for inspection to the small audience gathered there. The women were screaming now, in shrill voices, one after the other, as though they had agreed to go turn and turn about. The water moved around them and under them.

I do not know how they were rescued. Most likely somebody

from the boatshed rowed out to them and towed them in without much fuss. They were still stranded on the lip of the weir when I spotted the pale nurse moving down the riverbank towards us. I looked at my watch and saw that it was almost one o'clock. I stood and brushed off my trousers with the palms of my hands.

'I'd better get back, otherwise the boss'll give me the sack.'

The incident with the canoe and the Indian women seemed to have depressed my uncle. He looked up at me with eyes that the wind off the water had stung. 'Thanks for coming. It's good to get out once in a while.'

I nodded, embarrassed, shook his hand and said goodbye. I told him I might call in and see him again before he was discharged, but I never did.

As I walked towards the bridge the nurse was walking towards me. When I was still a couple of metres away I moved to one side to let her pass, but she moved at the same time so that we performed a chaste dance on the path. In the sunlight her uniform was a perfect white and the skin around her neck almost as white. I thought again about asking her out, but when we drew close I just said 'hello' and 'thanks' without breaking my stride.

I walked back towards the souvenir shop and the lunchtime crowd moved around me and past and I was caught up in their movement. The autumn weather was changeable and the day had become suddenly overcast, the clouds sliding in from the south in a dark smear. The first spits of rain fell. All around me people started to hurry, going back to their jobs with quick steps.

As I walked beneath the awnings I suddenly felt as though I were at a crossroad, but did not know why. Nothing spectacular had happened, or even particularly significant. I visited my uncle in hospital and we had gone and sat by the river. That was all.

The rain began to fall on the black asphalt with the sound of air leaking from a tyre. Pulling my jacket close, I put my head down and walked faster as the wind began to funnel down the street between the tall buildings.

JULIAN NOVITZ

The Bugger

ADAM GELLWORTH HAS BEEN LYING face down behind the couch for over an hour. The shearers or farmhands, whoever they are, don't seem to be going anywhere. They opened a crate about half an hour ago and every now and then he hears a tinkle of glass as they pull out another bottle. How many bottles do they have left to drink? How many crates? There's bugger all else to do out here besides drink; they could be at this all night. Adam hasn't been out in the country for a while and the smell inside the shed reminds him of visits to his grandfather's farm when he was a kid. Sheep dung, sweat and stale beer. Adam always hated the farm, hated the weekends with his grandfather. Mean-spirited old cunt. He'd be laughing now.

There are about three of them in the shed, Adam thinks — three at least, but not more than four. Two of them are sitting on the couch; he can hear the springs creak above his head. There is a portable TV on the table; they've turned it on to watch the match. The door is open and Adam can feel a slight breeze. The others must be out drinking in the paddock — he can hear them wander in from time to time to check the score. Adam wonders what happened to McCarthy and Garret. They must have been surprised — no time to send him a warning. Adam has switched off his radio, anyway; he doesn't want it crackling to life now. McCarthy and Garret must still be out there, he thinks, watching the shed from high up the hillside. There is bugger all they can do for him now.

This isn't the first time Adam ever got stuck. He is good at his job but you can't plan for everything, and over the past twenty years he's had to hide in wardrobes and under beds, leap out of windows at a moment's notice and leg it across suburban lawns. Stuff-ups are always a possibility but this is a bad one, almost unforgivable. He has no idea what sort of men he is dealing with — how much they know, how smart they are, what routines they keep. He and Garret should have watched the place for longer but they'd been cocky. Now Adam was stuck down on his belly on the filthy shed floor.

Hiding is not something they teach you. *Bugger all* is what they teach you — the rest you learn on the job, from experience. You stay still but try to flex your muscles every now and then so you don't get a cramp when you have to run. You take deep, regular breaths — no one will hear you breathing unless they're listening for you, and shallow breaths will just get you panicking. Adam's bladder has swollen over the past hour. He is not above pissing himself when he has to, but here they might smell it. He regrets not sending McCarthy into the shed now. He could have been in and out faster; he is good enough. And even if he isn't really good he is young, and he could manage lying still, face down on the floor for more than an hour. Adam isn't sure how much longer he can last.

You might be buggered, he thinks. The bugger is buggered. In the act of bugging he has buggered himself. If he makes a break for it they'd catch him. They are young men — younger than him, anyway — and Adam is out of shape. Too much time doing fiddly work with wires and electronics, too much time on the computer. His stomach gurgles beneath him. He wishes he could shift over onto his side, but he can't risk it. He has been looking at the floor for more than an hour now, at its warped wooden surface, the dust and dirt and flecks of wool. He has been looking at his forearms for an hour, crossed in front of him — bare, beefy forearms covered with ginger hair. So many hairs, so many freckles, dimpled spongy flesh around his elbows.

The wife took him to see a film the other month. Fucking *Mission Impossible* shit, fucking Tom Cruise. She thought it would be fun but it just pissed him off. Pretty-boy super-spies with their floppy hair, abseiling down skyscrapers, fucking explosions. Try lying on your gut in a woolshed and not being able to piss for over an hour, you alien-worshipping prick. We're not spies, Adam thinks; we're buggers. All we have is patience, all we're good at is staying still and not making any noise. Adam is a savant when it comes to not moving. He is a master at not saying a bloody word.

The wife says he doesn't talk to her and Adam knows he needs to make an effort now; he can't just piss off to the den and his computer every night, the way he used to when the kids were at home. He has to cook dinner once in a while, suggest a movie. And then the weekends, the trips to the market, sipping those lattes at an outdoor café, meeting friends in the evening, some other lonely-arsed couple with an empty nest. People have kids to stop themselves from getting bored, Adam thinks — sick of each other and themselves. There's no other reason, really, when you get right down to it, not with all the grief they give. The best you can say is that they're never boring.

One of the shearers on the couch leans forward to shout abuse at the TV. Adam thinks that if just one of the bastards gets off his arse, if just one of them decides he wants to have a stretch, take a wander to the east window, or pick up that motorcycle magazine he can see on the table behind him, it will all be over. Who knows what they'll do? Smartest thing to do would be to run him off the property quick as they can, then destroy any evidence. Keep their mouths shut and not do anything stupid. But the thing with this job, the thing that will always surprise you, is just how stupid your opposition can be. Adam still fondly remembers the time some idiots burned a DVD of themselves posing with all the loot they'd nicked, then forgot to take the thing out of a laptop drive when they tried to unload their haul at Cash Converters.

But sometimes you get the other side of that stupidity, and it must happen in an instant, in a flash of complete idiocy. Adam wonders what they might be keeping around here. Some bright spark might have thought to hide a shotgun on an upper shelf, because they're big-timers now, protecting their stash. But it doesn't take a gun or even a knife — all you need is any blunt heavy object you might find around the home. Fists and feet will do at a pinch; no one is too stupid to improvise.

Having dinner one night in a seafood restaurant, wearing paper napkins and eating mussels with the wife and some other couple he can barely remember, Adam had been asked a question about his job. His wife had smiled, because now there was a use for him after all — his job was interesting to the people she wanted to impress, the part-time interior decorator from her Pilates class and her real-estate agent husband. It was another world to those people, something off the tellie. They wanted to hear all about the case files of Detective Sergeant Gellworth — they couldn't get enough. 'The job?' he had said, looking up from his plate, his fingers and lips greasy from the mussel shells. 'When I'm on the job, mate, I'm untouchable.' And then that idiot real-estate agent had laughed because he thought Adam had made a joke, because an overweight, moustached fifty-something with a mortgage and a bored wife could hardly claim to be untouchable, not on the job, not in any capacity.

But untouchable he is, and that is why Detective Sergeant Adam Gellworth is still lying behind a couch on the floor of a woolshed, ready to piss his pants if he has to lie there a minute longer. The kids are gone, the wife is a lost cause — what else is there beside the bugs, the bugging, the bugger, the bugged and the buggered? There are other jobs for a man like him, of course: an older bugger in lousy shape with no leadership skills or management potential. There are a whole range of small, uncomfortable places for him: archives, admin, training, retraining, any number of desks and cubicles and out-of-the-way basement offices. Bloody old Currie, the old bugger Adam had worked with for years — what happened to him after he tired of stuffing himself behind furniture and under tables, wiring bedrooms and garages and buggering all manner of people with his tools of buggeration, those devices the size of a ten-cent, no, a five-cent piece, inserting them into the rectums of their lives with aplomb? Where is Currie now, that bugger of fifteen years' experience? At a computer in the corner of an office, click, click, click through his web browsers all day. Porn site after porn site, checking what they are showing and who is looking. Someone has to keep track of it all, and that someone is Currie, the poor bugger.

Adam isn't averse to pornography — there is still blood in his penis. But porn all day? Every day? Porn as your job, your life, for the five years you have to waste until retirement? No, Currie is buggered. But so is Adam, lying on his belly, looking at his fat forearms, his nose down close enough to smell his own skin. The fabric of his shirt and trousers have moulded themselves into the floor beneath his weight; he can't move an inch now without hearing them pull and stick.

The match is over; the boys sitting on the couch greet the final whistle with a groan and reach for more beer. Adam wonders who's been playing. He's never been much into sport, to tell the truth. His son had been good at soccer for a while, between the ages of ten and fifteen, and Adam had taken some pride in watching his matches. When people asked him about his son he could say he was good at soccer and that never failed to content the questioner. It was a fact uncomplicated by any qualification — good at soccer, good at kicking a ball past other kickers on some muddy field.

But the soccer fell away as the boy progressed deeper into adolescence, growing into a lurking, slouching creature. Adam wasn't an angry father — he lacked that kind of energy — and continued to say that his boy was good at soccer even after the ball had deflated in the garage and the boots had submerged themselves in the back of a wardrobe. Bad grades, late nights, sullen dinner conversations, cut classes, minor traffic accidents. The boy became more and more of an abstraction as he got older, just a wearisome thought in the back of Adam's mind. A lot of sneering, a lot of posturing, but not really anything to do with Adam, now that the soccer days were past. The girls had been easier. They just grew up.

Adam remembers a time when the boy had been seen at a party that got out of control; some cunt of a PC was joking about it in the cafeteria. Adam had gone home that night and not talked to anyone; sat in the den at his computer without really focusing on the images flickering on his screen. The next morning, a Saturday, he had gone into the boy's room and sat down on the bed. Adam wasn't sure how long he had sat there, watching the boy sleep, his face burrowed deep into the pillow.

Outside the sun was up; he could hear a neighbour mowing his lawn, could almost smell the grass cuttings on the hot flat air. After a while Adam had leaned forward, grabbed a handful of the boy's long, dyed black hair and tugged him upright. His son had been shocked, his face screwed up with pain, and Adam was almost touched for a moment — he had forgotten how the boy looked when he was afraid and vulnerable.

'Don't you embarrass me, son,' he had said, pulling harder. 'Don't you fucking embarrass me.' And they had looked at each other and understood each other then, and Adam had wished that the moment could have lasted forever, but eventually he had to let go and walk away, with a few long black hairs still looped around his fingers. The boy was up and about in an hour, all his rudeness and insolence flooding back, but he was a bit more careful around Adam after that, at least until after he moved out. Buggered off to university in some other city to collect his bloody Bachelor of Arts, his degree in Bugger All.

Shadows move across the floor of the woolshed; twilight is passing. Outside Adam can hear loud talk and laughter. If the boys on the couch would only get up and join their mates then he might be able to slip out through the other door, creep away around the hillside, moving unseen through the dark. One of them tears open a pack of potato chips and swears as they scatter over the couch. Adam's bladder has grown until he thinks of it as an entity quite apart from him, a swollen island beneath his skin, round and hard like a rock. His weight presses down on it and it presses back into him and Adam starts to believe that he is not controlling it but that two equally intractable forces are simply keeping each other in check. Despite his attempts to stretch and flex, his joints have stiffened, his knees feel sore and swollen. If he has to run he'll never make it, not in this state.

After another minute one of the shearers stands up from the couch. Adam hears him brush potato chips out of his lap, hears the springs creak. The man shuffles around, looking over to the window on the other side of the room. All he'd have to do is lean forward a little, let his eyes fall lower, but the moment soon passes and the man turns away. Adam hears him walk across the room and out into the paddock. He releases his breath in a long steady stream through pursed lips. Adam Gellworth is untouchable. For a while yet, anyway. For a little while longer, perhaps.

Two left on the couch. Three, maybe four out in the paddock. Six years ago he would have risked it, would have wriggled across the room, got the window open and rolled out over its ledge without anyone hearing a thing. Now he's not sure if he can stand up on his own. Adam thinks about Garret and McCarthy, up on the hillside with their binoculars, trying to guess what might be going on. He almost feels sorry for the poor buggers, then decides to feel sorry for himself instead. McCarthy made it out okay, scampered up to the tree-line without being seen. But the door was already opening by the time Adam realised what was going on and he was down on his knees, busy with his buggering behind the couch. In another minute he would have been out of there, but all he could do then was fall flat on his belly and wait for a chance to slip away, or wait to be buggered himself. Now his world has shrunk to the bare wooden floor beneath him, his forearms crossed in front of his face, the dirt, dust and curls of wool. This is his world and he is learning to live with it. Better to be here than anywhere else, he thinks. This is his job, after all, the only job. It is the one thing in the world that is indisputably his, and no floppy-haired Tom Cruise fuckwit can dispute his ownership. Fucking super-spies: there's no such thing. Just buggers like him.

Above the shed, on the hillside, Garret and McCarthy must be listening in, listening through his bug to the drone of the television and the mumbled commentary of the shearers on the couch. Maybe they can hear his slow regular breaths as well, and reassure themselves that he has not vanished entirely, that he will return from behind the couch at some point. This is the job, Adam tells himself. This is what I do.

It is dark outside. They have passed from twilight to night, and the voices in the paddock seem closer, as if they are moving back towards the door, drawn to the pallid light of the shed. How long can he remain undetected with four or five people milling around inside? He has been waiting for things to get better and now they are getting worse. He has been waiting for a chance, but perhaps he's missed it. What will the wife be doing now? Watching television probably, the pre-dinner hour. Dinner will be eaten with the news, then after-dinner TV, then bedtime, forty-five minutes with her library book before lights out. God, she must have been embarrassed when he talked about the job, when he claimed to be untouchable. A fat old man making out like some faster-than-fast super-spy. God.

They're not moving out but coming back in. All of them are inside now; the door to the paddock has been swung shut and the television turned off. More bottles of beer are produced — the last bottles; there is talk of opening another crate. Adam looks around and sees a couple of crates on the other side of the room, on his side of the room, over by one of the shearing stalls. I-spy-with-my-little-fucking-eye. Of course they may just be empties, from some earlier drinking session, but he can't quite bring himself to believe that, not tonight, not with the way his luck has been going. When he is on the job he is untouchable. Stupid. Fucking unbelievable.

Adam can't understand how he has not seen those crates before now. He doesn't understand much, really — not the wife as she declines daily, tottering bravely through a life of vague dissatisfaction; not the kids with their useless degrees and useless ideas, their smugness, their support for that lesbian bitch in the Beehive, their patronising glances at his solid, silent form. He doesn't understand any of that or any of them. But the job — he thought he understood the job, he thought it all made sense. Bug, bugger, being a bugger, we've bugged them and they're buggered now. Stuff-ups happen, but if you do the job, if you know the job, then you'll get through it. A bugger doesn't let himself get buggered.

Footsteps creaking on the wooden floorboards, someone moving around the side of the couch — he can see them looming up from out of the corner of his eye. Adam puts his head down, as if that will help. Stupid. Oh God. Stupid old man. Stupid fucking God. He doesn't understand a thing now, can't for the life of him understand how he came to be here. Everything is a mystery.

Above him, Adam hears a drawn-in breath. He lifts his head from his forearms but it seems to take ages for him to raise his eyes, up past muddy steel-capped boots and yellow pulled-up socks, past hairy bare legs and faded shorts, past the beginnings of a beer-gut and the turned-up collar of a dirty chequered shirt, to the face of the surprised young man. A rush of warmth overcomes him, then and Adam realises that the long battle with his bladder is over and in the end it hasn't mattered — nothing has. The man above has not shouted, not alerted his friends. His mouth is still wide with surprise; he doesn't know why Adam is here or what to do, not for the life of him, not yet.

It's okay, Adam wants to say as he looks up, you don't have to do anything because you haven't really seen me at all. When I'm on the job, mate, when I am on the fucking job I am untouchable. So don't take that from me, please, I'm not ready to lose it yet.

But the shearer would not understand, and Adam is not sure if he understands himself, and in fact, at that moment, neither of them can be said to understand a bloody thing. Two men, behind a couch in a shed in the hills at night-time, one of them looking up, one of them looking down, joined together by complete incomprehension. It is a beautiful moment, Adam thinks. He wishes it could last forever.

Velocity

I USED TO LIVE WITH a man called Jack Duffy. We were good together, me and Jack, for a while. I guess you'd call him a traveller these days. He drives around the country in a dark green 1978 Holden ute with an old Lilliput caravan towing behind. It's one of those little ones shaped like a white button mushroom. Reg GP9302. That's the caravan, not the ute.

Jack's got a road map of New Zealand in the glovebox, and he draws a black line along each road he takes. Some roads have two lines on them, from when he's backtracked. The silly bugger's been doing this for ages and the map's a smudgy mess — there aren't many roads, major or minor, that Jack has not driven along at some time.

I see him from time to time, when he passes through Tirau. That's where I ended up after things fell apart between us. I rented an empty building and set myself up a little second-hand shop. If you know Tirau at all, you'll appreciate it's become quite the little tourist Mecca of the south Waikato. So yeah, I'm settled, doing okay. Anyway, Jack calls in maybe two or three times a year, and it's always good to see him. He never stays long, though, on account of being on the run from a bird.

We met in Tokoroa, which is just down the road from Tirau. Back then Tokoroa was a lively sort of a place. Lots of people came for a few months, earned big money at the mill, decided they liked it enough to stay. Monday to Thursday everyone generally got on with their business. Come Friday, the boys would come in from the bush and there'd be the usual suspects pissed and fighting down at The Trees. You didn't have to drink there, though. There was the Toke Tavern, and the Timberlands if you felt like a change. I never did. I liked the old Toke Tavern.

I'd lived in Tokoroa all my life. Dad was a bushman and Mum worked in the canteen at the mill. I've realised since arriving in Tirau that outsiders actually looked down on Tokoroa, thought it was a rough sort of a place with nothing going for it. It amazes me that people saw it that way. To me it was just home, with a big mix of people who arrived all the time from God knows where — the islands, Europe some of them. Lots of

Dutchies. Where they came from was no big deal; it didn't have anything to do with the fighting. No matter what they turned up as, they ended up the same. Bushmen. Cutting down trees. Moving trees. Turning trees into paper. Turning paper into money — enough money to leave for somewhere else, or so they'd reckon when they first arrived.

At the time I met Jack I was a postie. It wasn't a career or anything; the whole career thing doesn't do much for me. But I was keen on netball and I needed a job that kept me fit and allowed time for training. So being a postie suited me down to the ground. I had the option of doing the round on a little motorbike the Post Office gave me, but I never used it; I either ran or rode my mountain bike. The job was all over by lunchtime, which meant I could go to the gym or netball training or whatever.

I had a dog, Lucy. A Lab something something bitser — I got her from the pound when she was a pup. Lovely dog. She'd come with me on the postie run and add twenty minutes onto the job because of all the attention she got. Anyway. She needed attention for some complaint so I took her to the vet clinic.

Jack worked there. Not as a vet, but a vet's assistant. Meaning he could tend to the little problems, like whatever it was that Lucy had, but not surgery and stuff. Well, nature took its course. Lucy came right and Jack and I went out a few times, had a laugh, ended up getting together. We rented a little two-bedroom weatherboard house and a couple of paddocks at the northern end of town: enough space for the recovering sick animals Jack would bring home from the clinic.

The thing that struck me about Jack was his amazing kindness to all living creatures. I mean, you just had to look at him to see that he was a kind man. He was tall and gangly and he had this sort of lovely pathetic aspect to him, like Hugh Grant at his most useless, if you know what I mean. Except Jack's hair was blond and frizzy, and it looked like a toilet brush when it got away on him. He wore little round silver-rimmed glasses, which sort of added to the pathetic impression, and he had these brown eyes that were huge on account of the magnifying of the glasses. They stared straight at you, like an innocent trusting animal does. So I suppose actually he didn't look like Hugh Grant at all, but overall it was a Hugh Grant sort of effect.

The funny thing was, because he was so kind and pathetic looking, everyone liked him. Even the thugs left him alone. A few times I remember we'd be at the pub and Jack would blunder on in — you know, tip someone's jug over accidentally or bump someone's cue when they were playing pool. And I'd think, *Shit, here we go,* but whoever it was would just look at Jack and sort of sigh and say, *Doesn't matter, mate, don't worry about it.* Half the time they wouldn't even let him pay for another jug. Honestly. I don't know how he got away with it. But he did.

You should have seen Jack with a sick animal. Honestly, it was a thing to watch. He was just so gentle — cared for sick creatures like he was a mother to a baby. I saw it immediately, that first time I took Lucy in. She was whining and snarling, and I lifted her up onto the vet's table and Jack just quietly touched her, felt around her body, and talked to her in this low voice he uses when he's trying to calm something down. Old Lucy just lay there, stopped growling, almost like he'd hypnotised her. She let him prod and poke and stick a thermometer up her arse and everything, not a whimper.

It ended up to be nothing serious — I think she'd eaten something dodgy and Jack just gave her some medicine to cancel out whatever was disagreeing with her. He didn't have to call in the proper vet. She was as right as rain the next day, and as a matter of fact she lived to a ripe old age.

But it was something to see, how he handled her that first time. It was hot, actually — I mean really sexy to see the power he had in his hands when he was with sick animals. Don't take this the wrong way, but it was almost like he was a lover, a strong, powerful lover, and the animals gave themselves over to him completely, knowing that he would work magic.

I'd see it over and over again, as I spent more time with him. Didn't seem to matter what the animal was. Dogs, cats, horses, the lot. They'd calm right down. I used to think that he had some sort of connection with them, some extra sense that most humans don't have.

So, yeah. A hell of a lot of animals ended up in our front paddocks, recovering from illnesses of some kind or another. I'd be cycling or jogging home from doing the delivery and hello, there'd be another beast there.

Jesus, you should have seen some of them. Goats with those funny bucket things around their heads to stop them getting at their wounds. They looked like old-fashioned lampshades. Horses and ponies with bandaged legs. Dogs all shaven and stitched in the big open-run kennels Jack had bought. I'd be laughing away, shouting out *Welcome* to these animals. They'd stay there a few days, then Charlie Boyd (that's the vet) would arrive out with the truck and the horse float and pick them up and take them away.

I wondered, in those early days, why Jack had never bothered to finish vet school. Once, just after he had calmed and treated some poor animal, I asked him.

He just said it wasn't for him, the whole university thing. You wouldn't believe what it was like, he said, unless you'd been there yourself. He said he couldn't handle the pressure of exams, everyone competing. And he was quite happy as a vet's assistant, even if he couldn't do everything.

I knew one thing for sure — Charlie Boyd was rapt to get him. Charlie was forever whinging how he couldn't get a vet to come and work in Tokoroa. He reckoned the vet school graduates got too much of a taste for the city life while they were at university, then they'd go soft and want to stay in town. Treating *small animals*, Charlie used to say: *rats and hamsters and gerbils and other fucking rodents.* When Jack applied for the job, Charlie was grateful. More than happy to do the big stuff on his own, let Jack do what he could manage. Charlie told me this himself.

Velocity turned up on Jack's birthday one year.

It was about five in the evening; there was a northerly breeze blowing the stink from the mill away from the town. It was cold, but a big red sun was going down over the back of the pine forest. That's a sight worth staying outside for, no matter how cold it is.

Jack was sitting on our back steps, picking mud off his boots with a stick. I'd brought us out birthday beers and settled down on the steps with him.

Roly Smythe came up the driveway in his new red Rodeo truck. Roly is Jack's mate. He's farmed all his life next door. We've never got on, me and Roly. He's one of those guys who hates women because they steal a man's friends. Consequently, Roly is a bachelor and a lonely soul.

He slowed to a stop and the driver's window went down. 'Happy birthday, mate. Gotcha something,' he said to Jack.

'New truck. Thanks, Roly.' Jack raised his bottle. 'Come and have a beer.'

'Na, mate. Something else.' Roly jumped out of the truck and walked around to the back. He lifted a cane hamper, just a bit smaller than a washing basket, off the deck and carried it over to where we were sitting. He put it on the ground at Jack's feet.

'What's this?' said Jack.

'Open it, see for yourself.'

Jack lifted the latch and opened the lid. Sitting inside was a grey bird, slightly smaller than a seagull. It had iridescent green feathers around its neck — the colour you see inside paua shells sometimes. The wings had a frill of black feathers near the edges.

'What's the problem — is it injured?' Jack leaned forward and gently lifted the bird out of the box. He lifted one wing, then the other, checking them over for damage.

'Nup. It's a pigeon,' said Roly, grinning away. 'A racing pigeon. Thought you might enter it in the competitions, have a bit of fun with it.'

'Christ almighty. Where'd you get it?' The bird sat calmly in Jack's hands, black eye watching him.

'At the saleyards today. Old fella had it, said it was a great racing bird. Said his wife had got sick of the whole pigeon racing scene and that he had to give the game up. He was giving her away, so I grabbed her for you.'

Roly smiled at me. Wanker.

'Cheers, mate. What the hell do you do with them?' Jack passed the bird to me. It crapped into my lap.

'Buggered if I know.' Roly went into the house, then came out with a beer in his hand. 'It's a girl, and her name's Velocity, the old guy said. He named her after the fastest pigeon to deliver mail between Auckland and Great Barrier Island, back whenever.'

'Shit, is that right?' Jack was impressed. He always liked to hear about animals' achievements.

'Yep. First ever pigeon airmail service in the world, apparently.'

'Jeez. Amazing, eh.' Jack stroked the pigeon's head again.

'Yeah, sure is.' Roly took a swig from the bottle, then clunked it against Jack's. 'Happy birthday,' he said.

Next morning Jack went off to the library for books on racing pigeons. He came back with a few, and a mountain of building materials on the back of his ute.

'The thing is, Sandy, these racing pigeons live in lofts.' He dropped the pile of books on the kitchen table and flicked open the top one. 'See, look at this. This is what I need to build.'

On one page there was a photo of a little house on stilts. It had chicken wire across the front, and inside were various pieces of miniature furniture — they looked like tiny chests of drawers — which turned out to be feeding and water equipment. On the opposite page were drawings showing how to construct this loft.

Jack settled into the task, which ended up taking most of the weekend. I went out and gave him a hand, passing nails, reading out measurements, that sort of thing. I was sort of hoping we would get it all done on the Saturday, but it was obvious by about five o'clock that it would be a two-day job.

We ended up finishing late Sunday afternoon. We put water in the little container, and Jack mixed some concoction of feed for the bird. Peas, maize, oats, rice barley; apparently you had to have the ratio just right to keep the bird healthy.

As he tipped this mixture into the feed container I lifted Velocity out of her hamper. 'There you go, girl,' I said. 'Welcome to your loft accommodation.' She tilted that head of hers to one side and, like lightning, nipped me on the wrist.

She drew blood. It oozed out of the wound, which was shaped like the point of her beak. It was surprisingly deep. I dropped her; Jack quickly scooped her up and put her in the loft. 'Jesus, Sandy, be careful.'

'She bloody bit me.'

'Well, you were probably squeezing her or something.'

'I wasn't. I was holding her just like you do. I've probably got some disease now. What do they get, these birds? Rabies?'

'Don't be stupid,' he said. He stayed outside, watching the bird strut around its new home, while I went inside and found a sticking plaster. I waited a bit, thinking Jack would probably come in and check I was okay. But he didn't.

Velocity and I quickly reached an understanding. I fed her; she attacked me. I didn't like her. It's hard to like something that wants to kill you.

The weird thing was, after that first time she behaved herself with me when Jack was around. He would give her to me, and she would sit quietly in my cupped hands, little black beady eye in its yellow ring looking up at me, sussing me out.

'See,' Jack would say, 'she's fine with you. My two girls.' His face would glow with a love that appeared to be divided equally between me and Velocity.

The night before Velocity's first race, Jack and I took her to the pigeon club and put her on the pigeon truck going south. The guy driving this truck is called the Liberator. Imagine that. Like some kind of superhero.

Anyway. Off the Liberator went, *da da da*, into the night with a truck full of pigeons. To Christchurch, where he would set them all free to fly home. Jack was beside himself, seeing her off. I was quite excited about it all too. Christchurch, I thought. Across Cook Strait and its howling storms. All that way.

Jack had calculated how long it would take her to fly back — ten hours, he reckoned, seeing as she would be flying into a head wind. The birds were due to be released at dawn. That meant we had most of the next day to ourselves.

'I've arranged something special for us,' I told Jack on the way home. 'Tomorrow morning. We're going through to Hamilton. We'll have a look at some new furniture, then have lunch somewhere nice.'

'You're joking.' The disbelief in Jack's voice twisted it, gave it an ugly, high-pitched tone I had never heard before. When he turned towards me he was frowning and laughing at the same time.

'No, what's wrong with that?'

'We can't go anywhere. We have to wait for Velocity.'

'Yeah, but she's not due back until four in the afternoon. We'll be back well before then.'

'Yeah, but she'll probably get back early. She's a bloody champion flyer, you know, Sandy.' His whine sounded stressed now, like a truck being driven too fast in low gear.

'What — so we have to sit around all day and wait for her?'

'Yep.'

'Well, I'm not spending all day waiting for that fucking bird.'

'Suit yourself. Though I thought you might care how she got on, in her first race.'

The rest of the drive home was one of those quiet, uncomfortable, stuffy ones, where you can't get enough air circulating, even with all the windows down.

I won't bore you with the details of the pigeon racing season. I'll just say that Velocity lived up to her champion reputation, and Jack spent a hell of a lot of time feeding, training and exercising her.

We argued a lot that winter — usually about the need for us to hang around home every weekend, waiting for the bird to arrive back from other places. When we weren't arguing about that, we found other things to disagree on. Anything, really. Jack laughed at me a lot, accused me of being jealous of a bird. *A bird!* And he'd crack up laughing in that new whiney voice of his.

Well, yeah, maybe I was a bit jealous. But it seemed to me that the magic Jack had — that power, the strength — was disappearing day by day, leaking out the ends of his lovely fingers every time he handled Velocity. She'd sit in his hands, looking at him and me at the same time, and she soaked up every little bit of that magic for herself. The bits left over for me were the dregs.

It was early afternoon, a beauty of a spring day, still and warm. I was biking up the driveway on my way home from the delivery run when I heard tyres spitting stones, a vehicle coming up behind me. I turned around and it was Charlie. He followed me up to the house, driving slowly all the way.

He got out of his truck and I asked him which animal he'd come to pick up, seeing as he didn't have the horse float.

'The crossbreed bitch in the kennels,' he said.

'You mean Jessie.'

Charlie laughed. 'Is that her name?'

I asked him if I could have a ride back into town with him. I had a doctor's appointment and I'd planned to meet Jack later at the pub.

'Sure,' he said.

So there we were. Me and Charlie in the front of the truck, Jessie in the back.

'Where are you dropping her off?' I asked.

Charlie looked at me. He's got big hairy eyebrows, Charlie, and dark stubble all the time, even first thing in the morning.

'What do you mean, dropping her off?'

'Who owns her?'

'No one. She's a stray, a mongrel.'

'So we're off to the pound.'

Charlie was looking at me hard.

'The pound.' He laughed. 'Shit no. They don't want her back. She came from the bloody pound. Came into the clinic with an abscess on her leg. No, what happened was, the pound thought they'd found a new home for her, so I treated her. Assumed the new owners would pay. But the new home's fallen through. I'm putting her down, Sandy.'

We pulled out onto the main road, both of us staring straight ahead. I didn't ask about the other animals. All the sick, sad beasts that had been in our front paddocks. And the times Charlie had turned up with his horse float and taken one away. We drove to town in silence.

Just before we got to the clinic Charlie asked me where I wanted to be dropped off.

'Is Jack at the clinic at the moment?' I asked.

'No, he's out all afternoon.'

'When are you doing it?'

'Right now. While he's out.'

We sat there for a minute, me and Charlie. Not saying anything. Not looking at each other either. We just sat and I understood some things about Charlie and Jack, about how it worked for them. One putting sick animals out of their misery, the other prolonging it. And how this had never come between them.

'Can I watch?' I asked Charlie.

Charlie kept looking out the front of the truck, at some invisible spot on the windscreen. 'Sure,' he said.

I stood under the harsh light over the vet's table, patting the dog. The place was clean and white, like a hospital. Charlie had gone out the back and I could hear doors opening and shutting as he moved through the building. I heard cats meowing, other dogs barking, but the dog on the table didn't stir. After a moment Charlie returned.

I patted her head — long, even strokes: her eyes closed each time.

They would open again when the stroke stopped. She was a perfectly healthy dog.

Charlie disappeared again, returned with a syringe and a long needle. He stroked the dog gently on its side, then inserted the needle and slowly pumped the liquid into the skin under her back leg.

I watched Charlie's face, looking for some kind of emotion. Sadness, or even pleasure — cruelty — as he killed the dog. There was nothing there. He was just doing his job.

'Bye, Jessie,' he said. The dog gave one long final sigh and then she was gone.

'That's it, Sandy. That's what happens.' Charlie put the syringe back on the counter behind him. The dead dog farted, expelling the last of its air; last laugh to her.

'It doesn't matter, you know,' Charlie said. 'Doesn't matter that he can't bring himself to do it.'

I didn't know what to say to that.

I asked Jack whether he wanted to move out, or whether I should go. Jack said he wasn't leaving — how could he, with Velocity at the peak of her racing season and all those other animals in the paddocks to care for?

Fair enough, Jack, I replied. Fair enough. It didn't take me long to pack.

Jack and Velocity did very well. I kept track of them through the newspaper. Ribbons, cups, cash prizes. Then Jack turned up in Tirau one day and told me, over a cup of tea, that there was a problem between him and Velocity.

'Oh?' I said.

I confess, I'd already heard. Charlie calls in from time to time too, and he'd told me. But I wanted to hear Jack tell the story.

Jack had had enough of pigeon racing, he said. But the problem was, Velocity had not had enough. Of racing, or of Jack.

He'd tried to sell the bird, then give her away. But she'd attack anyone else who came near her.

'Really?' I said. Then, just because I couldn't help myself, 'Maybe Roly might take her back.'

'Huh,' said Jack.

So there he was, in a bit of a fix about things.

Now you would agree, there was an obvious way of dealing with this problem, having exhausted other options.

But instead, Jack entered Velocity in a race that started in Invercargill. There was no race scheduled for Stewart Island, otherwise he would have sent her off there, he said. So he entered her in this race, and then he went out and bought that ugly Lilliput caravan.

Two days before the race he took Velocity to meet the pigeon truck. She was safely tucked in her travel hamper, sufficient food and water for the long journey south. Once he'd handed her over, he raced home, hitched the caravan to the ute and took off.

I know, I know — crazy, stupid plan.

Turns out he could run but he couldn't hide. Velocity had spent enough time eyeing up that caravan through the chicken wire of her loft to bond with it, or whatever it is those racing pigeons do. When she arrived home from Invercargill and found no one there, she simply followed State Highway One north until she spotted the caravan.

'Did you know that racing pigeons actually follow, from the air, roads that they have already travelled on by car or truck?' Jack asked me. 'That they will take left and right turns directly above the roads?'

'No,' I said, 'I didn't know that.'

So, that first day of playing fugitive, Jack woke up in a camping ground on the outskirts of Cambridge to find Velocity sitting on the bonnet of his ute.

He tried again. And again. He'd drop that bird off in Whangarei, run for Auckland. She'd track him down.

To this day, she tracks him down.

I've told Jack to bring Velocity with him sometime, when he's coming through Tirau. Told him I wouldn't mind seeing the little bird again, holding her tightly in my hands. He just does the Hugh Grant thing on me when I suggest it.

Never mind. It's always nice to see him, when he passes through.

SARAH QUIGLEY

In the Palace Gardens

THEY WALKED IN THE GARDENS of a palace, late in the afternoon. After three months of winter the snow had taken possession of the ground; it seemed that there was nothing in the world not touched with white.

'Just look at those hedges!' he said. His laugh sounded as if he were laughing for the very first time; it was full of surprise, and a kind of wonder, making other people look over and also smile.

Obediently, she looked at the hedges. So many of his sentences started with the words 'Look at —!' and she did always look, out of a combination of loyalty and genuine curiosity. Strictly speaking, there were no hedges to be seen. No foliage at all — only the raised curving lines of an ornamental garden completely blanketed in snow. It was possible to make out the pattern designed several centuries earlier, but only as white relief on a white background.

It struck her as remarkable that nature was able to bury a part of itself, like a child covering its legs over with sand. 'Don't you think it's remarkable?' she asked. 'As if nature is playing a game with itself, oblivious to us.'

'But Man has undeniably intruded in the game,' he contradicted her. 'The shape of the hedges is entirely artificial. Perhaps what Nature is doing — in this case, at least — is reclaiming her body, rather than hiding it.' He spoke of Nature in the classical manner, as he did with Mankind.

She said nothing, and fastened the top button of her coat, a gesture that might be interpreted as defensive. He often did this, picking up the loose trains of her thought and developing them until she could no longer recognise that their origins lay in herself.

I am beginning, she thought, to have less and less energy for debate. Perhaps this was due to the constant cold, which truncated her thought processes, cutting them short before they could unfold and expand into feathery leaves. 'You make the landscape sound like a cosmic cake,' she said lightly. 'A layer of Man between two layers of Nature.'

He smiled at this, although his smile was barely visible behind his tweedy collar, which was turned up high against the cold. It had been mid-afternoon when they left home, and now the chilly light in the gardens was turning to grey. Night was waiting, hanging in the branches of the trees, lying flat and watchful on the frozen river.

'You are fanciful,' he said. 'I like that.'

She was pleased. He was such a serious person, even when joking, that to amuse him felt like an achievement. 'What else do you like?' she asked, testing him.

'Your red hat,' he said without hesitation.

'Do you?' She had never liked hats, and had bought this one in defiance of an indifferent shop assistant who appeared to care more about having a phone conversation than making a sale. 'To tell the truth,' she said, putting her hand up to the knitted snowflakes, 'it makes my forehead itch. But this winter is so very cold, and forty per cent of body heat is lost through the head.'

'Is that so?' He didn't sound sure. 'You might be right.' He walked beside her with shortened strides because of the icy path: from time to time his or her feet would slide from under them, and they would grab at the other one's sleeve.

Was it forty per cent of body heat? She believed this was true. At least, this was what her father had told her when she was small, in spite of the fact that they lived in a country with hardly any snow and many beaches. Now, sometimes, it seemed as if these words were the only ones her father had ever said to her.

Why could she not hear him any more? She could see him clearly enough, knotting a feathered fly onto a fish-hook, or standing in his workshop, sanding a piece of wood until it became as smooth as skin. But never once did he speak, even when she most hoped for it. There were nights when she had lain in bed, knees locked together and hands clenched, her whole body tense with the effort of resurrecting her father's voice. But the only time she thought she heard him was when she superimposed this line about hats and body heat (this ridiculous piece of common sense, this possibly inaccurate fact) onto his closed, silent, long-ago mouth.

She realised she hadn't said anything for several minutes, and hoped she didn't appear sullen. 'I was one of five daughters,' she offered, as a sign of trust.

'You've told me before,' he said, looking slightly surprised. There was a short pause. 'However,' he added politely, 'I don't believe I know what your sisters are called.'

They reached a small bridge and took hold of the railings, one each side, so as not to slip. Her careful footsteps trod out the names of her sisters, one for each rising step. 'Tuscany, Paris,' she intoned. 'Lisbon,

Antalya.' The bridge's surface was mercifully gritty; someone — a caretaker or a groundsman — had sprinkled sand over the ice. 'And then,' she finished, 'there was me.' Standing at the top of the small wrought-iron curve, she felt like the youngest princess in a fairytale. Below her lay the river, silenced by ice, its surface veined like the skin of an elderly, still beautiful woman.

'Such names!' he said. 'Your parents must have been great travellers.'

'On the contrary,' she said. 'Neither of them ever left the town in which they were born.'

'And so their five daughters became their wish-list?' He raised a quizzical eyebrow. 'Perhaps that is why you are such an inveterate wanderer — a parental blessing?'

'A blessing, or a curse,' she said.

He bent to pick up a couple of stones, and threw them hard onto the surface of the river. They jumped and skidded, but failed to break through the many layers of ice. 'A proper winter,' he observed with satisfaction.

'And you are a proper male,' she adjoined.

'Why do you say that?' He was distracted, casting around for stones that appealed to his eye and passed his secret criteria.

'All men throw stones into water,' she said. 'Or, in this case, onto it.'

'All women sit beside water,' he replied, 'and look soulful.'

She laughed, but in a way it was true, and she couldn't help wondering why this should be so. Sometimes she thought that the many years of schooling, the lessons and the repetition, the classrooms smelling of sweat and stale sandwiches and desire — all this had been nothing but the most rudimentary of preparation for moments such as these. Standing on a bridge, exchanging inexplicable truths with a man who, this time tomorrow, would once more sit in his office and assume control over the multitude of problems belonging to this city (an authoritative man, a public figure of a man, but one who nevertheless was happy to spend the dying afternoon walking with her in a snow-covered garden).

She covered up her sudden uncertainty with words. 'Men of your importance,' she chided, 'are not supposed to have a sense of humour. It's bad for the image. Gravitas must be maintained at all times, even on a Sunday.'

He deliberately ignored this, throwing one last stone at the shuddering ice, and then they left the bridge, slithering back down onto flat ground again. Other people walked ahead of them, also moving with difficulty, bundled up in coats with scarves wrapped around their necks and hats pulled over their eyes. She wondered where the compulsion to exercise came from. Why were these people not resting in well-heated living rooms, allowing their leg muscles to grow slack and their arms to lie comfortably on padded armrests? She supposed it was one way to stop themselves thinking: a travelling to escape, in the same way that, once, people had boarded steamers and journeyed over oceans, or had walked for many months through meadows and mountain passes, simply to keep decisions temporarily at bay.

'But why walk?' she said out loud. 'Why are all these people so determinedly out walking?'

'For relaxation?' he answered. 'For health? It's good for the body and the soul to spend time in Nature.'

'But this is not nature!' she exclaimed. She looked at the white ground and the sombre black trees, and replaced them with a long, lizard-like peninsula, and blue dazzling water dotted over by many ships blowing fast towards the harbour mouth, towards freedom, space and the unknown. 'This is not what people in my country would call nature,' she said, almost angrily.

'It is as close to Nature as we, trapped in our city, can get.' He shrugged. 'I'm sorry if it does not meet with your approval, but there is only so far one can go in the space of a single afternoon, particularly when one leaves home so late.' It was difficult to tell if this was a reproof or merely an explanation.

'I didn't mean to criticise,' she said, but she was not sure if this were true. Her outburst had been caused, at least partly, by disappointment and a touch of comparative superiority — and, yes, together these might amount to criticism.

He glanced at her but said nothing.

'It's only that I get so tired sometimes,' she said lamely, 'of buildings and people. And of —' She looked at the graceful rows of trees stretching away to the right and the left, and at the parallel lines of statues with snow epaulettes lying on their stone shoulders. 'Of enclosed spaces,' she finished. 'All year round, with no escape.'

'You must remember that the people who lived here used this palace only as their winter quarters,' he said. 'In the summer they would leave the city and spend months in what even you might call real countryside.'

So he had not realised that she had been talking about herself; rather, he had picked her up as a contemporary example and placed her in the corner of a far wider picture. She tried to imagine herself in those times: wearing a heavy dress that swept the ground, walking out with a dog running before her, leaving behind the stifling air, the gossip, the rich smells of basting juices and the dark aroma of port wine. Leaving all that, with the fall of a heavy door, and walking out on a midwinter day like today, so cold that when the air fell against your face it left first a pain and then a numbness. She turned around, half hoping they would be out of sight of the palace, but still it lay behind them, long and massive like the body of a beached whale. 'I only wondered,' she said, 'if people in those days got claustrophobic. If they suffered from what we call cabin fever.'

'Human beings have not changed between then and now,' he said, swishing at the bushes with a long stick, making snow fly under his commanding hand. 'The nature of people does not change along with the century. You think you would chafe at palace life and its restrictions. But if you had been born into it, as a royal, then you would consider it normal. You would not even notice the fences around you.'

I would, she thought mutinously. *I would*. She sank her chin low into her scarf, but the wool had become stiff and frozen into folds, and it gave no comfort.

'You would not even notice.' He repeated his last sentence, as if answering her stubborn unvoiced thoughts.

An irrelevant discussion, she thought angrily. I am not a woman born several centuries ago, he is not a man from Renaissance times, that girl over there is different from —

'Look at that!' he said, interrupting her musings, taking her arm. Some distance away an old man was zigzagging through the trees. At first he appeared to be skating but, as he came closer, they saw that he was pushing himself along on very long skis. His thin legs were covered in shiny blue lycra and there was a sweatband around his thinning hair; he propelled himself about the gardens of the old royal palace as if he were miles from civilisation, on an alpine snowfield.

'Such an old man,' she said. 'So ancient, so shiny, and — skiing!' For some reason she felt uneasy at the sight.

'Yes, just look!' he said in admiration. 'To be so oblivious to one's surroundings! Now, that's really something.'

She watched until the old man had toiled out of sight, but she saw mainly a fierce and restless spirit that was willing itself elsewhere. 'Old men should spend their last years in peaceful pursuits,' she said with mock reproof. 'They should stay at home with their wives.'

'That old man doesn't have a wife.' He regarded her with a curious expression, half amused, half watchful.

'I bet he does,' she challenged, 'and three children and six grandchildren, all of whom are waiting for him, wishing he would spend what might be his last Sunday on earth at home with them, rather than sliding about on two sticks pretending that he's in the alps.'

'Well, if you care to *bet*,' he said, 'shall we wager champagne?'

'A bottle,' she agreed, with dignity.

'Wonderful,' he said, rubbing his hands.

'What makes you so sure of yourself?' she said. 'And how do we find out the truth?'

'I am sure of myself and of the truth,' he said, 'because the shiny old skier who has just disappeared behind that brick wall happens to work for the government department next to my office. Moreover, I have it on good authority that he is gay.'

'Oh,' she said. 'Oh.'

'Oh,' he mimicked, not unkindly. 'I thought people only said that in novels.' He pulled her towards him and kissed the top of her woollen snowflake head. The effect of his kiss fell through her body in a delayed way; it was like standing some distance away watching a building being blown up: first seeing the magnificent cloud of splinters and dust, and then hearing the boom.

'I *oh* you champagne,' she punned.

He groaned. 'For that joke, you do. Perhaps you can buy me tea instead, at the Belvedere.'

'The Belve-where?' she said. 'Just how far do we have to travel for tea?'

He pointed and, when she was able to draw her eyes away from his tired, chilled, humorous face, she saw among the trees a small domed building. Its walls, painted in the palest shades of blue and cream, were curved as if they had been shaped by a cupped pair of hands. 'Having a building like this in your back garden might satisfy your restless soul,' he suggested. 'Taking a carriage out here for the occasional party, dancing to a waltz by chosen musicians, flirting over your fan?'

She looked up to the gilt cockerel on the roof, its beak open silently against a snow-coloured sky. 'Perhaps it would satisfy me,' she said. 'Perhaps.' She followed him up the low stone steps, through a heavy door and some thick red curtains, and suddenly they were immersed in warmth. The air hummed with voices and was sweet with perfume; a huge cut-glass chandelier hung above the round room, casting flickers of yellow light over green palm trees. The world outside had been bleached of colour; here, there was almost too much. She sank into the nearest seat and opened her stiff coat. 'It's so warm,' she said. 'So unbelievably warm.' She pulled her hat off and smoothed her hair back: it was ice-cold to the touch, still holding the memory of where it had been.

He ordered cake. 'My treat,' he said quickly. 'My Sunday treat.' For a second, at the mention of the working week ahead, he looked bleak. She wanted to reach out and touch him, but the waiter was coming with cutlery, and a pile of serviettes on a tray, so heavy and starched that they looked like a stack of pure white books.

'Don't think upon the morrow, because the morrow never comes,' she misquoted, looking at him over the silver teapot, willing him to be happy.

He rallied, as he always did. 'Would you like to try the cheesecake?' he asked, holding a quivering forkful over the table to her. 'It's a speciality of this region.'

She leaned forward and opened her mouth like a bird. 'Delicious,' she said through a mouthful of soft yellow cream and gritty biscuit base. The elderly waiter, positioned discreetly by the nearest palm tree, tried to look unperturbed, though he was more used to fur-coated women slipping slivers of steak to their poodles than important public officials feeding slender, frozen-looking girls.

She raised a subtle eyebrow in the direction of the ornamental palm. 'Look to your left,' she muttered through expensive cake crumbs. 'You should be careful — that waiter could be your hanging voter.'

'I am tired of being careful,' he sighed. But he sat back in his chair and chatted to her about non-emotive topics. Later, he tipped the waiter with a large note. 'Thank you, sir,' said the waiter, bowing deeply. 'Nice to see you in our establishment, sir.'

She started gathering up her gloves and scarf, but as she stood up the room began to whirl around her. She sank back into her chair, holding the sides of the seat tightly with both hands, while her cheeks flamed.

'Are you all right?' he asked in alarm. He came around the table and crouched beside her, but in a discreet way so that nobody would notice.

'I'm fine,' she said, looking up, trying to smile. She was not used to a round room, this was it; she had never been in a room without corners in her life. 'And the heat,' she added, 'after such extreme cold.'

He told her to take her time, that he would wait, but he looked anxious as he watched her walk away. She brushed unsteadily past potted plants that scratched her lightly on her arms and face, past a row of fur coats smooth on her burning cheeks, and then through some swing-doors. Now the world became white again, smelling only of cleanness and water. She shut herself in a cubicle and leaned against the door, closing her eyes and pressing her forehead hard against the varnished wood. *We place our trust in upright things*, she thought. We lean against trees and walls when they could fall at any second; we ascend to the twenty-seventh floors of buildings, riding in elevators held in place only by swinging cables. But nothing is certain: not mechanics, nor memory, nor love.

She had a sudden vision of him sitting alone at the round table, waiting for her in the round red room. Turning, she pulled some paper out of the dispenser and wiped the sweat off her forehead. When she opened the door of the cubicle and saw her reflection in the mirror, her face was pale and inscrutable once again, which was how she preferred it. She washed her hands and splashed water on her face, and then she pushed her way back out into the restaurant, where she made a reassuring quip about the potency of the tea they had been served.

'You're sure you're all right?' he asked as they made their way back out into the black and white world, and felt the cold wrap around them again.

'I took sleeping pills last night.' She frowned. 'Sometimes, much later, they can make me dizzy.'

'I've never taken sleeping pills,' he said, as if making a confession. 'I'm lucky, I suppose. I can sleep at the drop of a hat.'

'But what about the stress of your job?' She felt the cold filtering through the weave of her coat and settling in a familiar way on her skin. 'Are you always able to forget about that at night?'

'The one night in my life when I was too stressed to sleep,' he said, 'was the night my wife left me. There were gaps all around where her things had been, like holes in the sky. It was . . .' he paused, 'disturbing.'

'And what did you do that night?' she asked. (She had also had a time — not one night but several months — when sleep had eluded her: when it had became so rare that she would have given all the money she had, sacrificed her beauty, forfeited her jokes, for just one hour of oblivion.) 'Did you go out walking?' she asked. 'Did you turn on the light and read?'

'Someone in my building had hung a punch-bag in the basement,' he said. 'I went down there and smacked it around, for hours on end, until the sun came up.'

'And then?' she asked.

'Then I ate breakfast,' he said, 'and then I went to work.' His face looked quite calm, even though he was recalling a period of emotional chaos.

'I had a time —' she began.

But suddenly he took hold of her shoulders and turned her around. 'Look!' he said. 'Look at that!'

It was the sun, making its last appearance for the day. It hung low behind the trees, a huge crimson disc, glowing through the black branches in an unearthly way. Around them, scattered through the gardens, were the small figures of human beings, all turned in the same direction like worshippers of one god.

'It reminds me of something,' she said. 'That nineteenth-century painter.' Her hand was tucked under his arm, so she could feel the way his ribs rose and fell with each breath he took.

'Caspar David Friedrich?' he said.

'That's right,' she said. 'The one with three names that could go in any order.' She saw the palace, far away at the end of the long frozen pond, blazing with reflected red light; its windows flared and merged together so the facade became a blur of fire. Then, just as quickly, the brilliance faded — the palace became a building once more, and people turned away as if they had been temporarily spellbound and were now returned to their own lives.

'You're funny,' he said, laughing.

'Why am I funny?' she said absently. She could hardly remember what she had said, nor what had come before: the stifling heat of the tea-house, her near faint, the return to the cold. Neither was she aware of her numb hands and tired feet. The sun and its sleight of hand had relieved her, for a moment or two, of her own weight.

'What you said about Caspar David Friedrich.' He tucked her hand more securely against his side. 'Maybe this is why you were put in my path — to make up for my own lack of humour.'

'But I'm not funny.' She was puzzled: her mother and sisters had always said that by the time she was born the humour genes in the family had been used up.

'Whoever told you that?' He didn't wait for an answer; to him it was irrelevant, for he had found her funny and that was all that mattered.

Turning off the narrow slippery path, they joined a wider one that ran parallel to the dark rectangular pond. At the end, like a fullstop at the end of a sentence, sat the palace: solid, uncompromising, impossible to place in any familiar context. In her country there were no such buildings. As a child she had believed moats and drawbridges existed only in fairytales.

'I need to ask you something,' she said slowly. 'Do you believe in memory loss?'

'One can hardly not believe in it,' he said. 'It is a clinical affliction, a medically proven condition. You would have to be a fairly inventive philosopher to circumvent its existence.' There was a pause. 'But I gather you are talking about a somewhat different thing,' he said.

'I have a problem,' she began. 'I've had it for a long time — long before I met you. A part of my past has . . .' She hesitated. 'Disappeared, almost entirely. And I can't seem to get it back.'

'Because of an accident? Or an illness?' He sounded detached, like a mechanic diagnosing the problem in a poorly running motor.

'Neither an accident nor an illness,' she said. 'At least, there was illness, but it was not one suffered by me. I fear that it is beginning to make me ill, though. There's a kind of white noise over that place in the past — a muffling, a deadening of sound, which makes it impossible to orient myself. Sometimes the disorientation becomes physical.'

'Ah.' He kept walking with measured steps, looking only at the ground in front of him. 'Perhaps it is stress,' he suggested, keeping his eyes down. 'Perhaps you need to be still for a while, stay in one place. And then whatever is missing will come creeping back?'

Was he offering what he really believed to be a solution, or doing nothing more than betray his own wishes? She hoped it was the former; she wanted to believe he was as altruistic as he had always seemed.

'When you are not trying to think,' he went on, 'thoughts often come. At least this is what I have found, when searching for solutions in my work.'

These words convinced her that he was trying to help her, rather than himself, and she lifted her head in relief. Under floodlights the palace appeared less forbidding and, for the first time, she was able to look at it without a sense of exclusion. 'Why is it yellow at one end,' she asked, 'and grey at the other?'

'That is because of me.'

She didn't understand. She scraped her boots on the low railing by the pond, ostensibly to rid them of their second sole of snow, but in truth to camouflage her non-comprehension and her silence.

'I ordered that the palace be cleaned,' he explained. 'The facade has been accumulating grime for over forty years. The ochre on the left is its original colour — the shade with which it started its life over three hundred years ago.'

Ochre, she corrected herself, *not yellow*. Suddenly she was irritated with herself for not knowing this kind of detail. Had she been born to a different family, in a different place, she would already have absorbed such things into her system of knowledge. Why must you say *yellow*, she mocked herself, and thus betray the depth of your ignorance?

'When summer comes,' he went on, oblivious to her embarrassment, 'it will be ochre all over, just the way it should be, and it will look splendid.'

Most of the time she forgot that English was not his mother tongue; it was only when he used words such as 'splendid' or 'smashing' that she remembered he had grown up speaking a different language from her. She had become accomplished at pushing this thought away, for it created a gulf between them — a gulf he did not even notice was there, which made her all the lonelier. She cleared her throat. 'If you

had not asked them to start cleaning,' she said, 'no one would ever have
questioned its greyness. People would never have known that another
shade lay underneath.'

'If the palace had remained grey,' he agreed, 'no one but experts
would know the difference. But restoration is important precisely because
of that. To show us more clearly where we have come from. To enable us
to look back and know the truth about our origins.'

'Origins!' Her voice was deliberately light, but the last syllable
dragged downwards like weed catching at the feet of a swimmer. 'You
people are obsessed with origins.' She pulled her hand free from his
and began to run. The snow was so heavy that she had to lift her feet
unnaturally high but, still, she managed to run. 'See you at the end of the
pond,' she called back to him. Her words flew in a straight line back over
her shoulder as if streaming from the circular mouth of a Japanese fish-
kite: See — you — at — the — end.

She didn't look around, nor did she expect him to run after her.
(He was not the type.) Sure enough, when she finally stood panting in the
thick snow and looked back, there he was, still walking at the same even
pace along the path. Despite his thick dark coat and square shoulders he
looked unusually small — but this, of course, was because of the distance
between them. When he saw she had stopped, he waved and broke into
a slow jog, and her heart lurched. 'Now look what you've done,' she said,
bending over, speaking into her frozen denim knees. When her breath had
come back and her heart had settled into its normal beat, she straightened
up and saw how close he was. She rested her hand in a deliberate pose on
the nearest statue — a naked boy who stood by the pond, lips pouted in
a stone spout from which neither words nor water flowed.

'You have come too late,' she said, shaking her head regretfully.
'You have been replaced in my affections.'

'Then I will simply order the immediate removal of my rival,' he
said. 'Just as I have ordered his ancestral home to be restored to yellow.'

So he had noticed! But she didn't mind; there was a kindness
in the way his grey angora scarf was knotted softly around his neck, and
in the slightly worn state of his suede shoes. There was nothing at all
pretentious about him, even though people recognised him and sometimes
pointed, even though he could walk into the restaurant not far from here
— a place frequented by movie directors and filmstars — and be offered
a table any night of the week.

'Oh, you are . . .' she said. But there was no way she could sum
him up in a word or two: words, on the whole, were quite inadequate
for capturing the essence of people. The Russian language, of which
she had learnt a little, was better for this. Echoes lay behind its flat face,

stretching back like interconnecting caves, and once you began listening to the many meanings lying behind one word, holding your breath so the fainter sounds of humanity were not obscured — well, there it was.

There it was. Another of her father's sayings! Out of the dusk, out of nowhere she had retrieved one more phrase — although still not his voice. He had handed this out to them all — to his five beautiful, often impatient daughters, and to his faithful wife — with a shrug and a smile as if to say, 'There's not a lot you can do about it, this is the way things are.' She raised her face to look for the sun, but already it had diffused itself along the horizon in a smeared orange line.

'I am . . .?' he queried, returning to her unfinished sentence with politeness but an undeniable curiosity. To have one's personality conclusively summed up by an acquaintance or a lover is naturally appealing, even for someone inherently modest.

She looked at the great dual-toned hulk of the building sprawled in the dusk. 'The Russian word for palace,' she began, in an apparent non-sequitur, 'is derived from the word for courtyard. Did you know?'

He shook his head. No, he didn't, and in spite of the cold that rose from the ground like smoke, it seemed he would wait patiently — perhaps forever — to discover the connection between this fact and his own quintessential qualities.

She spoke like a guide pacing through intricate linguistic halls. 'This means that in Russia, at least, the concept of the palace is linked to the ideal of a small, cosy place you can claim as your own. Grandeur is equated with intimacy, gilt with cobblestones. A monument can also be a hearth. Gilt-edged mirrors and balloon-backed chairs are the royal Russian equivalent of wooden-framed windows and a sofa.'

He shook his head, puzzled. 'But what does this have to do with me?'

'To put it quite simply,' she said, 'you are everything! You are both great and small. You are a public figure with the common touch, a man who combines supreme self-confidence with humility.' She announced this with the flourish of a magician pulling silk scarves out of a top hat; indeed, as she unfolded the definition, she had come to believe it.

He looked at her for a long while. The bitter cold crept from the ground and worked through the soles of their boots; both began to shiver, but neither moved. Then she shrugged. 'There it is,' she said, paraphrasing her father. 'There it is.'

'You are extraordinary,' he said, and shook himself as if he were a dog. 'Extraordinary.'

'Well, I see you find it easy enough to describe me!' she said. She felt a small smile spreading over her face. (*I am funny, I am extraordinary;*

see what this unfamiliar milieu can do for me!)

They set off across the snow at an angle to the palace, passing the side-wing with its long, elegant windows reaching from the eaves to the ground. 'Are you tired?' he said. 'Or shall we walk a little longer? Down that path is the mausoleum.' A straight and unforgiving line of trees led to a faraway shape, barely distinguishable in the dim light.

She peered at it and suddenly her sickness returned: the unease in her stomach, the shifting and whirling in her head, growing and overwhelming her. 'Should we?' she ventured.

'I'm game if you are,' he said. 'I assume you're not the sort of person who believes in ghosts?'

She could not answer; again, her stomach lurched. But she started to walk forward as if towards the guillotine. Her feet, crunching on the snow, seemed strangely distant from her. And then, up ahead, she saw a figure emerging from the gloom, weaving its way between the trees. It wore a long coat made of patched pieces of fur, and a hood covered its head. As it drew nearer to them, she began praying to a God she did not usually believe in. *Give it eyes*, she prayed. *Please, God, give it eyes.*

Just as the figure reached them and she felt she would scream, she saw a clearly visible human face in the depths of the hood. 'Nice evening for a walk!' said an ordinary human voice.

She started to laugh, very quietly and weakly. 'I thought it was a spirit,' she whispered. 'Risen from the dead.' She glanced back. Once past them, the figure had again become unearthly; the dim light made it appear too tall and thin to be human, and the sweeping coat seemed to glide on its own, forming a small arrow of snow in its wake.

'A spirit,' he agreed, 'or a doomed medieval necromancer, taking a last stroll before things got altogether too hot for him.'

'You mean a burning at the stake?' she said. 'The things people did to each other.'

'We still do them now,' he said sombrely. 'And with the same degree of self-righteousness, invoking the same legal powers. The only difference is the methods we use.'

'But we no longer execute for witchcraft — at least not in the western world, nor for conducting scientific experiments. At least we have outgrown that sort of superstition.'

'It doesn't matter what name it goes by,' he said, his voice as implacable as the stone walls looming before them. 'We kill and we sacrifice for exactly the same reasons as we once did, simply under different nomenclatures.'

'Why must you always see life as one continuous process,' she said, 'and people as one homogeneous mass?' She sounded exasperated, even to her own ears.

'That is not how I *see* it,' he said, 'it's how it is.'

'How it is?' she repeated in disbelief. She stopped walking and stamped her foot in the snow. (Perhaps this was another form of expression he believed to exist only in novels?) 'All periods of history are not the same,' she cried, 'and neither are societal problems. From the day we are born we live individual lives, and our fates are varied. Vastly, unavoidably, infinitely varied!'

'Yes, varied,' he agreed. He stood on the bottom step of the mausoleum and looked down at her through the gloom. 'Exactly. Variations on a theme. And the theme is one.'

'No,' she contradicted him. 'When this snow melts, the modern world will become visible again. Snow is like time: it muffles the divisions between eras, it disguises the cracks. Today may have been like stepping back into the past — palaces, fountains, alchemists in fur coats. But only because of this snow, this deceitful and lying snow. In a few weeks the ground will be running with mud and water, and then you will see the sweet wrappers and the drink cans, the condoms and the cigarette packets; you'll see the modern world.' She rushed on to stop him interrupting. 'I know you will say these are contemporary versions of objects dating back to Roman times. But that is only *your* opinion, and whatever you may think, you represent only one subjective mind. You may convince the people of this city that you stand for all men, but you do not convince me!'

'Once you calm down,' he said, 'you will understand that we are not on opposite sides of the fence. We are on the same side — standing slightly apart, perhaps, but nonetheless shoulder to shoulder and facing the same way. Once you stop being angry you will understand.'

'I will not understand!' she said, stamping again. (This was not a humorous way to behave, nor was it conduct worthy of an extraordinary person, but she no longer cared what he thought about her, not at this minute.) 'You are wrong! *You* see the snow as a solid, unbroken blanket. And I . . . and I . . .'

'Yes? What do you see?' He began to sound tired.

'I see pieces,' she finished. 'Separate pieces of snow. And that is the difference between us.' Now, once more, she thought she was going to fall. She put her hand on the railing of the steps and held on tightly, as if she were on the deck of a rolling ship.

He did not notice — or chose not to notice — her sudden dizziness. 'I understand what you say,' he said evenly, 'although I don't agree with your vision. You seem to regard the whole of civilisation as cut up in chunks — like icebergs, perhaps? Floating around independently of each other, with no connection whatsoever to where they have come from?'

Mutinously, she remained silent, but she held on to the rail like a life-line.

'Yes, icebergs,' he said, when she didn't reply. 'Perhaps you see the ancient Greeks existing on this chunk of ice, and the ancient Romans on that. The Renaissance era has broken away from the Middle Ages, and is drifting away to exist in its own separate context. And this new millennium of ours — perhaps you saw that as some kind of starting point? Many people did. But it was nothing of the kind. I stick to my point of view — which is certainly subjective, as you point out, but I think less flawed than yours. That human nature remains unchanged from one century to the next, and societal habits are influenced by those that came before, and also influence those after. There is very little difference between your instincts and those of a woman born a hundred years ago.'

'You're wrong,' she said, her grip on the railing giving her some stubborn foothold in the discussion. 'There has never been another me, and there will never be. There is only one thing we all share, this crawling human race of ours. Do you want to know what it is?'

He raised one eyebrow, which she took as an invitation.

'Dust,' she pronounced.

'Dust?' he said quizzically.

'Dust!' she said, her voice so loud it was almost a shout. 'We all end in dust. Look at what lies behind you! Look at that building, and imagine what it once contained. Bones and teeth, hair and fingernails, the cartilage of nose and ears — they've all crumbled into dust, and this is the only thing that unites us. We career towards some kind of future, we shed knowledge, we discard people, we lose all certainty that has been built up behind us. Nonetheless, in spite of our efforts, we end up there, and that is the only way in which we join what has gone before us.'

Just as she finished speaking there came the clear call of a bird: a firm, confident call, so that she turned her head to the direction from where it had come. Far off to the west a thin line of turquoise cut across the mass of dark grey cloud; it was as if the darkness had cracked open for a moment to expose its hidden heart. If I could only remember, she thought desperately: if I could throw off this long, deadening winter and get back to a time *before* — before I was left.

'You are entitled to your opinion, of course,' he said. He did not sound defeated, and she was glad about that. With an effort, she unwrapped her fingers from the metal bar; her hand felt as if it had become welded to the railing by the fierce powers of rust and cold. 'I think perhaps we should go,' she said, turning to look at him. With an equal effort she transferred her hold to the padded comfort of his sleeve.

'That's better,' he said, putting his other hand over hers. 'Are we friends?'

'Of course,' she said. But something had changed, and the realisation made her feel both lonely and a little optimistic.

Just as they were making their slippery way back along the corridor of trees, a guard materialised out of the darkness. 'We closed the gates fifteen minutes ago,' he said sharply. 'You'll have to go out the side exit.' His voice was a mixture of disapproval and satisfaction; at least their errant behaviour had justified his presence in the gardens throughout the long, grinding day. But as he peered at their faces, his reproving attitude dissolved. 'Sir!' he said. 'Sorry, sir! I didn't realise.' He gave a suppressed kind of salute and rushed away.

She laughed a little at this, but beside her he gave a small sigh. 'Tell me something,' she said quickly, to take his mind off his unwanted, ever-present status.

'If I can,' he said, courteous as ever.

'We talked earlier of memory loss. You know that many psychologists believe we retain no memories before the age of four?'

'I've heard that,' he said. 'And I believe it. That is, I believe we can store colours or sounds or impressions from our first four years, but real events seem to be largely reconstructed.'

'From photographs?' she said.

'From photos, or family stories.' He told her a brief account of how the taste of bitter cherry had always transported him back to an early family holiday which, it transpired, he had never been on. 'How could I have been?' he said with a laugh. 'I was not even born at that time. But I had seen pictures of the cottage and the orchard, had heard my brother talk of sitting high in a tree singing like a bird, and my mother talk of scrubbing cherry stains out of his clothes. And so, when I first ate a cherry, I connected it with that. In my imagination, which I confused with memory, I had also been there.'

He had never talked of having a brother, nor had he ever mentioned his parents. He seemed so self-sufficient that, despite the fact that she knew about his past marriage, she imagined him having always been free-wheeling and solitary, loosely connected to many satellites (connections through work and society), tied to none.

'So, hypothetically speaking,' she said, 'if you have no ability to retain memories before the age of four, and someone leaves you when you are five, you have known that person for only one year of your life?' She swallowed, finding it difficult to pass the saliva down her closed throat.

He considered this for a second, his boots breaking through the icy crust forming on top of the snow. 'One year of conscious knowing,' he agreed. 'One year of what we, as adults, would call real memories. Although I suppose you might also be left with four years of ingrained sights and smells, which can later be linked to photographs and stories.' He paused again. 'Perhaps erroneously linked,' he added, 'as with my brother's cherry tree.'

'Three hundred and sixty-five real days,' she said. 'That's not many.'

They trudged on through the trees. 'Speaking of memory,' he said, breaking the silence, 'I can't remember where the side exit is, can you? And I suppose that park man has disappeared.'

'He became invisible from overwhelming respect,' she joked. 'Isn't that an information board over there?' She stepped sideways to get a better look and half fell into a bush. 'Damn,' she said, brushing foliage and snow off her coat.

'A possible escape route!' He, too, peered over to where a lamp-post cast a dim circle of light about its base. 'I'll go and have a look at the board. Back in a minute.'

She stood picking twigs out of the weave of her coat, and watched him disappear into the darkness, his coat flying out behind him in a reassuring tweedy blur. After his footsteps had died away there was complete silence. And it was then that she heard the voice, coming from nowhere. *I have to go away*, it said. It was both clear and very distant, like a radio played in a car several blocks away.

She waited, but nothing more came. 'And what?' she said imploringly. 'What else?' But all she could hear was her own breathing, ragged and loud in the silence. Behind her the trees marched towards the mausoleum, now a monstrous black shape slightly darker than the night.

'Wait!' she said. 'Please, wait for me.'

She had never run in such blackness before. Her feet landed blindly, and sometimes crookedly, on the uneven ground. Every time she stumbled her arms flew out to save her from a fall that never came. Sweat broke out under her thick clothes, ran between her shoulderblades and down her spine. Her saliva caught in her throat; she choked as if from fear.

When she came once more to the steps, she fell, landing heavily on her hands and knees. Snow skidded up inside her gloves and down into her boots, prickling its way through two pairs of socks. But she was there, at least, and she half crawled up the steps to the mausoleum door. The pattern of leaves was backed by a thick pane of glass and, when she pressed her face against the combined coldness of glass and iron, her eyes smarted and ran.

'Tell me,' she whispered. 'Tell me the rest of the sentence.' She knew now that she should never have come to this land of blankness and whiteness: not yet, perhaps not ever. 'You never saw a palace in your life,' she said, under her breath. Her cheek grated on the sharp petals of a steel flower, but she pressed closer to the pain. 'You never heard the winter call of a bird in snow.' She waited for a moment. 'If you tell me the second part,' she promised, 'I will do the rest. I will remember you.'

She took her face away from the door and stepped back, cupping her hands around her eyes so she could see through the glass. The thin light of the moon slanted through a slit window on the side of the building, outlining the hunched shoulders of a stone body with two hands pressed together in prayer. Now the pain in her head became agonising, and she bit down hard on her lip until she tasted blood.

It was difficult, afterwards, to know how long she stood there: perhaps a minute, perhaps five. The concentration was what mattered, and it was not so much to do with seeing as a conscious not-seeing. Her eyes remained open, but she was staring backwards down the long barrel of her past. And then, at last, it became clear. The pressure in her head, which had been there for as long as she could remember, suddenly lessened, like the breaking up of a frozen river: a great shifting, a loosening and creaking, sheets of ice breaking free and floating downstream, revealing running water below.

'That's it!' she whispered. 'Those were your words. "*I have to go away, but I want you to know —*"' She felt as if she had not breathed properly for most of her life; now, she drew in huge lungfuls of icy air.

From far away down the avenue of darkness came a shout. She turned towards the sound, but pressed her hands against the door behind her in a parting gesture. Then she ran. When she met him halfway back to the palace, it seemed he had also been running; at least, he was breathing heavily. 'My God, I thought you were lost,' he said. 'I thought I had lost you.' She was glad he differentiated between the two; they were quite different things, and she valued mutual understanding above all else.

'Not lost,' she said, taking his hand. 'I had dropped my glove back on the mausoleum steps, that was all.'

'I would have fetched it for you,' he said. 'Weren't you scared?'

'Yes,' she said honestly. 'I was terrified.'

From studying the information board he had worked out where a side exit was. He led the way, cutting through the lines of trees on a diagonal, to a well-lit footpath leading to an archway in the wall. Pushing open the heavy green door, he stepped back to let her through. 'This is the way most of us leave life,' he observed. 'Entering with a fanfare, a roar and a fuss! And then, seventy or so years later, slinking out a side gate when the world has stopped watching.'

'Speak for yourself,' she retorted. 'I intend to leave as late as possible, and with the maximum uproar.'

'I would expect nothing less of you,' he said. 'Perhaps that attitude is the reason for you ending up here, so far away from home. It is your . . .' But as they stepped through the gate the world was once again lit by white electricity instead of gas-lamps, and the end of his sentence was bleached out of existence before it had been uttered. 'Time for a drink,' he said instead. He led the way around the long palace wall to the front entrance, where the huge gilt gates were wrapped around with chains and padlocks.

They picked their way like horses over icy tilting cobblestones, past a fountain, and suddenly found themselves on a flat pavement. Perversely, she now missed the hardship of snow; she had become attuned to uncertainty and, although she no longer had to concentrate, for a few moments she resisted looking up.

'We can cross over there,' he said, pointing to a four-way intersection. 'There's a little place I know a couple of blocks away.' Before them the wide road streamed with cars, tyres hissing in the slush and the mud; on the far side there were unlit apartment blocks and shops closed up for the night. Even the sex cinema was deserted, its neon pink heart turned off, its windows blank and shuttered.

'I can't stay too long,' he apologised, leading the way into a small overheated bar. 'My daughter's coming to stay and I promised I'd be home by eight.' They sat in a booth with floral upholstery and he ordered lager for both of them; only after the drinks had been delivered to their table did he look stricken. 'Would you rather have had wine?' he asked. 'That was high-handed of me.'

She would have preferred wine, but she could also see that he had become distracted. 'Beer's fine,' she assured him, picking a dried flower out of its vase and crumbling it over his head like confetti. He drank fast and she kept pace with him; when he kissed her, she tasted bitter white froth on his lips. Half his mind already seemed to be in tomorrow, while half hers was in yesterday, and all the many months and years before that. She answered his questions automatically; she was remembering, for the first time, the van that had taken her father away from her, was remembering running after the shrieking red blur, falling, crying, and the bony hands of her sister — the oldest of the five — grabbing her too hard and holding her back.

After a while the waiter reappeared and hovered politely: could he bring them more drinks? 'Just the bill,' they answered in unison.

'But I'd like to pay,' she objected. 'To thank you for today.'

He looked surprised. 'On the contrary,' he said, 'you have given me an afternoon to remember. Besides, I am paid too much for what I do, and you are paid too little. So until the world comes to its senses, the drinks are on me.' Putting down a crisp note, he helped her on with her coat.

The air outside was chilly and damp. They stood in the doorway of the bar, watching a few people hurry by, their collars turned up, intent on getting home. When he turned to her, half his face was in shadow so that it looked as though he spoke from one side of his mouth. 'As I mentioned, my daughter is staying tonight,' he said. 'But that doesn't mean I can't have house-guests.'

She already knew how he slept — quietly, peacefully, lying on his back with one arm flung above his head. 'I would love to,' she said, 'but I think not.'

'A moral decision?' he said. 'Due to a minor in the house? Or something more serious?' He had never pressured her in any way; the first time he had kissed her had been without embarrassment or haste, in front of the two doormen outside his office. He had suggested they meet the following day, and had then disappeared through the heavy glass doors to make important decisions for the citizens of his city.

'It's something more serious,' she confirmed. Because she had no choice, she felt no regret: only the less complicated emotion of sadness.

'I thought so,' he said slowly.

'What will you do tonight?' she asked. She wanted to know so that later, lying in her own bed and watching the headlights of passing cars sliding over the wall, she could imagine him as well as remember him.

'Watch the sort of movie I loathe,' he said. 'The sort featuring a high-school band, or a football team, or a group of people stranded on a beach in various stages of undress.'

She laughed. 'And what else?'

'Eat a pizza. Talk about school. Iron a shirt for tomorrow.' He looked at her inscrutably. 'What will you do?' he asked. 'A far less predictable question.'

'To tell you the truth,' she said, 'I don't know.'

'But you're thinking about going back,' he said. 'Going home.' It was not a question. A wind blew into the doorway, dragging old leaves and crumpled advertising in its wake, though underneath its stale breath she thought she detected a faint smell of spring. She nodded.

'You'll be all right,' he said. It sounded like a reassurance as much to himself as to her.

'I'll call you, of course,' she said. 'Before . . .' She didn't know what to say; nothing seemed enough for him. But this was all right; their relationship had been successfully based on reticence and courtesy, and had thus held itself clear of difficulties, while nonetheless acknowledging them. He sighed but said nothing. A bus roared past, its long, lit windows marked out with incurious faces. She waited until the sound of the engine had died away, and she took a deep breath. 'I have to go away,' she said, 'but I want you to know — I'm not leaving you.'

He looked sharply at her. 'That sounds like a quote,' he said.

'It is,' she replied. 'Something my father once said to me.'

'Can I give you a ride?' he said. 'At least let me do that. You're not familiar with this part of town.'

'Thanks,' she said, 'but I know my way home.' She looked at his divided face for a moment, memorising the dark eyebrows and straight nose, the reserved but tender mouth. Then she walked away, without looking back, towards the bus-stop. It was hard but bearable, like the burn of snow on skin.

DUNCAN SARKIES

from *Two Little Boys*

A novel in progress

Advice from God, and What I Did with my Hard On

DEAN

IN THE SHOWER I TALK to God. I don't know if it's actually God — it's just that the way the sunlight hits the water vapour makes for a real 'God' feel. I say to God, 'Any ideas of how we can get out of this one?' and God shrugs his shoulders. You can't see him shrug his shoulders because vapour doesn't have shoulders, but I can *feel* God shrugging his shoulders.

I say to God, 'Is this really happening, God?' and God says, 'Sure is,' and I say, 'Is it like a test?' and God says, 'Nah. It's just bad luck,' and I say to God, 'Or good luck, depending on how you look at it. There's a good chance that this whole experience will bring me and Nige closer together,' and God doesn't comment on that one.

I use conditioner in my hair but not shampoo, because you're supposed to let the natural oils in your hair clean itself. Like, your body knows a lot that you don't. Like, when a woman has a baby, her whole vagina gets larger and larger, and don't ask her how she did that — it just happened because her body knew more than her brain. I only know this stuff because one of my favourite porn stars got pregnant and she wrote about it all in gory detail in her blog. Put it this way, next time I have sex with a pregnant chick, I'll do it from behind, just to be on the safe side.

Anyway, where was I? Oh yeah. My hair cleans itself, much like a pregnant woman having a baby for the first time. But I put conditioner in because I might be going bald and I figure that might keep the wolves at bay, if you get my thrust.

God tells me I should have lunch with Nige today, just so we can get our story straight and make sure he doesn't say anything stupid to anyone. I'll get him a cheese and pineapple toasted sammy from Stewarts because he likes cheese and pineapple, and I'll get him a custard square as a treat for after he's finished his sammy. I'm picturing the look on his face when he sees I've got him a custard square. Nige loves custard squares. He loves all custard. He even made love with custard once, but he told me he got burns on his dick because he poured it out a bit too hot. He ran it under cold water and it was as good as gold but he had to put sex on hold, which was a pity.

I feel a real need to get in touch with Nige and check he's doin' okay, so I phone him even though I'm naked and I haven't even dried myself. If some chick wanted to have a perve through the kitchen window she'd cop an eyeful right now, and she might like what she sees.

The thought of it gets me goin' so I hold on to myself loosely with my right hand while I phone Nige with the other. When Nige comes on the line I say to him, 'So you wanna have lunch?'

'Yeah sure,' Nige says, 'as long as you think it isn't . . . you know . . . suspicious.'

'There's nothing suspicious about having lunch with your best mate of fifteen years,' I say, peering down at my penis, which is bobbing up and down hopefully.

'Hey Nige,' I say, 'are you acting normal?'

'Yeah. I thought it would be hard,' he says, and I have to admit as soon as he says the word hard the blood runs straight to you know where. 'It turns out acting normal is pretty easy, because if you think about it, we act normal every day so we get lots of practice.'

'Good boy, Nige. You have master criminal potential.'

Nige suddenly freaks. 'Ohhh . . . what if they tape the phone calls?' I'm lookin' around on top of the telly for that porno we got out the other week. All I can find is Sandra Bullock in that movie *Miss Congeniality 2*, so that'll have to do. 'Nige, don't worry about it. I've gotta go and wash the dishes. See you at twelve.'

'Okay, mate.'

I hang up and try to rewind the vid to a good scene with lots of beauty queens but a good car chase comes on and I'm pretty excited anyway so I work myself over while watching the car chase and I catch my reflection in the TV which puts me off so I close my eyes and do a mental picture of all of the girls I've ever slept with, but bloody Nige keeps popping into my brain — must be all the worry — so I finish myself off with a picture of Nige in my brain, which has happened before and hopefully will never happen again. I must be really worried about him, I guess.

Penguin Divide

NIGE

I'VE JUST GOT BACK TO sleep again when I get woken up and it's Gav sayin' 'Nige, it's dawn,' and I'm, 'Eh?' and Gav says, 'Let's go and see the penguins,' and I say to Gav, 'Nah, not this morning — I need a lie in,' and Gav says, 'C'mon, Nige! I wanna see the penguins!' and he pulls the covers off my bed.

I've been awake all bloody night worrying about shit and thinking about the body in the backpack and I just got back to sleep and Gav wants me to look at penguins. 'Nah, I'm not coming,' I say.

'Get up, Nige,' a new voice says, and I'm surprised to see Dean all up and ready. I don't get it. I hear a whistle coming from the kitchen and it's the jug. It's one of those jugs you put on an oven element and when it whistles it sounds a bit like a train screeching, just a bit quieter I suppose.

Gav's making the cups of tea and I say to Dean, 'I wanna stay in bed.'

Dean says, 'Nige, you know when you get one of those gut feelings that feel like you're gunna have a spew but actually it's your body telling you something? Well, my body just told me to get up and watch the penguins with Gav. I don't think we should let him out of our sight. That's what my body reckons, anyway.'

'My body reckons I should stay in bed.'

'Well, my body and your body disagree, Nige, but who's smarter, you or me? Answer me honestly.'

'You.'

'So what are we gunna do?'

I'm sitting in the lounge drinking a cup of tea from a tin mug. It's my old tin mug. The new people at the crib haven't thrown that out yet. I used to drink a lot of milk from that mug, and then when me and Dean got older I remember I drunk a lot of tequila out of that mug too.

Outside everything is still pretty dark, which is a bit weird. I'm used to going to sleep when it's light but I'm not used to getting up when it's dark. Doesn't make sense. My body thinks it's all a dumb idea, but Dean's body reckons this is the way to go so I guess that makes it a good idea. Besides, I do like the penguins.

When me and Dean were kids we went down there a few times and tried to scare them. Like, if a penguin is sitting on the egg it won't leave the egg so you can go right up close to it and it won't move. It's shitting itself but it doesn't go anywhere. Deano used to go right up to the penguins and make, like, penguin noises at them. We were pretty drunk, you know, having a laugh and that.

One time Dean took a penguin egg and he threw it into the sea, smashing it. He thought that was real funny but I felt a bit weird about it. Dean told me it was just nature. Survival of the fittest and that. He was stronger than the penguin as a human being, so he was just letting the penguin know who was boss, by chucking out its egg to teach it a lesson or something. Dean reckons that animals were put on earth to give us meat — nothing more and nothing less, and he has often said to me, 'I wonder what a penguin would taste like.'

I'm driving us to Nugget Point and Gav pulls out his peace pipe and suggests we have a few cones and lights up in the van. I kind of watch Dean decide whether he'll smoke drugs or not. He says drugs have no effect on him whatsoever but I reckon that's not true. I reckon he goes a bit weird, kinda slower but more dangerous. He thinks when he's stoned that he's actually still as straight as a die, which is weird because when Dean's stoned he's definitely a bit different.

Anyway, Dean decides to partake. When Gav offers the pipe to him he says, 'What the fuck,' and goes for it big time.

'Don't Bogart the joint,' I say after he's been at it for a while.

'Don't what the what?' he says. 'Firstly, Nige, this is not a joint, and secondly, what was that word you said?'

Gav goes, 'He said Bogart, after the famous actor.'

'Well, he can't be very famous cos I haven't heard of him.'

Gav seems pretty keen to talk about Humphrey Bogart. 'You know Humphrey Bogart? Here's lookin' at ya, kid,' and Dean goes, 'No, Gav. The only actors I know are famous ones, like Tom Cruise. He was excellent in *Top Gun*. You like *Top Gun*, Gav?'

'Kind of.'

'I like how the Ice-Man who is the bad guy becomes Tom Cruise's friend in the end as they bond together to fight the real enemy, the Russians.'

'How come the Americans always get to be the good guys and the foreigners are bad guys?' Gav says, and I say, finally getting a toke, 'Yeah, why is that?'

The view is opening out in front of us and it's like one of those views that you would take a postcard of if you knew how to. You can see the mountains and the lighthouse flashing in the distance and the sea is roaring and as we drive up the steep dirt road it feels like we're about to drive over a cliff. Me and Dean used to rally drive on this stretch so I pump the accelerator and take us on a joyride just to scare Gav a bit, because I reckon he might get a kick out of that, and I'm goin, 'This van handles good, Gav.'

We pull up to where the penguin bit is.

'Okay, is everyone wasted enough?' Gav asks, and I say, 'Yeah, I'm pretty fucked. What about you, Dean?'

'I don't feel anything,' Dean says.

See what I mean? Dean thinks he's too strong in the head for drugs.

We hop out of the van and the wind is going nuts, like it's real loud — so loud it like whistles in your ears and knocks you around a bit.

'Fuck, I love this place,' Dean goes, taking a piss at the first bush we get to. 'Watch out for friendly fire,' he says, shooting a little burst of warning-piss our way.

Then another van pulls up at the carpark.

'Ahhh, fuck. Tourists,' Dean says.

'Backpackers,' Gav says, eyeing up their van. It's one of those rentals that the rental company has drawn lots of patterns on. We listen in and hear them speaking in German or something. I start to feel a bit sick.

Dean spots this and he says to me, 'Nige, it's understandable for you to develop a fear of backpackers, but you need to get over it. Come on,' and Gav says, 'What was that?' and I say, 'Dean just told me a joke,' to cover up, which was pretty smart thinking of me.

We head down to the path and come to like a crossroads in the path. There's like the main path that goes to the hide, which is this big wooden peephole thing where you can watch the penguins from. Then there's the little path that goes down to the beach where the penguins are.

'Dean, we're not s'posed to get close to them,' I say, and Dean says, 'I forgot, Nige — when was it exactly that you turned into a fuckin' square?' and Gav goes, 'I'm heading to the hide,' and heads the opposite way from Dean.

I don't know which path to take. Do I go with Dean or do I go with Gav? It's like one of those real hard decisions, especially when Dean hates me hanging out with Gav so much, but Dean does want me to pretend to be friends with Gav, so I figure maybe I should go with Gav.

'I'm goin to the hide with Gav.'

'You fuckin' pussy,' Dean says. 'Fine. Do what you want,' and he heads down the hill without me.

DEAN

A LOT OF THINGS ARE running through my head. Obviously there is 'When do we get rid of the body, and how do we get away from Gav to do that?' I figure an opportunity will come our way, but we have to do it today. The longer that backpacker sits in the boot the bigger the stink and the more Nige'll freak out, so today is the day, and I think Jack's Blowhole is the perfect spot.

And I'm also thinkin' 'What exactly am I doing all this shit for Nige for when he almost ignores me? He treats me like shit. Like, why did he go with Gav and not me? I mean, here I am, his best friend for fifteen years, and he's known Gav for like a few months and Nige goes, 'I'll go with Gav.' Now those words might seem like little words, but to me they say a lot more than the words themselves. They say, 'I choose Gav' to me, and that makes my stomach bubble with anger.

I try to tell myself that Nige is just pretending to like Gav, but something deep inside my body is telling me that Nige is pulling away from me, and into the arms of Gav.

It's like a kind of warmth that is missing from him when I talk to him. I had this dream once where I looked at him and I thought to myself, 'Where have you gone, Nige? Where's the real Nige? Where are you?' And it was one of those dreams where he could hear my thoughts due to ESP and he said, 'What do you mean?' and I said with my thoughts, 'You never smile to me, or laugh at my jokes any more. You never phone me. It's always me phoning you. How come you don't phone me?' And his brain says, 'I dunno, I'm just tired,' and I say/think 'Oh yeah, well, you don't seem to be very tired around Gav. You don't seem to be very tired around Monica. You don't seem to be very tired around my Mum even. How come you're just tired around me?'

That was the end of the dream but I picture it again and again as I head down the hill toward the penguins.

I stare up at the hut where I know Nige and Gav are and I can feel the bile in my stomach leaking into my bloodstream. About a hundred metres away from me there is some movement in the ocean and the first couple of penguins come to shore. They're all kind of chatty like they're happy to be in from the cold and back on dry land after a hard night catching fish and shit like that. More penguins start to come out and they're all chattering away like they are real happy birds.

My brain is doing a lot of weird things at the moment and the way the penguins are making so much noise and seem real happy makes me feel sad and makes me feel angry at Nige for even letting Gav into our lives. I figure that Nige has no idea what friendship is. Like, Nige thinks friendship is like a relationship — you know, you move on when you get bored — but I think you have to ride out the bad times in order to see the good again.

I haven't changed. I'm still the same old Deano, and I don't know if he gets that. Sometimes I think 'fuck him' — ya know? But then I think of living my life without Nige and I think that Nige is more than my mate; he's my family — especially since I don't have any brothers or sisters and I wouldn't want any even if I did have a brother or sister because I would have Nige.

I don't know. All I know is that he better start treating me better, otherwise why do I risk everything for him? Why should I take a bullet for someone that doesn't laugh at my jokes any more? Why?

But I would. I would take a bullet for him. I would take a bullet in the heart.

More penguins are coming to shore so I try to light up a cigarette and watch from a distance, but I have a hard time shielding the cigarette from the wind. I can't get the flame up and running so I just sit there trying to light the cigarette again and again and again as the penguins come to shore. They're makin' a real racket. I don't know if it's my mind playing tricks on me but I get a mental vision of me and Nige frolicking among the penguins. I can see it all. I pick up a penguin egg and I say, 'Hey, Nige,' and I throw it at him and yolk goes all over his face and he laughs and says, 'I'll get you!' and I say, 'No you won't,' and he runs after me in slow motion and tackles me to the ground and we playfight while millions of penguins get in one of those circles around us, watching us and making penguin sounds.

The thought of that makes me smile quite a lot.

My cigarette still won't light. I see two love-bird penguins in front of me. They do that thing where they stick their heads together like they are kissing and it's real lovey-dovey chunder material but I know my mum would get off on it. I wish she could see through my eyes sometimes, and then she could see the penguins up close and personal. I'm glad she can't see through my eyes all the time though, like when I'm vomiting or having a wank.

Eventually I head back to Gav's van and wait for the other two, thinkin' they would have got bored by now, but they're takin' ages. And cos I'm alone, I start crying. I guess I'm going through a lot and I don't know how I can deal with it all. My tears are not tears of joy — they are tears of doom and tears of sickness: that sick feeling where you can feel your best mate of fifteen years pulling away from you like the Picton ferry setting off for the North Island.

One of the side doors is unlocked so I head into the van to get out of the cold and I wipe my nose on Gav's mattress. And then in front of me, I see . . . a suitcase.

Gav's suitcase.

And I think to myself . . . why not look? There's a lot that me and Nige don't know about Gav. I've always been a bit of a snooper anyway. I used to look through Mum's undies drawers. Not that I wanted to have sex with my mum or anything. Nothing like that. It's just that I knew she kept a stash of chocolate there quite often so I would scoff it. I think Mum knew I was looking in her drawers but she never asked me about it, so I kept on scoffing a little bit of chocolate. Like, if there was a chocolate bar there I would break off only one bit at a time so she wouldn't notice — that sort of thing.

Same thing with Nige. I always would snoop through his drawers, but that was different because I started telling him I was doing it and that I didn't mind if he had a look through my drawers. I'd leave some porn under my side of the bed sometimes and I know he watched it because he never bothered rewinding it to exactly the same spot, and I knew it wasn't the tooth fairy watching those vids so that left Nige by the process of like elimination and that. And that brought us closer together and that.

So I'm staring at Gav's suitcase and I'm thinkin' should I or shouldn't I?

And then I think to myself . . . 'Fuck it. Why not?'

I find out a few things, like the fact that Gav's BO is riddled throughout his clothes and is the sort of BO that no scientist could ever wash out, no matter how many chemicals they tried . . .

And I find out that Gav has like a set of those aromatherapy candles, which is a bit gay, so, you know, more ammo, I guess . . .

But the best thing I find out . . .

Is a little black book. And what's inside that black book?

I have a feeling Nige might be lookin' at Gav in a whole new light in a few hours' time . . .

Incident in the Middle of the Night

DEAN

I WAS FURIOUS. BLOODY FURIOUS . . . Words can't describe the emotions I felt when Gav told me off for flushing the toilet.

It was in the middle of the night. I'd gone to the toilet, just for a piss because my bladder had got a bit full in the night, and when I go back to me and Nige's room, Nige whispers to me, 'Gav's not gunna like that.'

And I'm like, 'What? . . . What, Nige?'

'Gav doesn't believe in flushing the toilet,' he says.

'You're kidding me.'

'Gav believes that we flush too much. Because of all the water.'

'What water?'

'The whole planet depends on it.'

'Eh? Nige?'

'If the planet had no water on it, we'd all be dead, wouldn't we?'

'According to who, Nige?' I say, and I have to tell you, words will never descibe the emotions I'm feeling as Nige is talking to me like one of those guys from the Bible that followed Jesus around and then just said all of Jesus's stories for him after Jesus snuffed it.

I go to the hallway and stand outside Gav's room. 'Gav,' I say.

'Don't wake him up,' Nige goes, but I say quite loud, 'Gav! Gav! Wake up, ya cunt!'

I hear a voice groan and say, 'Come in,' and I turn on the light and the fat prick puts his hands over his eyes because they weren't ready for me to suddenly turn on the light. It's actually quite fuckin' hilarious watching him be such a pussy.

'Hey, Gav,' I say. 'Nige has been telling me you've got a problem with the way I flush the toilet.'

'Eh?' Gav goes.

He's probably just woken out of some gay dream where he was bumming a wild pig or something so I refresh his brain back to reality. I say, 'Something to do with water, Gav. The way I'm flushing the toilet is going to cause everyone in the world to die. Something like that. Nige didn't explain too well.'

Gav sits up. 'Well, ya know, yeah. I just think there is clearly a water problem —'

'What water problem? We're in New Zealand, Gav. We're surrounded by water. There's fuckin' lakes and rivers and glaciers and —'

'It's a world problem, Dean.'

'Oh, I see. So when I flush the loo it affects some poor starving kid in Ethiopia. Is that what you're trying to say, Gav?'

'You're simplifying it.'

I do the siren sound. 'Woo-oo-woo-oo-woo-oo it's the big-word police,' and Nige laughs.

'What's the big-word police?' Gav says.

NIGE

I CAN'T BELIEVE GAV HAD never heard of the big-word police. I try and explain it to him. 'It's like, if you use a word with more than three syllables, your mate can do a big siren sound, and you get a fine, or you have to scull. It started out as a drinking game but we've adapted it into life.'

Dean looks real pissed off at Gav, standing over him with a crazy look in his eye, you know, like that crazy look King Kong does when he's got that woman in his hand. Gav says, 'Okay, you're right, I'm wrong. I wanna go back to sleep,' and Dean goes, 'Did you hear that, Nige? Flush the loo as much as you like.'

I know Gav didn't mean it, because Gav just wants to get back to his dreams and that, so he'll say anything. But Dean is really rubbing it in like he's just won an argument with fuckin Einstein or something.

Dean's goin', 'Fuck, well, you probly want to go back to sleep, Gav. Would you like me to turn out the light?'

And Gav says, 'Sure, thanks.'

Dean goes, 'Well, you'll have to say, "I was wrong and you were right."'

'I was right and you were wrong,' Gav goes.

Dean says, 'If you're gunna take that attitude the light stays on,' and he storms out of the room.

I go, 'Jesus, Dean,' and I turn off the light and say, 'Sorry, Gav,' and Gav goes, 'Hei aha. No probs,' because he's so easy going. Nothing ruffles his feathers. He's like one of those surfers, except I guess Gav's a bit too fat to surf. But it's an attitude thing.

Anyway, the lights are off and you'd think that would be the end of it, but no. The toilet flushes. And it's obvious it didn't flush by itself. So by a process of insemination I know Dean flushed it.

I go to the toilet and say, 'What are you doing?'

Dean says, 'Nothing, Nige. You go back to bed.'

So I go to bed and there's this flushing noise again. And then one minute later another flush. And one minute later another flush. I look at the digital alarm clock and he's flushing about once a minute. And I just know he's tryin' to get Gav's attention, I just know he's tryin' to turn it into a fight, tryin' to wind up Gav. I lie there and put the pillow over my head and watch the clock. And twenty minutes later he's still doin' it.

Fuck, Gav must be sleepin' like a fuckin' dead person because the cistern on that toilet makes a real high-pitched squeak and that just makes the whole thing worse, especially when you've heard it for the thirtieth time.

I get up and I say, 'Dean,' and Dean doesn't look pissed off any more; he's hunched on the floor staring into the toilet. His nose is probably getting wet each time he flushes. I say 'Dean.'

I hear an echo from the toilet bowl say, 'I'm tired, Nige.'

I say to him, 'Come back to bed, dude. You need to chill out,' and he lifts his head out of the toilet and stares at me. The top of his hair is wet from water from the toilet. I hope there's no piss in it. He looks at me and shakes his head slowly. I say, 'Come on, Dean,' and he follows me back to the bedroom.

Before he crashes out he says to me, 'Betrayal isn't an easy thing to take, Nige,' and I don't say anything because I just want to get to sleep. Dean says, 'I love you like a brother, man,' and then I don't hear boo from him until the morning.

TRACEY SLAUGHTER

a working model of the sky

THERE ARE MANY DREAMS THAT rise from that summer when the woman fell. Her fall is somehow the background for all of them. For instance, there is the frequent dream: I'm a child returned to a classroom where I am kneading a torso of dough. The hump is glutinous, sultry, and at first I love the feel of it under my fingers. I've punched it until it's a sleek, rough jelly: when I sink in my hands it puffs out around my wrists. But then something changes: the mass begins to alter, I feel its bulk shudder and curl. I feel some identity move in it, dilate, throb. It grows. It takes me into its bulges, until I feel it press through my mouth, roll into my eyes to take a soft and appalling mould there.

In another dream, one that comes less often, I stand in our dining room of those days, and I see my mother, who sits at the wide round table, silent, watching the window. There is no sudden pang or slump: she simply leans forward and lays her head down, tilting it carefully onto its side on the flat, bare fan of her hands. She has taken her rings off, but the table is covered with ring after ring: I remember this tablecloth, a pale red at the outer circle, progressing through darkening hoops to the red in the centre, so rich it is almost black. The cloth is plastic-coated, so it shines and ripples, and the dimming bands seem to lead down and down, in gleaming logic to the core, the well that my mother's hair slides towards.

So, that summer a woman fell, on our farm. It sounds easy, commonplace when I phrase it that way. It sounds as if the woman might simply have slipped down the back steps, or blundered on the clay bank; as if her foot might have quivered away from the fence or grazed at a trunk she was trying to climb. Rational images seem to fit, not fatal ones: the limit of rooflines or trees, known structures, human and definite. I almost see her when I write that sentence: hoisting her flimsy body, clinging, skidding down in a flutter, laughing as she brushes at light wounds, picks away at adhesive leaves.

But she did not fall like this.

She fell from a plane.

From the field I watched her, splitting my sky, becoming its axis.

I would date myself as a writer from that summer. But I've tried many times — and failed — to write of the moments when I watched her fall. The memories are there: I've never lost *them*, those pictures, those flashes and stills, both exact and warped. I don't know how a memory can be both . . . this *trauma* of iridescence, a mangling of sound and light through nerves, a rush against throat and iris . . . and a scene, composed and detailed, held in a strict lens, the edges of each component, textures and voices, crisp, objective, distanced. But it can, it *is*. That summer is clear, its images finite, intricate; I should be able to frame it, locate a line of story, set it down scene by scene, control it. Sometimes it hovers just outside my reach; I almost see it there, that story divided into a grid, that summer explained in lucid sections. But always, along with this order, comes the rising vibration, the crash of radiance. There's no perspective that does not come with the pressure that bursts along each sense until the story comes through the skin, myself and the memory plunging, entangled, memory sucking my focus away, no body left outside the disaster to watch it.

That is a misleading, *selfish* paragraph. I know my husband would agree with *selfish*. For, as he has frequently pointed out over the years, it was *not me* who fell. Nothing is gained by my repeated attempts to write of it: nothing except his frustration. And how could an act of imagination ever draw close to the real act of falling, the scrape and lapse of the body through space, the body squeezed and stripped by the air, its terrible cadence? The woman who jumped was unknown, a stranger; the day she fell I was a child, alone, in a field. And yet sometimes I think *she* was selfish. I doubt she paused to wonder who was below her, who might incline their eye, so that after that moment the watcher could never keep the horizon entirely clear of a body inscribing on the sky its gaunt and terminal graffiti.

Of course her fiancé, the pilot, insisted that the fall was not an issue of choice. He used the word selfish himself as he sobbed through his testimony: *She could never have done anything so selfish.* He kept to this version of his lover, despite the fact that it deepened suspicion of him. There were claims of sinister or clumsy omission, things malignantly or stupidly left undone, allowing *chance* to swing on the door, *accident* to slip under loosened straps, to dislodge hinges. On the day I was taken to the inquiry I remember staring at him: I could not account for so much water coating a male face and hands, for the ugly structures of muscle that moved in his neck as a prefix to each cry. He choked all the way through my story, explicit sobs that jerked and hollowed him. I had always thought of the male body as a kind of fortified place; I felt shocked as I listened to it dismantled. Yet also . . . culpable. And the court wanted details. If I stammered or delayed I was only made to repeat myself: I was made to launch the image of that woman's body, direct and mechanical, again and again, across the room. I knew the vision hit her lover like a grenade. His grief was sinewy and beautiful. My father led me out when I had finished, and this time I chose not to grope for his tough hand. He cleared his throat coarsely several times on the drive home but never began to speak to me.

I thought of the woman, soft and grotesque in her trench, and wondered how she had managed it.

In the days immediately after the fall my father decided the best plan was to keep me attending school, keep me occupied. (My mother had passed away earlier that year.) That summer (as in the dream) we were in the process of moulding figures from dough. We loved the project: we bumped and thumbed the sludge across the emptied tables; we scratched great bubbles of mix from the vats, and paddled out trunks and slimy club limbs, tore and rolled noodles of hair that stuck to our clothes. We squelched our knuckles into the vegetable bodies that smelled like soda and dirt, and bashed them flat, each of us shaping a self to slip into the oven for drying. When they were hard we glued them onto board and painted clothes on them, trying to dab in our teeth or freckles, a special hair-tie or flick of eyelash or scar. I remember it was hard to make one body stand out from another . . . to give evidence that this creature, crooked and rancid, was somehow distinct, unique. I think it was *that* that made me cry: they had been such work, these crushed little people — there had been such slick and mellow joy in the making of them — and now they were ordinary. The paint with which we tried to infuse our identities into them had disappeared through the cracks.

It had been three days since the woman fell, since I sat in the field and watched her falling. Search parties had combed the bush on our property but her body had not been found. When I cried, the teacher and the mother-helper leaned over the table, murmured and patted at me, and hissed at each other: *coincidence* they hissed.

When I got home that afternoon I went to the dictionary and looked up *coincidence*. I had heard the word many times, slithering between adults, in the past three days. Everywhere around me adults seemed to mingle, alert and grim, the muscles of their faces rigid as they muttered consultations, dropped their heads to nudge them covertly at me. The word *coincidence* was whispered so many times I thought it might have been a curse.

In the dictionary I read: from Latin *cado*, I fall, and *incido*, I fall in.

That seemed, to me, the strangest coincidence of all.

One word, with two women falling in it.

On the fourth day, when they still had not found her, a larger, darker group gathered around me, this time bending down to me, talking in active, organised voices, expert and firm. My father stood, remote, behind the crouching officers, and when they left gaps in their steady, reasonable speech, he nodded methodically, his chin crunched up in agreement, his eyes fixed on a distance somewhere behind my head or through the sundress which, as the task became clear, I clutched and wet.

Last year, at my husband's conference, they loaded us all into small helicopters. The flight was unexpected, a bonus: we had all been standing in the hotel grounds, in the tight, immaculate grasses that money outlined from the other bald, grey fields. We heard the surprise approaching us. Some of the women gave gleeful jumps, waved their coloured nails up at the crafts, patted their heads with their crinkled haloes of lacquer. I did not consent. But it happened too fast: my husband governed my elbow, steered with his hip. He said something politic, some instruction, his mouth impinging on the skin behind my ear. When the pilot rushed forward, my husband handed me to him.

The pilot said nothing, but ran with me through that coagulation of air. He installed me and I sat and stared at the air, its terrible gloss and abundance.

Then the door was shut.

The walls of the capsule were clear, a pure curve of plastic. At shoulder, at knee and along the left side of my skull I pressed against the dome. The land diverged and swung, and I felt its suck in my abdomen.

There are hells that are convex, transparent. The heart, fixed in its own container, recognises them and crushes itself.

Two weeks ago now, the pilot whose lover fell came here to visit me. He had seen my father's death notice, and found out from it my married name. It was years, he said, that he'd wanted to see me.

I've often thought, he said.

And repeated it.

I took him out to sit by the pool, and I watched his face mottled with holograms of water. Leaves dropped in spirals into the pool and moved in shrinking, oily trails.

He said, your father seemed like a good man. But you were so little.

His eyelids were the dregs of skin, shrivelled and tender. Beneath them the pupils were pale, the whites traced with tiny haemorrhages.

I thought, he continued, he oughtn't to have let you go up that day. When they said. And I oughtn't either. But I wasn't thinking. Or not of you. Only of finding her. If I could've thought beyond that, I'd have known it was no place for a little girl.

Around his eyes the skin moved in radii, wet now. His neck formed channels, thrumming and loose, above his shirt. I reached across for his hand, steadied it.

Oh, he said. It's a long time. I have wanted. Your pardon.

His ribcage staggered in his chest. His grief was how I remembered it.

I said, I could see you loved her. When I saw you, I thought, that was a reason. I thought that made it worth it. In a way. Because I could see how much you loved.

A thick membrane of leaves had floated to rub at one edge of the pool. I watched it rustle, and I thought for the first time that there might be a pattern somewhere. I stared at the veins descending through the old man's hands, fluttering, and it almost seemed palpable . . . some correlation with the sky retracing itself across the water, the apparition caught in the flickering leaves.

But then he said, what's made it so bad all these years is the things I can't answer. What's so awful is I didn't notice. That's the reason I couldn't say . . . because I wasn't noticing. The door was just open. And she was gone. It must have been an accident. It was love, I know that much, for both of us. But already . . . I wasn't noticing her. I don't know how that could've happened.

He looked at me. The soft raft of black leaves pushed and chafed at the poolside, rotting and tranquil.

My husband appeared at the back of the house then. He strode out, hesitated, extended his ratifying hand. But when I made the introduction I saw his hand flinch, uneasy in the grasp of the old man's.

I realised that for all these years he may never have wholly believed my story.

Before the pilot left he said, Were you with your father, at the end?

No, I said.

So you didn't talk then, before . . .

No.

He said, I've often thought about your father. Not that he didn't seem like a good man. Really a very good man, of his kind. But I suppose you learn that people show their love in different ways.

I said, but you also learn the ways they show their lack of love. And they're the same ones.

A child does not have a map. When they took me up and tried to make me outline where the woman had dropped, I had lost any sense of how to make objects relate, how to pinpoint place, measure distance: it seemed to me that the land and the sky were plasma, still pouring through my closed lids. The only thing I knew was that *wherever* and *whenever* I was then, I felt the pressure of the woman falling, her rush and scream suspended in me. We coincided. But as for any other co-ordinate . . . all maps had slipped into permanent flux. A woman and I were joined, determined, a dark recurrent gradient, but I had no means to transpose that onto the land. I may as well have tried to map the sky between us.

They also asked me to show them, again, where I was when I'd seen the woman fall. Once more I said I would not be able to take them back to the place. But my father should, I cried. I said my father should have known where I was.

I had been there, hunched there, disappeared there every day since my mother's death, since my father collected me from school and drove us home with the same slow rigour, and sat across the table from me and informed me that my mother had died, his explanation dull and staunch.

He would have known where I was if he'd ever looked. But every day, just like the first day he told me, he'd turned to his farm and trudged through his tasks, his body blank and massive and stoic, his work clothes hardened with oils and hung with tools or sour with animal life. I'd watch him function, his movements so habitual his body seemed almost to be uninhabited. He fed me — pale, reliable cans oozing onto clean plates; he formed a routine of low, neutral grunts that signalled my time for sleeping or dressing. It was not that he was a bad father; it was simply that he was . . . a horizon: however I tried to move towards him — and I did, hovering, creeping — the space between us stayed impassable, fixed. My mother was no longer there to fill it.

Once, when I asked him, he briefly touched the place on the cold round tablecloth where my mother's head had rested, deliberate, while her vision dimmed. The way I had always measured my world was through my mother. Some days I seemed to have no map left but the red circles formed on the darkening table, the grooves in the dense practical plastic like rings sent out from a dream where my mother vanished into its target, ridge on sleek ridge marking her body, still trying to uncurl from somewhere in that blood-black core.

After I watched the woman fall I sat for a long time in the field.

I think perhaps I wanted to keep her for a while to myself: I've never understood my motives for concealing my location, but certainly, in the days following, I often thought of her, hushed and cupped in the moist black cradle she'd cut for herself, and the knowledge glowed with some haunting, sordid kind of comfort.

Other times I've wondered whether my intention was to punish my father. Childhood wishes can be ugly: my father was in the search party that eventually located the body, and his presence there, at the edge of her ditch, seemed right to me, seemed satisfying.

Mostly, though, I think back through that summer and get no closer to answers: but I do know I sat on the hill that my mother and I rolled down together on an earlier summer day. That day remains clear. She'd lain alongside me on cool, long grass, her head slippery by my head, her instructions giggled, silly and winsome. She'd squealed at the nestling of tiny crickets, crackling and frantic over our hair and skin, whole nets of their crisp bodies pinging at once. She'd braced there one rigid moment longer, then roared out and rolled, and I shuddered down after her, thrashing the bleached grass, tasting the jolt and slur of the thick earth through every pore, coming to a crazy halt against the warm cove of my mother's hip, still squirming with laughter, my cheek grazing studs in her cowshit-crusted jeans. The jewellery of crickets still snapped above us and trickled skinwards as we calmed and sighed. And the sky was above us, squirming as much as we did, matted as our clothes and hair, streaky and dusted and luminous as my mother's face tilted up, quivering with joy that started to run then, run down into the bare and secret coil of her ear.

There are nights, as I lie asleep beside my husband, when I dream we are in flight. It is the same dream, or some model of it, I've had since my first days with him, but over the course of our marriage it has altered many times. In its earliest form, our movements are fierce and scattered. His knuckles plunge across at me, my hands blunder and rake the metal, the door repeatedly smashes and cleaves until I finally swing out into the sky. A later variant takes place without struggle, its structure impossible as all dreams are: my husband simply depresses the disc on my chest and, soundlessly, I become cargo. The execution has become cleaner, more dispassionate as years progress: straps release, latches slip open, my husband acts without hatred and I don't hinder him, don't scratch or cling. There seems no reason to impede him.

More recently the flight merely glides on beyond the point where I normally fall. Beyond us the sky is bland, a dome as featureless as the clear cabin. In and out of our mouths I hear the steady expulsion and influx of breath, the blotching of it coating the screen with mist. I watch those images drift from us, disperse and recollect, but they resemble nothing. If his hands or my hands lift to change our course, neither of us notices.

C. K. STEAD

A War Story

HER NAME IS INGRID, SHE comes from Malmo in southern Sweden, a widow (once, long ago, married to a Frenchman) aged seventy-eight who might pass for fifty-eight. Every year since 1970 she has come for a few months of the summer to this little rural village in the Langue d'Oc where she has a house. She has a French daughter and a Swedish daughter, grandchildren and great-grandchildren. She is handsome, energetic, enthusiastic, warm-hearted, and smokes cigarettes which she rolls from French tobacco with a machine. Recently, when the village celebrated *quartorze juillet*, she sang karaoke in the square and danced with M. le Maire. She is our neighbour here and we have become friends.

From time to time we have drinks together in the evening, or dine at Chez Suzy, the little café-restaurant in the square. She tells stories of the village thirty years ago, when there were still donkeys to carry loads up and down the narrow streets, horses to plough and harrow the surrounding fields and pull loads in the vineyards; when there was a *boulangerie*, an *alimentation*, and, two or three times a week, a visiting butcher's cart, a fish cart, a cheese cart. Those were the days (she tells us) when what is now Chez Suzy was a café where the locals met. It was run by a woman said to have made her small fortune as a prostitute in Marseilles and retired, with her husband, to respectability in the provinces. Now there are no little shops, no visiting carts, no donkeys in the village or horses in the fields, just a supermarket ten minutes' drive away — and Chez Suzy is full of tourists.

'Like us,' we say.

'Like you,' she says, grabbing our hands across the table, squeezing them and smiling, dismissing nostalgia. 'How lucky I am to have met you.'

We (husband and wife) tell her we are the lucky ones. Our conversations are like that — full of small explosions of good feeling. Her English is halting, as is our French, and we go back and forth constantly between the two languages.

She talks often about the fact that I am a writer, that she has many stories, that she should have written hers but will never do it now. One night when we are sitting, the three of us, having eaten an excellent meal and drunk a little too much wine, as the twice-over clock in the *mairie* strikes its second ten (the last it will sound until seven in the morning), she grasps me by the wrist. 'I will tell you a story.' There is something breathy in the way she says this, a catch in the throat. 'It happened more than fifty years ago and I have only ever told it once — to my grand-daughter.'

It was 1946. Ingrid, a schoolteacher aged twenty-one, was engaged to a Dane but wanted, before she married and 'settled down', to see something of the world that had been closed to her during the war. She persuaded a girlfriend to come with her. They travelled *auto stop* — hitch-hiking — and headed for Paris, which she remembers now as if recalling one of the French black and white movies of that time, full of drama and romance, accordion music, poverty and noble sentiments. When their money was almost gone and it was time to return home, she knew she would have to find a way to come back. Her appetite for France was aroused, not satisfied. Her planned future — teaching small Swedes, marriage to a Dane, the life of a conventional housewife — seemed remote and unromantic.

They had seen nothing of occupied Germany and thought they might return via Hamburg and Kiel. No one was permitted to cross into that country without special papers, but a truck driver hid them in his cab and got them over the border. Their next pick-up was by two American soldiers who said they would take them to Hamburg. As the afternoon wore on they seemed to be taking more and more remote roads. It began to get dark. The Swedes were nervous, the Americans silent.

They came to a village or small town and in the half light could see that, like so much they passed through, it was in ruins. One of the soldiers, the driver, whose name was Chase, was large, loud and strongly built. 'Here,' he said, 'we'll introduce you to a nice family. Good Germans — you'll see. They'll give us something to eat.'

The four climbed a steep stair. The apartment they came to was scarcely more than one large room. There were a young husband and wife and two small children. Like all Germans at that time they looked strained and undernourished, but they offered food to the travellers — dark bread, cheese and a little dish of cabbage. The Americans gave them chocolates and cartons of cigarettes, which were at once hidden away; also a stack of tins of food, army rations. Cigarettes and chocolates, Ingrid knew, were used as a dependable currency.

Not much was said. The children were awake but unnaturally round-eyed and silent. The German woman looked uneasy; her husband seemed kind, but he too was anxious, and there was something desperate, avid, about the way he watched the gifts being unpacked and hidden away. There were halting exchanges in English and in German, but no warmth. It was all a transaction.

When they returned to the car the German man came too. Ingrid thought he had come down to say goodbye, but he took the wheel.

'Let's go,' Chase said. As they drove, he sang songs of that time, some with strange words that didn't sound to Ingrid like English or anything else — 'Mairzy Dotes and Dozy Dotes' and 'Chattanooga Choo Choo'. He sang tunelessly and without enthusiasm, as if to fill the silence.

Ingrid was squeezed between him and the German. In the back her friend sat with the other American. It was dark now, and they seemed not to travel on major roads. But what was a major road in ruined Germany?

She felt fear taking hold of her. 'Where are we going?' she asked. Her own voice sounded weak, childlike.

'Honey,' Chase replied, 'we are goin' to Hamburg, aren't we?' And he laughed as if she too should enjoy the joke.

She gripped the driver's thigh. His face had been reassuring. It was as if she knew him — enough to be sure he was a good man. She spoke to him in German, which she knew much better than English. 'Please help us.' She said it quietly but urgently, leaning towards him. 'I'm afraid.'

He didn't reply, except with the faintest shake of his head.

After a time she appealed again. 'Please help us' — squeezing his leg so hard he flinched and nudged her away.

They turned off one dark road into another, even darker. The silence in the car was terrifying. Ingrid began to appeal once more, again in German. She was stopped by a sharp blow to the face.

'That's enough,' Chase said. 'Stow it.'

Her nose bled. Her eyes filled with tears — not weeping tears, but the kind that spring from pain. She was beyond fear now. Shock had put her into what she later thought of as 'survival mode' (though she didn't expect to survive) — a kind of stillness.

'I'm crazy because of the war,' Chase said. He spoke fiercely. 'You understand?'

Through tears and blood she told him that yes, she understood.

'Good,' he said. 'So let's get on with it.' He gave her a cigarette, lit it, and lit one for himself.

In a village that seemed more than half destroyed and entirely deserted they stopped outside a building. 'Come with us,' Chase said.

Ingrid made one last appeal to the driver. 'Please . . .'

'Go with them,' he replied in German. He kept his hands on the wheel and his eyes ahead. 'You won't be hurt,' he said.

She took this to mean they would not be murdered, and she believed him. She and her friend went into the dark building. On dank mattresses they were raped. Later they were dropped in a small town, not far from a railway station, and the army car sped off into the dark.

At the station they were told there would be no trains until morning. They found a hotel nearby and told the man on the desk what had happened.

'He gave us a room,' Ingrid said, 'and water. He charged us nothing. In the morning we caught a train to Kiel.'

And afterwards?

'Afterwards,' she said, 'my friend and I were the same. We went together to see a doctor. We had tests. We were not pregnant and we had caught no disease. It was over. We spoke of it to no one — not even to each other. It had not happened.'

'And yet, after all this time . . .'

'Nearly sixty years,' she confirmed.

'You remember.'

'Oh, but of course. I remember. Especially the fear.'

'And you told your grand-daughter . . . as a warning?'

She thought about that, looking up from the terrace into the sky that still, even in darkness, managed to be blue. 'No, I don't think so. Not so much . . . it was a little gift — that's all. And a gift to you also. It's a story, isn't it? You can write it.'

I had to think about how to ask my next question. 'If you wrote it yourself . . . would there be a point?'

'It was war, you mean? Or had been war . . .' She tailed off for a moment, then began again. 'Yes. Yes, it was the German. That is the point. I was so convinced he was a good man, that he would not . . .'

'Allow you to be murdered?'

'He loved his wife and children. For him, you see, I think it was a calculation. We would suffer and survive, as they were suffering and surviving. That's all. They needed those things — the cigarettes, the chocolates, the tins of food.'

'And the Americans?'

'Oh, the Americans.' She shrugged, dismissing them. 'Well, they had won the war.'

JUDITH WHITE

Crash

YOU WANDER OUTSIDE, BLINKING IN the sun. The day is bright, intensely bright, with the bluest of skies. There is a cold ruffly breeze and you can hear the lazy donging of windchimes. And a bird. A blackbird. The busy complication of its song. You sink down into the dewy grass and look at the sky. Your vision is framed by leafy branches wavering lightly, and beyond that, blue. You would like to determine the edge of it, the outer edge where clouds are gathering like the intestines of a child's abandoned stuffed toy, and above, the dissolving fluid frenzy of blue nothing.

But still you continue to stare, until you see the busy throbbing skin of your own eyes, and it's a relief to find and be able to focus on a single high fluff of fairydown sweeping haphazardly across the day. And the darting shadow of fear.

> *This is the sky, the unfathomableness of it.*
> *This is the sky of love and loneliness.*

In the house is a man named Tom.

He lies in bed, sleeping, one leg hanging over the side, his mouth open to allow the gentle passage of breath, to and fro. The gentle passage of that same stuff that feeds the sky. Above the duvet covering him, his back almost imperceptibly rises and falls, rises and falls. From time to time a foot twitches.

Two days ago you arrived here in a little rattling grumbly plane, flying through that vast open space, with no dotted lines, no meridian lanes, no traffic lights and, it seemed, no rules. You saw the minusculeness of everything, the white fringe of waves, of ragged froth, coming in upon one another in a leisurely way. You saw streams of tiny wiggles of water and the great shapes of green hills. There was a sense of not moving, of being suspended there in a capsule of roar, the vibrating in your head like a dentist's drill. And all around you the sky. Nothing. You were held from the ground by the very stuff of breath.

You hear a muffled cry, and you twirl through the grass to your feet and rush inside to find him sitting up in the bed, his hands dredging his hair, perspiration like rain on his face.

You sit alongside him and take him in your arms, his cheek sticking against yours. He is limp, passive, but nonetheless this is a man whose dreams leak into the air, infusing the ordinary with his own particular vision, casting doubt on everything you know.

If you didn't love him you would walk away; for your own survival, you wouldn't have come in the first place.

He pulls away, and then slips back onto the pillow, tossing the duvet from his shoulder.

You fetch a bowl of cool water and a facecloth, and start to wipe his brow, but he pushes you away, gently enough, turning over to face the wall.

'Go away,' he mumbles.

You sit there, uncertain, twisting the last drops from the cloth into the water.

'Go away, please,' he says again, this time with more emphasis. 'Go back to Lover Boy.'

In another town far away in another country is another man, Oliver.

You left him to come here. You left him five days before the holiday, the very first holiday you had planned together.

As you sit on the bed you think of the discussion in the kitchen. Oliver was doing the dinner dishes, his sleeves pushed to his elbows, froth competing with the hairs on his arms. You were drying a cup, slowly, deliberately, rubbing at a persistent tea stain with the towel.

'I can't believe this,' he was saying, shaking his shaggy head. 'I just can't believe it.'

He flinched when you placed your hand on his arm.

'It's just for a few days. I'll finish my packing tonight. I'll be all ready to go when I come back.'

'*If* you come back.'

'Don't be ridiculous. You're being —'

'Silly? Unnecessarily dramatic? Unreasonable?'

You hated the hurt in his eyes but it was not enough to prevent you coming.

'You know I love you. I truly love you,' you told him.

He scooped the cutlery from the sink and crashed it on the dish rack, two of the knives landing over each other on the bench. Knives crossed: a fight, your superstitious mother would say.

'I thought you hated flying.'

'I do,' you said, picking up the knives.

'And specially small planes. Connecting at the other end with a small plane . . .'

'Believe me, it's not what I want to do. There are time constraints. In this case I don't have a choice.'

'You could choose not to go.'

'There is no choice,' you repeated.

Later, you could hear him strumming his guitar behind the closed door of his study while you packed for two journeys. He crept stealthily into bed after you had turned out the light. The night was spent without touching.

Early the next morning, when the shuttle arrived to take you to the airport, he walked behind you to the gate in his blue towelling dressing gown. During the night a spider had cast a thread from one shrub to another across the path, as if in a feeble attempt to prevent you going. It broke like a sticky whisper upon your face.

'Look after yourself,' he said, kissing you firmly on your forehead. You held him tightly, your head finding his warm morning chest through the parted dressing gown, hearing his good steady heart, breathing in the comfort of him . . . before the driver took your suitcase and you turned to clamber into the van.

And now you sigh and stand up from the bed to go back outside, to let yourself down into the cool welcoming grass.

He asked you to come and you came. He has told you to go and you should now feel free to return to Oliver, who waits for you so uneasily.

But you know that as soon as Tom hears the first sharp zipping of your suitcase, he will implore you to stay again.

This has happened before.

Until death us do part.

You hear another nightmarish cry from the house but you stay there. You are testing yourself this time. You are a mother whose breasts are bursting while the child screams for sustenance. You are the farmer standing with a gun while the wounded dog bleeds. You are withholding the vodka from the alcoholic. The needle from the white mottled arm.

You can feel the sky pressing upon you, the very weight of it.

It is not as if you haven't already witnessed a plane crashing to earth, a long time ago now. You know it can happen, whatever the odds. You can still recall the silver wing lifting from the grey sloshing sea, like a last stiff wave from a drowned bird. And from along the beach as your father tugged you away, you caught a glance of fully dressed men in the sea hauling at the lifeless body of the pilot, their trousers clinging to their legs.

You know it can happen. You know that people can die. And you know that love is a tangible but invisible force that takes on the qualities of the air around, but that it never dies. Love has tendrils that weave into the heart, simultaneously giving nourishment to and sucking substance from life itself, sometimes not in equal measure. When the balance is out, the symbiotic relationship becomes parasitic. It is up to you. You should be able to control it. And control the battling that now seems to be taking place between the relatively new love for Oliver, and the battered, weathered love for Tom. Between the giving and the receiving.

You could stay here and never have to step on a plane again. You could be the one, finally, to save him. You could be the one who set his life in motion again, unlocked the door to his studio to start him painting again. If only you could stand before him, upright, like a snarling stiff-armed commandant in brown uniform, guarding him from the next bottle, the next fix.

But instead, you are pretty and plump and vulnerable.

The visiting support worker told you about the difference in him since you arrived. They'd been worried about him, but then he was so buoyed by the thought of your coming.

You could set Oliver adrift like the fairydown drifting above you.

You could stay here and look after Tom and let your juicy pumping heart shrivel once more.

You sense the plod of footsteps and turn your head in the bowl of your clasped hands to see him moving towards you, his fists clutching the duvet at his shoulders in a fat cloak as it trawls through the damp grass behind him. His skinny chest is naked and pale, and the band of his maroon satin boxers sits across peaks of pelvic bone. He flops down beside you on the grass.

'I was looking for you,' he says, and he rolls onto his stomach, reaching beyond the island of his duvet to pluck a shiny green stem of grass.

'Are you feeling better?'

'I was looking for you. I thought you'd gone. I was panicking. Thinking of what it's been like without you.' He's staring at the blade of grass, twirling it to catch sleek flashes of sun. 'Without you all this time.'

'Yes, it's been nice, being here,' you say. You haven't moved, and your hands are still locked behind your head, safe. 'I'm proud of you. You're doing well.'

'Because of you,' he says.

He flips the duvet to fold it over his back in a cocoon. His fingers scrabble in the grass, parting it to expose the earth, and he peers closely at some moving creature there.

'No, because of *you*. You're the only one who can help yourself.'

'Don't give me that crap,' he snaps.

'And on Thursday I go.' You feel yourself cringing as you say it, although he's known from the start that this was the plan. He pulls his arms up and folds them under his forehead.

'Stay,' he mumbles into the duvet. 'Stay. I'll never drink or take anything ever again. Look. I'm already ten days down the track.'

'I can't,' you say. 'We both know that.'

'Well, why did you come, then?'

'I came because you asked for help. Because I care. You knew from the beginning it would be for just a few days.'

'If you *cared* you wouldn't go.'

'Come on. Let's not fight. You know I care.' You wriggle amicably closer to him.

'Care. What does it mean anyway? It means *nothing*.' He rapidly scrambles to his feet, scoops up the duvet and drags it back inside, like a child with a cuddly blanket, a pacifier. When he reaches the porch he shouts, far too loudly, 'You'll be sorry.'

You lie there, the sky heavy on your chest. You make yourself stay there; you use every iota of your strength not to stand up and follow him, to cajole him. You make yourself stay there until the cold finds your bones, and then you get up and go inside. You walk down the clean, neat, empty hallway, peering into each vacant room as you make your way to the front door, open wide to the path that runs between the flowers to the open gate. You cast your eyes down the suburban street, where all the little houses sit with closed gates and closed doors and closed windows, and you see only a cat, and a small boy swinging from the branch of a tree. You wonder if those words will be the last words you'll hear from him, and meanwhile the sky presses around you and you are astonished by the density of it.

Behind you, from his house, the phone rings. You turn but it stops, and then as you walk back down the hallway you hear his voice. He must have been there all the time, concealing himself from you. You stand by the lounge door.

'No, mate, sorry, she's not coming back. Hasn't she said . . . she was going to tell you herself.'

You barge in. 'What are you saying? You have no right . . . give me the phone.'

He is sitting, still wrapped in the duvet, in the big threadbare armchair by the window, and as you stride in he covers the mouthpiece with his hand. His eyes are large and innocent, a deep wipe of bruised shadow under each one. His curly hair flopping, his skin porcelain white.

'What?' he says to you. 'Excuse me?'

'What are you doing? Tom. Give me the phone.'

He blinks exaggeratedly as he rather archly places the phone in your waiting palm.

'Oliver?' you say, suddenly unsure, and indeed, a strange voice replies.

'Pardon? Sorry?'

You return the phone to his own outstretched hand, and flop across the room to curl into a corner of the sofa. You clutch a cushion to your stomach.

'Sorry, mate,' he is saying. 'My wife. She's expecting a call. Well, ex-wife, actually — she left me, but that's another story. Anyway. No, sorry about the other. Yeah. Yeah. No, I can't help, sorry. Bye.' He places the phone on the arm of the chair, lifts his eyes to you, smiles defiantly.

'Trying to track down a friend of mine. Hadn't turned up at the bakery.'

'Friend?' you say.

'Yep. Frankie.'

'Why would they look here?'

'Because she lived here once.'

'Lived here?'

'Yes.'

'Why isn't she here now? Instead of me?'

'She isn't here now because she has her own problems. *We* have our own problems.'

You clutch the cushion more tightly. You look around the room, the jumble of soft easy chairs, two heavily shaded sketches of Tom pinned onto the faded wall paper, the convex mirror in the ornate brass frame sucking in the distorted reflection of the whole scene. You are looking now for evidence of a woman's touch. There is none.

'Who did the drawings?' you ask him.

He twists his neck around, above the cocoon of duvet, and stares at the drawings as if he too has just noticed them.

'They're not too bad, are they? And her paintings . . . are amazing.'

'Why haven't you ever mentioned her?'

'Why should I have?'

You suddenly, inexplicably, unreasonably, feel furious.

'Did you love her?' You can only bring yourself to use the past tense.

'Not like I love you. Listen. Let's start again. I'm better. I feel better. Look at my hand.' He holds out his fingers, long and pink. 'Not a quiver. Look. Let's have babies. Go travelling. Like we were going to. Buy a house. Let's get it together and start again.'

'As always, back to front. As always, the clichés. As always, we both know we have tried and tried and that any hope for anything better is a lie.' You have to voice these words to remind yourself that they are true. You have to say them out loud so that you don't crumble once more into his dream.

As if on cue there is a subtle chilling of the air, and a long spluttering grumble of thunder. The sky has found you, has moved in to engulf you, crushing you like a small bird.

You remind yourself that you have Oliver, though you can't conjure any real sense of him. He is diminishing, and you discover you can't retrieve any substance of your love for him beyond, say, that of a fond uncle in a photo on a mantelpiece.

'If you hadn't come I would have been dead by now.'

You look at him enfolded in the duvet and see that his eyes are filled with tears. You stand up, walk across the wooden floorboards and rest your cheek on his tousled hair.

'No, you wouldn't, don't be silly.'

'Yes, I would have. I'd decided.'

'I'll fix something to eat,' you say. 'It's dinnertime.'

'I'm not hungry.'

'Everything will be all right,' you tell him, though you have no idea what that means.

The next day you greet each other in the kitchen with a warm, uncomplicated hug. He is looking healthier, you note. There's a flush of pink under his skin. Today he seems shy, awkward, and this endears him to you. You return to your task of cutting tomato and avocado. Eggs are boiling in the saucepan, and bacon is sizzling under the grill.

'Sorry,' he says hesitantly, 'for all that fuss yesterday.'

You smile at him. 'I hadn't thought of it as fuss.'

He stands pressed against the kitchen table, watching you, towel around his waist, water dripping from his hair onto his bony shoulders.

'That smells good. Thank you for coming over. I just want you to know that I appreciate it.'

'Oh. I'm really happy to be here. Truly. I just want you to be better. And happy.'

'I'll get dressed,' he says, and he whirls away and is gone.

And for some reason it is you who whistles brightly as you lift the food onto each plate, turning the bacon, and spooning each egg from the pot in the sink.

Later, the two of you decide to go for a walk. You make ham and mustard sandwiches with fresh white bread you bought from the corner store, and head out into the world with a small pack on his back. Linking arms, you walk briskly together with a good rhythm. You can smell the white crispness of his shirt. His headache has shifted, he tells you. He feels more normal than he has for years. This time everything will be different; he can feel it. He'll get back into working again, and painting. He wants to show you his paintings. And he'll get back into a routine. One day at a time.

You reach a park where a stream runs alongside a grassy bank, and spread a rug under a tree. You both sit with your backs against the trunk, alongside each other, not touching, watching the flowing water. On the other side of the stream there's a dirt path meandering through the trees. You open up the sandwiches and are just starting to eat when you both notice a ragged woman clad in a heavy coat shuffling along the path. Each arm is weighted with a number of bulging plastic bags. From where you are, you can see her purple complexion, her fat lumpy legs under her skirt, her despair. She heads for a rubbish bin on a post and, without dropping her bags, leans over the bin, searching with her eyes before she moves on again. As you watch, it strikes you that she is the embodiment of the clichéd outcome of all this.

'She's terrifying,' he says. 'Look at her, she's so . . . ugly. Why doesn't she just . . . get it together? Let's go, anyway. It's getting cold.' He grabs the rest of the sandwiches, bundles them in their wrapping, then stuffs them back in the pack. He stands, tugging at the rug as you take your time to haul yourself upright.

'What's the hurry?' you say. The woman is out of sight now.

'I just don't want to be here any more, that's all.'

Back at the house you open the sandwiches and eat them at the kitchen table.

'Sorry,' he says grumpily. 'I just freaked out. It just hit me, that's all. I don't want to be like that.'

'You won't be,' you say.

'No,' he says determinedly, his mouth bulging. 'I won't.' He swallows, awkwardly. 'Wait,' he says, getting up from the table. He disappears down the hallway and you can hear shoving and shifting sounds from his bedroom. He reappears with his arms outspread behind a large painting, which he props on the window-seat before you.

He folds his arms tightly and waits. 'What do you think?'

The painting is mainly a spread of blue, the perfect blue of a summer's day, with a couple of tattered wisps of cloud drifting to one side. Off centre is a tiny brown bird in flight, almost lost in the blueness. You imagine you can hear it singing. You stand up to examine it more closely.

'It's beautiful,' you say, turning to him, and you mean it. 'It's so . . . lonely, somehow.'

'I did it after you left. It's the last painting I did. Eighteen months ago now. Anyway, it's yours.'

'No, I couldn't.'

'It's yours. I did it for you.'

You step towards him to give him a hug. He keeps his arms folded, but rests his chin on your head. 'Stay,' he says.

You feel a deep stab of ache in your heart as you tell him that you can't, and he pulls away and walks up the hallway and you hear the front door closing quietly behind him. You follow, opening the door. He stops by the gate as you call.

'What?' he says with an innocent expression.

'Where are you going?'

'Out. Why?'

'Wait for me, I'll just get my coat.'

'Sorry . . . I need to think. I'd rather be alone.'

'I'd like to come. Please. I'll be quiet.'

You move towards him as he pauses, hand on the gate.

'Come back inside,' you coax. 'Let's really talk. We need to talk, properly.'

You see him hesitating, prevaricating. You almost tell him, heart pounding, that you've changed your mind, but he says, kindly and evenly, 'Don't worry. I won't be late.'

'Late? What does that mean?'

'I don't know. Anyway,' and now not so kindly, 'what's it to you?' And he turns on his heel and once more you are torn as he trots blithely down the street, jauntily almost, his head high. You don't know how long you can stand this. Tomorrow you are scheduled to leave and you don't know whether you will be able to. Back inside, in the kitchen, you stare at the painting and marvel at the way he has been able to capture that sense of absolute isolation and loneliness.

You busy yourself at the bench preparing a chicken with garlic and rosemary, and put it in the oven to cook. You peel vegetables and throw them in with the chicken. The last supper, you think.

Then you head outside to lie in the grass. The sky is hidden by a thick layer of messy cloud — a nasty colour, brewing something.

You wake up to the door slamming and, as you sit up blearily rubbing your eyes, he bounces from the porch to greet you.

'Hi,' he says brightly. 'You like it out here, don't you? When you go you'll be leaving your imprint in the grass. I'll be able to say, *there rested my wife*. It's a nice spot, that's for sure.'

'Oh, hi,' you say, smiling at him. 'You're happy.'

'Come inside,' he says, beckoning with his head, joggling from one foot to the other. 'There's someone I want you to meet.'

The kitchen is infused with the smell of the cooking meal. A woman in a long flowing dress is leaning over with her hands clasped behind her back, studying the painting as you had earlier in the day. A shaft of late sunshine has found its way through the French doors across the room, giving the picture a transparent vibrancy — it looks like a framed entrance into the sky itself.

'Frankie,' says Tom, his voice a little nervous. The woman turns and faces you, a hint of hostility in keen intelligent eyes.

'Hello,' you say.

'Hi,' she says and shakes your extended hand. She's handsome and strong, her bare arms sinewy and tanned. Tom is scrabbling around in the cupboard, bringing out glasses, and you're suddenly aware that he's breaking the screwtop off a bottle of red wine, and now pouring. You grab his arm, wave your hand over the glasses, wine spilling through your fingers onto the table.

'What are you doing?' you whisper sharply.

He meets your gaze mutinously. 'I'm having a drink,' he says.

'Stop it.'

'A man's allowed to have a little lightness in his life sometimes.'

'Stop it now.' You look at Frankie. 'Stop him.'

She shrugs. 'I don't own him.'

'Tom, stop it. Think of the old woman.'

'Don't spoil everything,' he says to you coldly. 'Anyway, it's too late; we stopped at the pub on the way.'

You flop onto a chair, your head in your hands. The woman and Tom sit at the table with you and he pushes a glass your way, nudging your arm.

'Cheers,' he says, and you take the glass and stare at it, shattered. Tom and Frankie clink glasses, and Tom reaches over to clink yours too. You look at him and for a moment his cockiness wavers, then he shifts his eyes away from yours. His cheeks are flushed. Everything is easy now. You are free to leave. You did your best. You sip the wine and start to make polite conversation. Already you are pulling away from this scene, in a little frightening plane, making your weary way into the lonely blue of the sky, into all the breathing of the world, on and on away from here into your other normal life.

An abrupt loud thud at a window hurtles you back to the present. You all jump up and group around the French doors to see a sparrow flailing on the porch. Gradually it settles to rest in a limp heap, beak open. Frankie runs outside. You and Tom watch from the window as she scoops up the bird, cupping it in her hands, stroking its head with her thumb.

'She's good with birds,' he says.

'I hope so.'

'Don't worry.' He squeezes your shoulder. Frankie comes inside, shaking her head.

'It'll probably come right,' she says.

She and Tom huddle over the stunned bird. You can see its little stick legs quivering, the grey skin of eyelid closing. You turn away and go to your room to pack.

Notes on Contributors

MICHELLE ARATHIMOS is a Wellington writer who completed a Masters in Creative Writing at Victoria University's International Institute of Modern Letters in 2006. She has written a book of short stories and is working on a novel about a Greek New Zealand family. She is an English teacher and currently teaches writing at Victoria University.

    * 'The Free Box' was inspired by my creative friend Airini Beautrais. I was at her house one day and she was making patches, and we went for a walk to an op shop down the road that had a 'free box'. I loved the idea of a free box — a box that would give you things for free but that perhaps also had magical 'freeing' qualities. I also credit Airini with a line of dialogue in the story: 'I would have been good in the depression.'

SANDRA ARNOLD lives in North Canterbury and teaches foundation studies at Christchurch Polytechnic Institute of Technology. She was founding fiction editor of the literary magazine *Takahe* and has had two novels published: *A Distraction of Opposites* (Hazard Press) and *Tomorrow's Empire* (Horizon Press). Her short stories, travel articles and essays have been widely published and her work has been broadcast on Radio New Zealand. After teaching in Oman in 2003–04 she completed a Master of Letters and is currently working on a doctorate in creative non-fiction.

    * The genesis of 'The Stone' lies in the death of my 23-year-old daughter in 2002. From the moment her very rare cancer was diagnosed a year earlier, through the intense year of caring for her until her death, and the year of numbness that followed, I lost the desire to write and the ability to dream. As a friend once described her life in a desert country: 'There were no seasons, just a drifting.' It may not have been coincidence, then, that my husband and I were drawn to leave New Zealand for a while and work in a desert country in the Arabian Gulf.

    Our life in Oman was characterised by the unexpected, the bizarre and the hilarious, and included our astonishment at the stark beauty of the landscape and the ability of the inhabitants to survive in one of the most inhospitable deserts on earth. It was the gift of this 'out-of-time' that re-awakened my senses and led to the re-assertion of my need to record and describe. Soon I began writing a few travel articles. However as the Iranian writer Azar Nafisi says in *Reading Lolita in Tehran: A Memoir in Books*, 'The ordinary pebble of ordinary life can be transformed into a jewel through the magic eye of fiction . . . what we search for in fiction is not so much a reality but the epiphany of truth.' Through the shape-shifting power of fiction it becomes possible to make sense of a place where 'normal' is merely a construct. Thus, I abandoned the idea of writing a travel book and instead began a novel in stories. 'The Stone' forms part of this work.

BEN BROWN is the author of the critically acclaimed memoir *A Fish in the Swim of the World* (Longacre Press, 2006) and several children's books including the award-winning *A Booming in the Night* (Reed, 2005), which won Best Picture Book at the 2006 New Zealand Post Book Awards, Children & Young Adults. His work has also been twice shortlisted for the LIANZA Book Awards; in 2005 with *Fifty-five Feathers* (Reed, 2004) and 2006 with *A Booming in the Night*. He has also published several short stories and the occasional freelance magazine article. He lives in Lyttelton, Banks Peninsula with artist/illustrator Helen Taylor and their two children, Connor and Sophie.

* I've always been intrigued by the Pai Maarire faith (literally *good and gentle*), in the sense of it being one of those spiritual world view constructs — a kind of hotch-potch blend of biblical and traditional references — that Maori seemed readily able to accommodate. My grandfather was an adherent and, indeed, to my memory's eye he also bore a passing resemblance to Ray Charles, whose song 'Tell Me What'd I Say?' has long been a favourite of mine. But the old man of the story is not Pai Maarire. His 'faith' is his own. It suits his needs, which are simply defined as the maintenance of mana, whaanau and whenua. Once again, this could be a description of my own grandfather. As to the young men of the story, well, they are what they are: indifferent to all needs but their own, in it for the buzz and the bucks and constantly missing the point. I might have been one of them myself once, and someone like my grandfather would have bailed me out.

DAVID EGGLETON lives in Dunedin, where he is a writer whose articles, reviews, essays and short stories have appeared in a variety of publications since the late 1980s. He has published five books of poems and a book of short fiction, and has written or contributed to a number of works of non-fiction.

* Novelist William Golding once claimed that 'human beings

secrete evil as naturally as bees produce honey'. I wanted to write a story about someone from a disadvantaged background struggling with the ethical issues that surround wealth and power — and the lack of it. The starting point was observing some of the homeless people in inner-city Auckland and wondering how they got there. In a sense my character is on that path, but he still could go either way.

CHARLOTTE GRIMSHAW is the author of three critically acclaimed novels — *Provocation* and *Guilt*, published in Britain and New Zealand, *Foreign City*, published in New Zealand in 2005 — and one short-story collection, *Opportunity*. In 2000 she was awarded the Buddle Findlay Sargeson Fellowship. She has been a double finalist and prizewinner in the Sunday Star-Times Short Story Competition, judged by Owen Marshall, and in 2006 she won the Bank of New Zealand Katherine Mansfield Award for short fiction. Her short stories have appeared in, among others, *The Best New Zealand Fiction* volumes 2 and 3, edited by Fiona Kidman; in the *New Zealand Listener*; in the *Sunday Star-Times*; in Reed's *Myth of the Twenty-First Century*; and in *Stand* magazine in Britain She lives in Auckland.

* 'The Body' is about a death in a family, and the way family members react to it. Each character has his or her individual perception of what lies beyond death, 'beyond the sky'. Each section of the story corresponds to the one before it; together they form a closely unified whole.

EIRLYS HUNTER was born in London but has lived in Wellington for over twenty years. She has four children, only one of whom is still a teenager. As well as short stories, she has written several books for children and a novel for adults: *Between Black and White* (Random House). She is (still) working on a novel that is set largely in the Philippines.

* I wrote this story last summer at the family bach. I often find my way into a story by establishing the time of year, the place and the weather, and relating this to a mood; with this story I borrowed the environment I was actually in. Then I invented a family and their visitors and watched their relationships unfold. I never plan short stories; events arise out of the interaction of the characters as I get to know them.

Often I'm not really aware of what's gone into a story until it's written. I love the way that the subconscious process works, mining memories, ideas and observations and connecting them together. For instance it wasn't until the first draft was finished that I realised the parallels between Alejandra and Janet (the 'aha' moment that I gave to Molly), and that realisation led me to rewrite the ending.

In retrospect I can see that the elements that make up this story are, as always, a mixture of the imagined and the experienced. For instance, one of my daughters had bad internet withdrawal symptoms when we made her come on holiday with us when she was younger, an attribute I borrowed for Molly. And we once spent a weekend with a woman who flirted with my husband as Janet flirts with Roland. The bach in this story is not our bach, and the family is not my family, but our bach is on the edge of phone reception, and the mess in the sleepout is very familiar.

To begin with the story was only from the mother's point of view, but I realised that I also wanted to show Molly's view of what was going on. I can remember being that age, feeling awkward, and wishing I could be the person I was in my imagination. I like teenagers. And I love how different they can be, not only from each other but also from the person they were yesterday.

WITI IHIMAERA was born in Gisborne in 1944. His first book, *Pounamu Pounamu* (short stories) was published in 1972; he became the first Maori novelist with *Tangi* in 1973. His subsequent career has primarily been focused on the short story and the novel; he has written twelve novels, and his sixth short-story collection, *Ask the Posts of the House*, is due out later this year. His books have won a number of prizes in New Zealand; *The Whale Rider* (1985) was made into an internationally acclaimed film in 2002.

    * This story arose out of a conversation I had with a publishing colleague who remarked on the difference between my early lyrical work as a short-story writer and the more political vein of my later work. He challenged me to write a short story of the lyrical kind that I used to write thirty years ago and so I wrote 'I've Been Thinking About You, Sister'. At heart it's a fictionalised and expanded version of a story I related in a session on the Maori Battalion with co-panellists Patricia Grace, James George and Mick Brown at the Auckland Writers' and Readers' Festival in 2005. But along the way I interrogate the story from a postcolonial political perspective and try to explain why I couldn't write it in quite the same ingenuous and lyrical manner that I was asked to do. The story is a companion piece to 'Meeting Elizabeth Costello', which appeared in *The Best New Zealand Fiction Volume 2*.

STEPHANIE JOHNSON is the author of seven novels and three collections of short stories, many of which have been published internationally. She is also a playwright and poet and writes for television and radio. For many years she has taught creative writing, most recently a three-year stint co-teaching a Masters in Creative Writing at the

University of Auckland. In 1998 she founded the Auckland Writers' and Readers' Festival with Peter Wells. She lives in Auckland with her partner and three teenage children.

* My contribution to this anthology is the opening pages of a novel in progress. The book is about a deep friendship between two very different men that begins in 1905, when Lyn and Norman are seven years old. For a period of some twenty years their friendship is interrupted, the reason for which is the mystery at the centre of the novel. In my historical novels, I have often examined changing notions of sexuality and spirituality. It is rich, sustaining territory.

TIM JONES's short fiction and poetry have appeared in magazines and anthologies in New Zealand, Britain, the US, Australia, Canada and Vietnam. His published books are a short fiction collection, *Extreme Weather Events*, and a poetry collection, *Boat People*, both published by HeadworX. His poem 'The Translator' was included in *Best New Zealand Poems 2004*.

* Arthur C. Clarke's science fiction stories were very popular in the Soviet Union. Although he is often thought of as a prophet of the technological sublime, the stories in his excellent collection *Expedition to Earth* are full of dying falls; of inscrutable mechanisms, their meaning long forgotten, waiting for new orders. By the declining days of the Soviet Union, that's pretty much what the Soviet system was like. Mikhail Gorbachev and his reformist-minded mates tried their best to shake the system up, and failed. And I'd done my time in meetings: facilitating, taking minutes, reaching consensus. Local environmental group, Soviet Politburo — how different could they be?

FIONA KIDMAN is a novelist, short-story writer and poet. She has published over twenty books, including the novels *A Breed of Women*, *The Book of Secrets* (winner of the New Zealand Book Award for Fiction) and more recently *The Captive Wife*, which was Readers' Choice in the 2006 Montana New Zealand Book Awards. She initiated and edited the first three volumes of *The Best New Zealand Fiction*. She was the Meridian Energy Katherine Mansfield Writers Fellow for 2006, and visited France in November with eleven New Zealand writers, as part of *Les Belles Etrangères* tour. She is a Dame Commander of the New Zealand Order of Merit (DNZM).

* Late last year I was on my way to the supermarket when I saw the meteorological phenomenon described in 'Heaven Freezes', which created a shaft of intense icy blue light over Wellington. At first I supposed I was imagining it, or that it was part of some more usual weather pattern

I had simply failed to notice before, until I saw others also looking up with puzzled stares. The next morning the newspaper reported the light with a headline that read 'Heaven Freezes City Skies'. I loved the first part of that headline. I thought how aptly it evoked those signs and portents that sometimes make people think they are at a crossroad in their lives, a moment of truth. The particular supermarket I was heading towards is the haunt of particularly fashionable shoppers, so I gave an imaginary one his moment of truth. The story came together when I put these particular elements together, including how difficult it can be for an outsider to break into Wellington's tight social networks.

SUE McCAULEY has written four novels, two collections of short stories, a non-fiction book and drama for radio, stage and screen. She lives with her husband in Waitahora Valley, east of Dannevirke, and is working on a novel about — among other things — the impact of Rogernomics.

    * In 2006, after fifty-three pet lamb-less years, I acquired two pet lambs — Jackson and Freddy. They are the lambs in this story, but I changed Jackson's name in case he took offence or sued.

        The story set out to be about Jackson's (Norman's) attempt to rejoin his flock while dressed in recycled tights — which was entirely true and both funny and sad to observe. But it seems to have turned into a story about the moral conflict of being a farmer.

        Jackson and Freddy are still with us; Jackson is getting a chance to prove himself as a ram, but only the falling price of lamb has saved Freddy so far. Should his story be snatched up by Hollywood, I fear he will not be around to give interviews.

PAULA MORRIS (Ngati Wai) is the author of three novels, *Queen of Beauty, Hibiscus Coast*, and *Trendy But Casual*. She is a graduate of creative writing degree programmes at Victoria University in Wellington and the University of Iowa, and currently teaches at Tulane University in New Orleans.

    * In 2002, while staying with my parents in West Auckland, I got to experience the madness that is the inorganic rubbish collection. My parents were selling the house they'd lived in for thirty-five years and were trying to clear out a lot of stuff. In the hazy dusk, as we carried things up the driveway, I became aware of vans cruising by and of people waiting to pounce. We threw out an old shower door, and within minutes it had disappeared.

        Not long afterwards, I moved to Iowa City and began work on my second novel, *Hibiscus Coast*. The title of 'Red Christmas' came from my upstairs neighbour, who was from Iceland. The main character, Ani, also features in *Hibiscus Coast*. In the novel, she's at university, trying to escape her mother; their benevolent neighbour, Uncle Suli, has died, and her younger brothers, Tama and Henry, have been taken into care. Above Ani's work table in the Art School, there's just one picture: 'two barefoot Maori boys leaning against the back door of a decrepit van'.

In the story, she's still at school and the family still lives in the small house in Henderson. Although she doesn't know it, this is the last time Ani and her brothers will borrow Uncle Suli's van and go on an adventure together.

CARL NIXON is a full-time writer who lives in Christchurch and has two young children. His recent work for theatre includes an adaptation of the Booker Prize-winning novel *Disgrace* by J. M. Coetzee. His new play, *The Raft*, recently premiered at the Court Theatre in Christchurch. Carl's collection of short stories, *Fish 'n' Chip Shop Song* (Random House) received outstanding reviews and went to number one on the New Zealand Best Selling Fiction list. His first novel, *Rocking Horse Road*, was published by Random House NZ in July 2007.

* This story was written at least five years ago, although it has never been published. It has been rewritten and tweaked at various points over that time. It is true to say that, of my own work, it is one of my favourite stories. It brings together a number of ideas and themes that recur in my writing: ageing and the regrets that lost opportunities leave behind; the importance of water, in this case a river; illness and hospitals; and a young man's search for meaning and place.

JULIAN NOVITZ was born in Christchurch in 1980 and currently lives in Melbourne. He is the author of a collection of short fiction *My Real Life and Other Stories* (2004) and a novel *Holocaust Tours* (2006).

* A few years ago an acquaintance told me how his father had been a surveillance specialist in the police force. He and his co-workers apparently referred to themselves as 'the buggers', and something about that pun stuck in my head. I was also attracted to the incongruity of rather ordinary middle-aged men putting themselves in what sounded like bizarre and dangerous situations (the situation Adam finds himself in the woolshed is loosely based on a true story). When I came to write the story the only thing I had decided was that it would begin and end behind the couch, and the voice of the character just took me from there. Anyway, I'm glad it has made it into this collection — 'bugger' is such a great New Zealand word.

SUE ORR has been writing short stories for two years. In 2006 she completed a Masters in Creative Writing at Victoria University's International Institute of Modern Letters. She worked on a collection of short stories that included 'Velocity'. Her work has been published in the *New Zealand Listener* and in *Turbine*, and features in *Sport 35*. Prior to writing fiction, she worked as a journalist, technical writer, editor and speechwriter. She is relieved that it is okay, at long last, to make things up. Sue is a Wellingtonian but currently lives in Devonport, Auckland, with her family.

    * American writer Catherine Brady has said she can never get started on a short story until she has two different tales to tell at the same time — the way one disrupts the other is what drives her to write. When I started 'Velocity', I wanted to explore perceptions of strength and weakness, and how such perceptions can test a relationship. Around that time I was sidetracked and seduced by the true tale of Velocity, the fastest bird to deliver mail between Great Barrier Island and Auckland for the Great Barrier Island Pigeon-Gram Service in the late 1880s. I set the story of Jack and Sandy in Tokoroa because I lived there for a short time in the 1980s, flatting with two vets. They would sometimes bring animals home overnight to recuperate from illness or an operation. Unlike Jack's poor patients, most of them made a full recovery. The tale of Jack and Sandy might have had a happier ending, had it not been disrupted by the arrival of Velocity.

SARAH QUIGLEY is a novelist, columnist and poet, with a PhD in Literature from Oxford University. Her most recent books are a novel, *Fifty Days* (Virago) and *Write: A 30-day Guide to Creative Writing* (Penguin). She is currently based in Berlin, and is working on a new novel.

    * A real winter's walk inspired this story: a cold February afternoon in Berlin, walking in the gardens of a city palace. It took me over a year to write. The two main characters are very private, and I felt as if I had to listen carefully to understand their personalities and work out their different pasts.

    While I was writing the story, a friend asked me what it was about. 'Snow,' I said. The whiteness and silence are important to the story, where nature is like an enduring backdrop for small human histories. To me, the story has stayed slightly dreamlike and mysterious. I can read it many times and still not feel sure how it will end.

DUNCAN SARKIES is best known in New Zealand for writing *Scarfies*, the country's sixth-highest grossing film. Before that he worked extensively as a playwright. His first play, *Lovepuke*, has been performed all over Australia. Another, *Saving Grace*, was the New Zealand Play of the Year in 1995. In 2006 he was invited to perform in the New Zealand International Arts Festival in a music-theatre show called *Instructions for Modern Living*. This show has subsequently been invited to the Barbican Theatre in London in 2008. His book of short stories, *Stray Thoughts and Nose Bleeds*, won Best First Book at the Montana New Zealand Book Awards in 2000. *Two Little Boys* is his first novel.

  * I need to explain something. It has never been an ambition of mine to write a novel. When I wrote my book of short stories people repeatedly said, 'When are you going to write a novel?' as if short stories were some kind of step toward being a grown-up. This riled me a touch. I've never seen it that way. Many of my favourite writers are short-story writers. So, to prove I'm not very grown up I've written a novel featuring the most juvenile, immature and uncouth characters I have ever written. I'm scraping the bottom of the barrel here. My writing is hitting a new low and I'm proud of that.

  The characters Nige and Dean have been haunting me for the last five years. I like their company, even if they leave a mess wherever they go. Nige and Dean started writing their own story, and they chose to write it as a novel. Who was I to disagree?

  Two Little Boys is a crime story. But the question is not 'How will they get away with it?' The real question is 'When will they get caught?' Someone told me *Two Little Boys* is a bit like Barry Crump, but *gayer*. It is a bit gay. It's also a bit bogan. So maybe it will be filed in your bookstore under the section entitled 'Crime Stories that are a Bit Bogan and a Bit Gay'.

  It is going to be published by Penguin in 2008. I'm bloody excited. As Nige or Dean might say, 'I'm really wetting my pants about it, you know, in a *good* way.'

  I've chosen some extracts that don't follow on from each other, because I don't want to give anything away. But I will say that as you read this you should keep in mind that Nige has just run over a backpacker, and the person he turned to for help, Dean, is not the sort of guy you want in a crisis — he's a bit of a psychopath.

TRACEY SLAUGHTER's first collection of poems and short stories, *Her Body Rises*, was published by Random House in 2005. In 2001 her short story 'Her First' won the Bank of New Zealand Katherine Mansfield Novice Writers' Award, and in 2004 'Wheat' was awarded the Premier Katherine Mansfield Award. In 2002 she won the Aoraki Festival Poetry Award and was the featured poet in *Poetry NZ*. Her work has been widely published in literary journals in New Zealand and in Britain. In 2006 'Wheat' was translated into French for inclusion in the journal *Europe*, the story 'A Tree Full of Angels' appeared in the anthology *Myth of the 21st*

Century, and 'a working model of the sky' was highly commended in the Sunday Star-Times Short Story Competition. Tracey studied at Auckland University and went on to teach at both Auckland University and Massey University, and in 2001 she completed her PhD thesis, an exploration of New Zealand women's autobiographical writing. She now writes full-time, and lives in Thames on the Coromandel Peninsula with her partner and two young children.

     * To try to retrace the beginnings of a story is as difficult as trying to piece back together the shade, the textures of vapour that hovered in the sky on the day that story first brushed through the mind or passed onto the page. The sky above childhood is an equally strange and distant place . . . but once a woman did, in fact, fall through the sky above mine. Unlike the child of my story, I did not *see* the woman fall, but the haunting knowledge that she had somehow dropped from a plane sighted over our land, and that her body lay undiscovered somewhere, was enough to keep me 'seeing' her fall repeatedly, descending through dream after dream. Looking back, I think I was learning things about the adult world at the time: perhaps she seemed to me like a bleak angel from that world, an image of the kind of simple atrocity with which adults could crash unthinkingly into, and out of, other lives. Her fall struck my imagination, as did her eventual location only a few fields away — or in my mother's shivering words, 'just across a few fencelines'. But despite this source in one wild and dreamlike fact of childhood — or perhaps because of it — 'a working model of the sky' is entirely *fiction*.

C[HRISTIAN] K[ARLSON] STEAD was born in Auckland in 1932. He has published thirteen collections of poems and two of short stories, eleven novels and six books of literary criticism, and has edited a number of texts. His novels are published in New Zealand and Britain, and have been translated into several European languages. He was Professor of English at the University of Auckland for twenty years, before taking early retirement in 1986 to write full-time. His novel *Smith's Dream* became Roger Donaldson's first movie, *Sleeping Dogs*, and Sam Neill's first movie role. He has won a number of literary prizes, including the Katherine Mansfield prize for the short story, the Jessie McKay Award for poetry, the New Zealand Book Award for both poetry and fiction, and the King's Lynn Poetry Prize. He was awarded a CBE in 1985 for services to New Zealand literature, elected Fellow of the Royal Society of Literature in 1995, and Senior Visiting Fellow at St John's College, Oxford, in 1997. He was awarded an Honorary Doctorate in Letters by the University of Bristol in 2001. His latest novel, *My Name was Judas*, was published in 2006, and his latest collection of poems, *The Black River*, in 2007, when he was awarded the Order of New Zealand, an honour he and Margaret Mahy are currently the only writers to hold.

    * There is little I can say about this story that it doesn't say itself, because (unlike many I have written) it is very close to fact. My wife and I do stay in a village in the Langue d'Oc in southern France, we did meet an elderly Swedish woman there, and she did tell us a story so like this one it would be difficult to remember how the two versions differ. I'm sure there are differences, because something essentially intuitive and therefore difficult to explain happens in making a 'true' story into a fictional one. The differences are subtle but real, and have to do, I suppose, with nudging the particular in the direction of the exemplary. This is a story that recounts real events in their historical context — and yet it has been re-imagined in such a way that the events contain (or so the writer hopes) something about life in general, about the nature of victory and defeat, and the different kinds of damage it does to those who experience one or the other. What kind of harm has the war done to the Germans, the Americans, the young Swedish women, and which is more serious? I have my own answers to such questions, but I did not write the story with answers in mind. I wrote it, I think, to arrive at the questions.

JUDITH WHITE's collection of short stories, *Visiting Ghosts*, and her novel, *Across the Dreaming Night*, were both shortlisted for the New Zealand Book Awards. She has won the Sunday Star-Times Short Story Competition twice and was third runner-up for the same competition. She teaches various creative writing courses in Auckland.

    * I started writing a couple of paragraphs for this story ages ago, after I'd had my first flight in a tiny plane. At that stage I didn't have any characters for the story except for a woman who was frightened of flying. When I took it up again this year I had to ask myself where, what or who she was flying to, and where, what or who she was flying from. I decided she was leaving a man she loved to visit another man she also loved. Then I had to ask myself why she would reasonably do this. I decided she was visiting an ex-husband whom she'd had to leave for her own survival, but to whom she still had an emotional attachment. I thought this would give the story a nice dramatic tension, especially when she had a niggling tendency to want to stay and help the ex-husband because he needed her, and because she felt, once again, that she might be able to make a difference. Meanwhile the current lover was waiting for her return, as they had planned their first holiday together. This was to give a finite timeframe for her visit, to create added pressure. The title, 'Crash', was an obvious one . . . her fear of the plane crashing, the man crashing emotionally, and the final crash in the last paragraph.

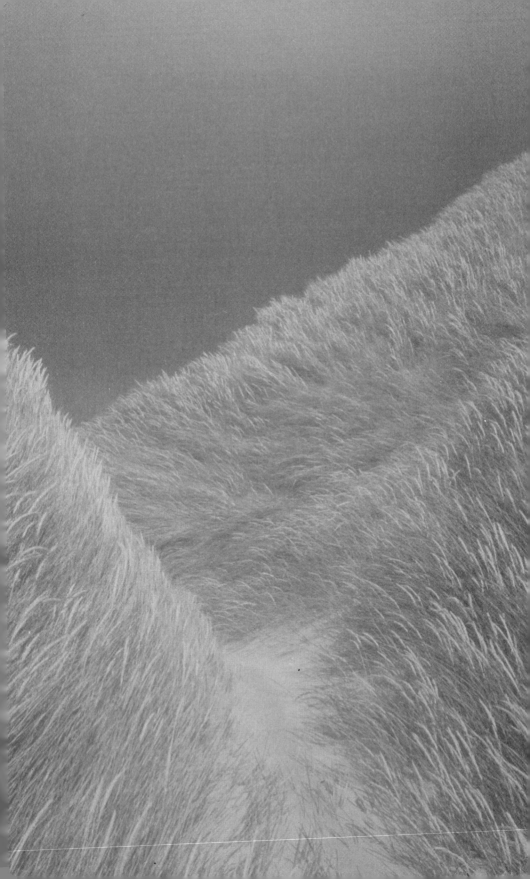